How to Read the
New Testament

The Crossroad Adult Christian Formation Program

**The Crossroad
Scripture
Study Program**

How to Read the Old Testament
How to Read the New Testament

**The Crossroad
Theology and Church
History Study Program**

How to Read Church History: Vol. 1
How to Read Church History: Vol. 2
How to Understand the Creed
*How to Understand Church and Ministry
in the United States*

**The Crossroad
Christian Living
Study Program**

How to Understand the Liturgy
How to Understand the Sacraments
How to Understand Marriage
How to Understand Morality and Ethics

**Crossroad
Special Interest
Courses**

How to Understand Islam
How to Read the World
How to Understand God
How to Read the Church Fathers
How to Read the Apocalypse

Some "How To. . ." texts, and accompanying study guides,
may be in preparation. For complete up-to-date
information, please write: The Crossroad Publishing Company,
370 Lexington Avenue, New York, NY 10017.

Etienne Charpentier

How to Read the
New Testament

Translated by John Bowden

Crossroad   New York

1997

The Crossroad Publishing Company
370 Lexington Avenue, New York, N.Y. 10017

Originally published as *Pour lire le Nouveau Testament*
© Les Éditions du Cerf, 1981

English translation copyright © John Bowden 1981

Nihil Obstat: Rev. Anton Cowan
Censor

Imprimatur: Msgr. John Crowley, VG
Westminster, 28 May 1985

Printed in the United States of America

Library of Congress Cataloging in Publication Data

Charpentier, Etienne.
How to read the New Testament.

Translation of: Pour lire le Nouveau Testament.
1. Bible. N.T.—Test-books. 2. Bible. N.T.—Introductions.
I. Title.
BS2535.2.C45 1982   225.6'1   82-13028
ISBN 0-8245-0541-7

A Guide to the Bible

'Do you understand what you're reading?' 'How can I, if there is no one to explain it to me?' This brief exchange, which Luke imagines in a conversation between Philip and the Ethiopian official (Acts 8.30), is a good indication of what I have set out to do in this book. It is a modest attempt to help others to read.

A travel guide

When you visit a monument with a guide – which may be either a person or a book – you expect the guide to be unobtrusive, to allow you to see the monument so that you take in all its essential features. This book is meant to be a guide of this kind to the New Testament, which will take you through it and be an unobtrusive help to understanding the texts.

Travel guides usually offer a number of options: 'If you only have a few hours to spare, see this and that. . . If you have three days. . .' The same is true of this one. It is impossible to cover every aspect of the New Testament in so few pages. So I shall try to keep to essentials and give you a general idea, while at the same time pausing over important texts. If you can only spare a short time, you can't see everything, so make your own choice. It's not a matter of steeping yourself in every detail, but of getting to know your way round. During this visit you will make friends with Luke, John, Paul and others – and you can go back to see them another time.

Second part

It's always fascinating to begin a book with Volume 2: you can exercise your imagination, wonder what happened earlier. However, inevitably that's not the easiest way of understanding it. The New Testament is the second part of the Christian Bible; Volume 1 is the Old Testament, and it's better to start there.

You can begin with this book, *How to Read the New Testament*, if you wish, but many things will be clearer if you first look at *How to Read the Old Testament*. In any case, I shall refer to it often.

How to use this guide

When you visit a town, you may find buildings which have been constructed in stages. The cathedral, the castle, old houses have some parts which are Romanesque or Gothic, additions which were made in the Renaissance and the eighteenth century, and so on. Usually, you visit such buildings one after the other, and it is only afterwards that you get a general impression of the Romanesque atmosphere of the town, or the way in which it developed at the time of the Renaissance. A more technical approach is to go round the buildings once, looking only at the Romanesque parts, then moving on to the Renaissance sections, and so on.

This guide has been designed in such a way that you can visit the New Testament according to either plan. You can use it by yourself, or for study within a group. That's why it's been divided into eight chapters. A group meeting just once a month could go through the New Testament within a year.

The first section presents the work of a New Testament writer (Paul, Mark, John, for example). First comes a page of introduction to place the author and the work in its setting; then an overall view of the work; then suggestions for the study of certain specific texts; then (in the case of the four Gospels) the passion of Jesus; and finally the portrait of Jesus shown by that particular work. You can read through the whole of the section, and then return to any particular part in which you are interested. However, you will be advised to study the texts indicated by this sign ♥ .These have been chosen because they are significant for the work in question. I have taken care to see that in this way you will be able to read the most important passages in the New Testament.

The second section of each chapter, which is indicated by a grey border around the page, traces right through the New Testament writings a theme about which the primitive community is concerned, such as preaching, miracles, parable, worship.

The two part form a whole, but they can also be studued separately. So the guide can be approached in two possible ways.

You can read it straight through, which is the easier approach. Alternatively, especially if you are in a group with an experienced guide, you can begin with a visit to the primitive community, in which case you will start by studying the second section of each chapter. Then, next time round, you will work through the first section.

You will understand these two different ways of approaching the book better when you've read the introduction as far as page 15. However, no matter which approach you choose, you should read all of the first two chapters as a start.

Which Bible?

This book can be used with any edition of the Bible. If you have a Bible, you can use this guide.

If you don't, then the two most useful translations are probably the Revised Standard Version (from which all the texts quoted in this guide are taken), or the Jerusalem Bible; the Standard Edition of the Jerusalem Bible also has introductions and notes to each book, but it is expensive. (If you have an old Bible, and don't want to go to the expense of buying a complete new one, you could buy a paperback edition of the New Testament and use your old Bible for the Old Testament.)

When it comes to studying the Gospels, you will find a Synopsis very useful (this is a book which puts the Gospels in parallel columns so that you can compare them). B. H. Throckmorton (ed.), *Gospel Parallels*, Nelson 1967, is probably the best.

Have a good journey!

It only remains for me to wish you a good journey through the New Testament, and to thank all those who have helped in the writing of this guide: the countless biblical scholars who are my friends, and from whom I have stolen so many ideas or pictures; all those who in the course of meetings or conferences have delighted me as we shared in reading these texts, including the groups in Chartres and Chateauroux who bravely agreed to act as guinea pigs by working with photocopies of the text of the guide.

THE JEWS SAID IT IS NOT LAWFUL FOR US TO KILL

ANYONE SO THAT THE WORD OF JESUS MIGHT BE
FULFILLED

SHOWING BY WHAT DEATH HE WAS

TO DIE THEN PILATE ENTERED THE PRAE-

TORIUM AND CALLED JESUS

AND SAID TO HIM YOU ARE THE KING OF THE

JEWS

...FOR THIS I WAS BORN

AND AM COME INTO THE WORLD TO BEAR

WITNESS TO THE TRUTH WHOEVER IS OF THE TRUTH

HEARS MY VOICE PILATE SAID TO HIM

WHAT IS TRUTH AND AFTER

HE HAD SAID THIS HE WENT TO THE JEWS

AGAIN AND SAID I FIND NO

This papyrus fragment, discovered in the sands of Egypt, belongs to the John Rylands Library in Manchester (hence the name which it has been given, the Rylands papyrus); it was published in 1935. The illustration above shows both sides of it; the text contained on it is John 18.31–33 and John 18.37–38. Alongside the reproduction of the papyrus, the same size as the original, I have put a literal translation of the verses so that you can have some idea of the words which the papyrus contains.

Scholars date it to some time before AD 150, because of the style of the writing. This is the earliest text of the New Testament that we have. Since John wrote his Gospel about AD 95–100, the papyrus shows that soon after its composition this Gospel had already spread to Egypt.

Getting Ready for our Journey

Before we set off to visit a foreign country, we usually learn something about its customs and way of life, the way in which the people there think and talk, so that we don't feel too lost and don't commit too many blunders. We may also look at a map, and bring ourselves up to date with the political, economic and social situation.

The New Testament is still something of a foreign land to us, even if we are very familiar with some passages. So our first stage will be to read the Acts of the Apostles, to learn about the world in which the first Christians lived.

Before that, however, we shall remind ourselves quickly of what the New Testament is, how it came into being. (It is worth your re-reading pp. 8–10 of *How to Read the Old Testament*, to remind yourselves of how the Bible came into being.) That will set the scene for this course, and also explain why I chose the particular stopping points that I did. You will also be able to see how there are two possible ways of using this guide (see p. 15).

This is what you will find in the following pages:

1. **The three stages in the formation of the New Testament**
   You can find these stages, along with a brief summary, in a diagram on pp. 10–11; pages 12–17 take it further and show how important the stages are.

2. **The literary genre of the Gospel** (pp. 18–19)
   Our good fortune in not having 'photographs' of Jesus.

3. **Literary genres in the Gospels** (pp. 20–21)
   A first introduction to the models and the styles that we shall be meeting.

CHILDHOOD OF JESUS'

Jesus lives at Nazareth as a good Jew practising the spirituality of the Pharisees

PUBLIC LIFE 28 – 30

preach

celebrate

teach

'Council' 50

51 PAUL

63 preaches

writes his letters

The disciples reread the life of Jesus on the basis of their life, in the light of the resurrection

Official Judaism rejects the Christians

JESUS OF NAZARETH (6 BC to AD 30)

Jesus was born in the reign of Herod, in all probability six years before the beginning of what we call the Christian era. He lived, in Nazareth, as a pious Jew, practising the Law in accordance with the spirit of the Pharisees, who were the most religious of the Jews.

About 27 or 28, his baptism by John the Baptist inaugurated the two or three years of his public life. He chose disciples and, with them, proclaimed the coming of the kingdom of God: by his words, and even more by his actions and his life. He never wrote anything. (That's not quite right. He did write something once, on the sand. . .)

He was condemned by the religious authorities and crucified by the Romans, almost certainly on 7 April 30.

THE COMMUNITIES (between about 30 and 70)

The resurrection of Jesus and the coming of the Spirit at Pentecost enabled the disciples to begin to discover the mystery of Jesus. These disciples remained Jews, but they formed an amazing group within Judaism: they were the witnesses to the risen Jesus.

(The grey area in this diagram is meant to represent the Judaism from which Christianity was born.)

The disciples sought to be faithful in two directions: to Jesus, and to a life which raised a great many questions.

It was in an attempt to answer these questions that they began to recollect what they remembered of Jesus. However, they did this in the light of the resurrection. These memories were focussed on three main points.

The disciples *preached*, to proclaim the risen Jesus: first to the Jews and then to the Gentiles. Here we have an announcement of the faith of the first Christians;

The disciples *celebrated* their Risen Lord, in the liturgy and above all in the eucharist. The eucharist determined the form of many memories of Jesus;

The disciples *taught* the newly baptized, and in order to do so recalled the actions and the words of Jesus.

Others soon joined the first disciples: Barnabas, the Seven (including Stephen and Philip), and above all, Paul. Paul was converted round about AD 36, and went on to bring the good news to Asia Minor, to Greece, and finally, to Rome. From that time Gentiles were able to enter the church without first becoming Jews: that was decided at the 'council' of Jerusalem in AD 50.

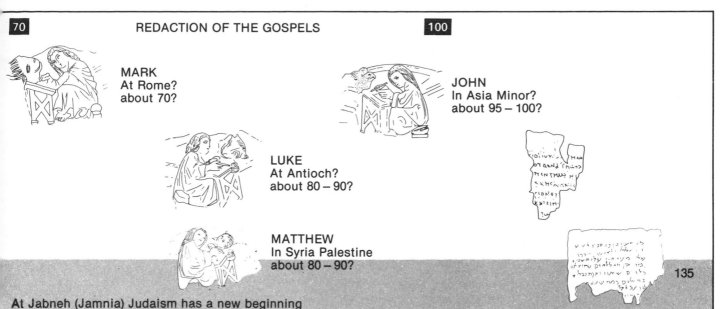

REDACTION OF THE GOSPELS

70   100

MARK
At Rome?
about 70?

LUKE
At Antioch?
about 80 – 90?

MATTHEW
In Syria Palestine
about 80 – 90?

JOHN
In Asia Minor?
about 95 – 100?

135

At Jabneh (Jamnia) Judaism has a new beginning

Between 51 and 53 Paul wrote letters to various communities.

Throughout this period, official Judaism gradually began to reject the Christians.

In 70, the Romans destroyed Jerusalem. Pharisees who met at Jamnia (or Jabneh, the Hebrew spelling – the place is south of modern Tel Aviv) gave Judaism a new life, which has continued down to our own time.

THE REDACTION (or editing) OF WRITINGS (between about 70 and 100)

Four theologians bore witness to Jesus, bringing together traditions which had already been edited in various ways.

Round about AD 70 the Gospel according to St Mark put down in writing what was almost certainly the preaching of Peter in Rome. It seeks to show that Jesus is the Christ, the Son of God, especially through his actions and above all his miracles.

The Gospel according to St Luke was written about 80 or 90, for communities principally made up of former Gentiles. It shows how in Jesus God has visited his people and manifested his loving-kindness towards them.

Luke wrote a second volume, the Acts of the Apostles, in which he shows how the good news, carried by the apostles under the guidance of the Spirit, began to spread all over the world.

The Gospel according to St Matthew was probably produced about 80 or 90 also, in a community of former Jews who had become Christians. Matthew attacks the Pharisees of Jamnia and shows how Jesus fulfils the scriptures.

In their enquiry into the mystery of Jesus, Matthew and Luke go back to his childhood, which they present in the light of his life and resurrection.

The Gospel according to St John is a very profound meditation on Jesus as the Word of God. Written perhaps between 95 and 100, it shows how the crucified Jesus is still alive today and gives us his spirit. Through the signs performed by Jesus, we must believe if we are to see.

In Revelation, John – whether the same John, or another one – presents Jesus as the goal of history.

In the meantime, John, Peter, James, Jude and other disciples wrote letters to various communities.

In 135, after a second rebellion, the Romans decimated the Jews. For centuries the Jews were not allowed to enter Jerusalem. Christians had already left Jerusalem and were settled all round the Mediterranean basin.

In a very schematic way, the diagram on the previous pages shows the three main stages in the formation of the New Testament. It is so important that we shall keep returning to it. We shall do so by means of images and comparisons; that may be rather a dangerous way of going about things, but it will be more interesting, and you will know where to add a pinch of salt!

The most murderous woman. . .

One day I met the most murderous woman in the world. While visiting an archaeological site in Iraq, we were welcomed by the archaeologist's wife. It was only later that we learned that she was Agatha Christie, the author of so many famous detective stories. If only we had known at the time, we would have paid more attention to her; now, we were reduced to reconstructing our scant memories, the few words she had spoken, the way in which she was dressed, and so on.

We will all have had similar experiences.

So, too, did the first disciples. They followed Jesus simply because their master, John the Baptist, suggested that they should. They did not really know who he was. They listened to him attentively, as one might listen to a prophet. They even came to think that he might be *the* prophet, the Messiah. But it was only after Pentecost that they began to discover who this man, their friend, really was: the Son of God! Their memories of the few years which they had spent with him then took on a new importance, and they began to try to reconstruct them.

This became all the more important to them as the years went by. Towards the end of Jesus' life, they had begun to believe that the kingdom of God had dawned with him, and according to the beliefs of the time, that meant the end of the world. Yet months and years went by; they kept on waiting, but they had to get organized. Now every society needs rules to live by; and Jesus had left no writings.

Jesus never wrote anything

Jesus never wrote anything – except on one occasion, in the sand! He spoke, he lived; and that's all. It's important. Look at the Greek philosopher Socrates and his disciple, Plato. Socrates didn't write anything, either, and it was Plato who put the teachings of his master into writing. So we study Plato's works, although Socrates is the person in whom we're interested.

This is even more true in the case of Jesus. At the source of the good news, the gospel, we find the person of Jesus. Had he produced writings, we might have been tempted to regard him only as a master of wisdom. But because he lived, simply, to the full, as he did, we have to go back to his person.

And it is this person, with all his mystery, who made an impression on the disciples.

A photographic laboratory

The disciples were 'impressed' by the person of Jesus. The word 'impression' is also used in photography: when we take a picture of something, an impression is made on the film, the image is recorded on it, but we cannot see anything. For this image to appear, the film has to be put into a developing tank. (The French have an evocative word for this; they call it a 'revealer'.)

We might say that in the same way, the disciples had an impression made on them by the person of Jesus, by his way of living, by his words and his actions. However, at the time they were not aware of the fact, and after Pentecost everything remained dark. To bring to light the multiple image which they had retained of Jesus, they had to be subjected to a process of development, consisting in the life of different communities.

We know that the development of films in a laboratory is a tricky business: there will be more or less contrast in the photograph depending on the length of the original exposure or the materials used; the colours can be changed, different details can be highlighted. In the same way, the images of Jesus that we have differ, depending on the way in which they have been 'developed'; depending on the communities through which they passed, the questions which were raised.

Thus during the years after Pentecost we might compare Palestine, Asia Minor, Greece and so on to an immense photographic laboratory in which the various communities led the disciples to develop the many different images of their master. Some communities were made up of former Jews who had become Christians, some of former Gentiles, some of poor people and slaves, some of traders, craftsmen and other professional people.

Life as a process of development

Thus the life of the communities was the developing tank which made it possible for these images of Christ to appear. This came about above all as a result of three main activities.

1. Preaching

From the beginning, the disciples proclaimed their faith in the risen Jesus. They did so in brief phrases which summed up the essentials of the good news. Scholars use a Greek word, kerygma, to describe this preaching. Kerygma is the cry of the herald, of the local town crier. The disciples said, 'You crucified Jesus, but God has raised him, exalted him, made him Lord, and we are witnesses to that. He sends us his spirit. Believe in the good news and you will be saved.'

A collection was also made of the various beatitudes which Jesus could use to proclaim this good news: from now on the poor are no longer poor, since God has come to establish his kingdom. People told of the miracles of Jesus, which show his victory over evil, suffering, sickness and death.

They also took up parables, that form of teaching by stories which expresses well and simply the happiness which Jesus has brought, and the need to make a choice.

2. Celebration

The disciples re-enacted Jesus' last supper, which gave a significance to his death. To begin with, when only the first disciples were involved, there was no need to recall the last supper in detail; they knew what they were doing. Each one could still say how he understood it, and add details: we can imagine Peter telling how he had betrayed his master, John saying what he had felt at the foot of the cross. Soon, however, there were other disciples who had not known Jesus; they had to be told the significance of these actions of breaking bread and drinking wine from the cup. This is probably the way in which, very soon, a first passion narrative came into being.

However, when they told this story, the disciples were describing the suffering, the passion and the death not of a man now dead, but of someone who was still alive – and that made all the difference. We know that we do not talk about the illness of a friend or relation who may be in hospital, hovering between life and death, in the same way as we do later, when they are cured. In the celebration of the eucharist, Jesus makes himself present to his community, and it was in his living presence that his disciples told of his death. The passion narrative, like all the other stories about Jesus, is told in the light of the resurrection.

In this liturgical context people also brought to mind certain actions of Jesus which enabled the meal to be understood better: for example the feeding of large multitudes, where Jesus made a few loaves and fishes go round so many.

3. Teaching or catechesis

Now those who had newly been baptized had to live as disciples of Jesus. To discover how to live in community, to answer the many questions raised in everyday life, they kept returning to the life of Jesus, his words and his actions. They took up the parables and adapted them to their new situation: they had to watch, keep vigilant, become the good earth in which seed could grow. . . New teaching was looked for in the miracles: the tiny community had the feeling of being a frail boat tossed by storm and tempest; they could survive only because the risen Jesus stood up to the tempest in response to the prayer of his church, 'Lord, save us!' How were the authorities to act? They remembered that Jesus had said to them, 'You are the servants of others', and had left them only two rules, mercy and forgiveness.

Thus wherever Christian communities came into being, images of Jesus were developed in the disciples' memory. These images, these snapshots, were quickly formed into sequences. Before we see how this came about, we must recall one important event: the Jewish theologian Saul, or Paul, became a Christian.

Paul the theologian

The first disciples, Peter and John, were people without any great religious education. Paul was a rabbi. He spent his youth studying the scriptures. On the road to Damascus, the risen Christ seized hold of this Jewish theologian and made him a Christian theologian, one who reflected on the mystery of Jesus, on his role in God's plan. For fifteen years, from 36 to 50, he preached and founded communities; for the last fifteen years of his life he also wrote letters to his communities, which sometimes are real theological treatises. That helped other disciples to reinterpret their memories of Jesus.

Arranging slides

In the winter evenings, you may decide to bring out the slides which you took during your summer holidays and put them in order. Let's look at the various ways in which you might go about this.

The slides

During your holidays, whether you were at the seaside, in the mountains, or in the country, you will have taken pictures of things that appealed to you: landscapes, monuments, family scenes. These photographs were developed in a laboratory and have now become slides. To put them in order you will have to arrange them in some kind of sequence.

Sequences

At this point, you may pause. In what order do you want to keep them? You might arrange them according to place: pictures of mountains, of the sea, and so on; or by types – family photographs, whether they were taken in the mountains or by the sea; or you might simply want to keep them in the order in which you took them, to retrace the course of your holiday.

It is the same with the various images of Jesus developed in the various communities. They, too, were rearranged in sequences. For example, miracles and parables were collected together; isolated sayings of Jesus, arranged one after another, became speeches. Or the Christians of Capernaum or Jerusalem remembered everything that Jesus said and did among them. When we open the Gospels, we have the impression that one day Jesus said to himself, 'What should I do today?' He looked at his diary: 'Miracles today.' And Matthew shows Jesus performing ten miracles one after the other. The next day it was a new programme, parables. Obviously things didn't happen like this; we can see that the Gospel writers incorporated into their work various sequences (parables, miracles, discourses) which had been constructed at an earlier stage. Again, at the beginning of Mark's Gospel, we find what has been called 'the day at Capernaum': Jesus calls the first four disciples by the lakeside, goes into Capernaum with them, preaches at the synagogue, drives out a demon, heals Peter's mother-in-law; in the evening the whole city gathers together and Jesus performs miracles; that night he goes into a desert place to pray, Peter goes to look for him and they go off again to preach. All these images of Jesus' activity in Capernaum have been brought together in a single sequence.

So you've collected together sequences of holiday photographs. Now some friends are coming round and you want to give a film show.

The show

You bring together all your different sequences. Perhaps you may add one or two pictures taken the previous year or slides bought at a shop (for example, of a monument which it was difficult to photograph). This show will be a good indication of what you thought of your holiday in retrospect. If parents and children each gave their own commentary on the same slides, the result would obviously differ but in either case it would show how one or the other felt about that particular time.

In the same way, at different times and in different communities, four disciples (whom tradition has called Matthew, Mark, Luke and John) set out to make their own presentation of Jesus. To do so they brought together various sequences which had already been constructed, added episodes about which they had gathered information, and made 'films': four films, each of which presents a particular way of seeing Jesus, the way in which the author and his community regarded him. So the Gospels tell us about Jesus, but they tell us just as much about the communities in which they were formed. An illustration may help you to understand this better.

Two books about Luther

Suppose we were to take two books written by Catholics about Luther, one in 1900 and one in 1980. The former, unfortunately, would go something like this: Luther, an unfrocked monk, seduced a nun and as a result of his pride subjected Europe to fire and the sword. . . The second would say: Like all of us, Luther had his weaknesses, but above all he was a very devout monk with a passion for God and for man's salvation; he had seen that the church had to reform itself, return to scripture – and by refusing to do so, the church forced him out. . . In these two books we shall learn something about Luther, but we shall above all discover the ecumenical attitudes of Catholics in 1900 and in our own day. In talking to us about Luther, these books also tell us just as much about the time in which they were written.

Similarly, the Gospels present Jesus to us, but they tell us just as much about their communities. To take just one example, when we hear the terrible words which Matthew's Jesus addresses to the Pharisees, we have to ask whether this is primarily the Jesus of the 30s opposing the Pharisees of his time or the risen Jesus, living in Matthew's community, about 80–90, opposing the Pharisees of Jamnia.

The way ahead

The diagram on pp. 10–11 and the explanations which I have given (don't forget that these are only comparisons) set out to identify the three main stages in the formation of the New Testament: Jesus – the communities – the redactors (who were editors – and more) who put together the New Testament books. How are we going to deal with them in this study? There are two possible approaches: research or exposition.

Think of an archaeologist excavating a site. In his work he begins at ground level, digs down, and gradually discovers various civilizations which have followed one another in this place: he goes back through history. If, however, he is giving a lecture, he will do things the other way round: on the basis of his discoveries he will trace the development of the various settlements from the earliest days down to modern times.

Here, too, I might have chosen the method of exposition: the first chapter could have presented what we can know of Jesus, and then, as a second stage, I could have tried to reconstruct the various sequences formed in the communities, ending by reading the Gospels and other texts.

Instead, however, I have chosen the order of research. What we have now are the Gospels and some letters – i.e. texts. What we read now is our starting point. At each stage, however, we shall try to discover what sequences existed earlier. To make it easier, each chapter will contain four pages (in a different typeface and with a grey border, so that you can find them quickly), presenting one of these sequences: miracles, parables, discourses, worship, and so on.

So there are two possible ways for you to use this book.

You can follow the order in which it has been presented; i.e., you can follow the order of research.

You can begin at the end (with what we know of Jesus), study the pages devoted to the sequences, and then those about the New Testament books themselves; i.e. you can follow the order of exposition.

The synoptic problem

A synopsis is a book which presents the Gospels in parallel columns, in such a way that you can read all similar texts at a single glance (Greek *synopsis*). The first three Gospels are similar enough for us to be able to put them in columns like this all the way through; that is why Matthew, Mark and Luke are called the synoptic Gospels (or just 'the synoptics', for short).

This similarity has raised the question whether these Gospels are not based on one or more *written* sources. For centuries scholars have produced one solution after another, sometimes extremely complicated and always hypothetical. To simplify things in the extreme (which inevitably means distorting them), one might say that it looks as though those who produced the Gospels as we now have them resorted to two 'quarries' of material. Matthew, Mark and Luke had access to one of these, which is referred to as the triple tradition; only Matthew and Luke had access to the other, which is often called the Q source (from *Quelle*, German for source). This source is seen as a collection of logia (from a Greek word *logion*, plural *logia*, which means words, sentences). This might be summed up in a diagram:

It is difficult to say whether Matthew and Luke had direct access to the first 'quarry', or whether they knew of it only through Mark. At all events, it is accepted that Matthew and Luke knew Mark's work, but are independent of each other.

Mark seems to be the inventor of the literary genre of the Gospel; in this way he provided a geographical and chronological framework for the story of Jesus. Matthew and Luke followed him.

Matthew and Luke made different use of what they discovered in the second 'quarry': Matthew ground it all up before incorporating it in his Gospel; Luke preferred to insert it into the framework he took over from Mark in two great blocks of material.

Both Matthew and Luke have texts which can be found only in their Gospels; Mark has very few of these.

On this double page, we shall be getting used to synoptic study by means of a very simple example. You can either read it now or skip it for the moment; we shall come back to it later.

A text: the healing of Peter's mother-in-law
This healing is reported in all three Gospels. This is how you will find the story in a synopsis.

Matt. 8	Mark 1	Luke 4
14 *And when*	29 *And immediately they left*	38 *And he arose and left*
Jesus entered	*the synagogue*	*the synagogue*
Peter's house,	*and entered*	*and entered*
he saw his mother-in-law	*the house of Simon and Andrew.*	*Simon's house.*
lying sick	30 *Now Simon's mother-in-law*	*Now Simon's mother-in-law*
with a fever;	*lay sick*	*was ill*
	with a fever,	*with a high fever,*
	and immediately they told	*and they besought*
	him of her.	*him for her.*
15 *and he touched her hand,*	31 *And he came and took her*	39 *And he stood over her*
	by the hand and lifted her up,	*and rebuked the fever,*
and the fever left her,	*and the fever left her;*	*and it left her;*
and she rose and served him.	*and she served them.*	*and immediately she rose and served them.*

The first thing we must do is to compare the texts. A simple way of doing that is to underline each word with a particular colour. There are naturally three primary colours: red, blue and yellow; mixing them produces all the rest. Red and blue make purple, red and yellow make orange, blue and yellow make green, red and blue and yellow make brown. Since there are three synoptic Gospels, simply give each of them one of the primary colours.

When a word is peculiar to Matthew, underline it in red; to Mark, in blue; to Luke, in yellow.

Underline a word common to Matthew and Mark in purple; to Matthew and Luke in orange; and to Mark and Luke in green; if it is common to all three, underline it in brown.

This work might seem very academic to you. But try it for yourself! It will help you to make discoveries, and you will have to read the texts very closely.

This brief study already enables us to note one or two things in the text as a whole. It is clear that Matthew is the shortest account and Mark the longest, but the three stories seem the same. You will have coloured few things in brown (common to all three): entered, house, mother-in-law, fever, left her, she served. There will be a good deal of red, blue and yellow, i.e. the words peculiar to each Gospel, and also green, words common to Mark and Luke. We might suppose that underlying what we have now is a common story which has been worked over by each evangelist.

The comments on each story will become clearer when we have looked at each of the Gospels in detail.

Mark is very specific; we can almost hear Peter talking. Do the words peculiar to him come from the earliest story? Have they been added by Mark, who is a skilful narrator? It's hard to tell.

However, Mark is also a theologian. 'Jesus and his disciples' is a characteristic way of talking about Jesus in this Gospel, hence his 'they', not 'he'. The expression 'lifted her up' almost certainly recalls the power of Jesus' resurrection: 'lift up' and 'raise, resurrect', is the same word in Greek. And Mark twice uses 'take by the hand' in a miracle story (5.41; 9.26–27).

Luke improves the text from a literary point of view. He stresses the power of Jesus: immediately.

Above all, Jesus rebukes, threatens the fever: this is the word used for driving out demons, and Luke uses it three times in a very few verses (4.35, 39, 41). We shall come back to this.

Matthew, as often in his miracle stories, keeps only two people: Jesus and the person concerned. He suppresses all secondary details, and this brings out the person of Jesus: he is the one who takes the initiative in coming to Peter's house, in seeing the sick woman.

She rises (again the same word as resurrection in Greek) and serves Jesus. We shall see that in this way she becomes a symbol of the church which serves its Lord.

Presenting the texts

In this diagram I have simply taken the titles of the texts that you would find in a synopsis, and I have limited myself to just a few chapters. That will enable you to see how the evangelists make different presentations of the same texts which have come down to them from the tradition. The arrows indicate the different positions of certain passages; we shall come back to them later.

A dash – in a column indicates that this Gospel does not have the episode which occurs in another. Thus Matthew and Mark do not narrate the coming of Jesus to the synagogue in Nazareth which is described in Luke 4.16–30.

A reference in brackets indicates that this Gospel has the same episode, but puts it in a different context. Thus the call of the four disciples put by Matt. 4.18–22 and Mark 1.16–20 before the day in Capernaum is put after it by Luke (5.1–11); the references in brackets opposite Luke 5.1–11 in the columns for Matthew and Mark recall where they included the episode.

For the moment, let us look only at the position of the story of the healing of Peter's mother-in-law.

Mark has constructed Jesus' day at Capernaum as a summary of Jesus' activity (see p. 14). Miracles form part of it, including the cure of Peter's mother-in-law.

Luke has taken up the sequence of the day at Capernaum, but he has included it in a much larger collection which extends from 4.16 to 4.44; thus we have not only a summary of the ministry of Jesus, but also a summary of the welcome which he receives, at first enthusiastic (4.16–22) and then hostile (4.23–30). In his programmatic sermon (4.16–21) Jesus announces that he brings liberation, but he does not say what this is. By writing that Jesus *threatens* the fever, Luke transforms the healing story into an exorcism similar to the stories which precede it and follow it; thus these three exorcisms show us that Jesus has come to bring liberation from demonic powers.

Matthew puts this healing story in a collection of ten miracles which follow the great Sermon on the Mount. By this presentation he shows that Jesus is powerful in both word and deed.

2. The Literary Genre of the Gospel

We are so used to talking about 'Gospels' that we don't see how novel this kind of literature was when it first appeared.

The gospel and the Gospels

To begin with, people had only the 'gospel' (in the singular), the good news which Jesus proclaimed, the coming of the kingdom of God, the blessings offered to the poor. Paul also uses the word gospel in this sense.

Mark was probably the inventor of the literary genre of the Gospel, which is quite unlike any other type of literature. With him the gospel becomes a text, a story: the story of Jesus' activity. Until then Jesus had been the one who proclaimed the good news; now he became the one to be proclaimed: he himself was the good news.

However, Mark does not talk about Jesus in the past: it is interesting to note how rarely he uses the past tense (the Greek aorist, broadly speaking the equivalent of our simple past tense); he uses the present. This is not so much literary clumsiness as his theological conviction: the Jesus whom he portrays in his text is always present in his community; in particular, he is alive in the eucharist. For Mark, to remember Jesus is both to say that he is absent (his earthly story is in the past) and to say that he is present in the ongoing life of the community which believes in him and celebrates him. The Jesus of history continues to live in the form of the word, written and proclaimed, and in the form of the living Christ in whom the community believes. It is through the church's Christ of faith that we can get back to the Jesus of history.

> The word 'gospel' (Greek *euangelion,* good news) was known to secular authors. It was used above all to announce a victory or great events in the life of the emperor. An inscription from 9 BC, found at Priene in Asia Minor, celebrates in this way the birth of Augustus (Luke may have been inspired by it in presenting the birth of Jesus: Luke 2.10–11):
>
> *Everyone may rightly consider this event as the origin of their life and existence. Providence has marvellously raised up and adorned human life by giving us Augustus . . . to make him the benefactor of mankind, our saviour, for us and for those who will come after us. But the birthday of the god (Augustus) was for the world the beginning of the joyful messages which have gone forth because of him . . .*

No photographs of Jesus

At one time or another we have all dreamed of having photographs of Jesus, recordings of his words: we feel that if we had them, we would really know him. But all we have is texts composed by his disciples, 'paintings' or 'mosaics' representing him. However, surprising though it might seem, this is merely a matter of chance; if we had only photographs of Jesus, we wouldn't know anything about him. Suppose I see, in your home, a photograph of a man looking rather strangely at a woman. It's a photograph, so I know that it records a particular occasion (unless it's a trick photo); but what else can I say? Nothing! Was the man looking into space when the flash went off? Did he look away because he didn't want to see the woman (he's got a sad air about him)? Does he love her? You have to tell me. And you say, 'Oh, that's a picture taken at Michael's engagement party. Just look at his face, though! You wouldn't know how happy he was. And to think of all the years they've spent together. . .' While you're talking the photograph comes alive: the faces bring home to us a life of expectation and hope; I can imagine the day. . . And all that happens because you, who were there to witness their joy, can interpret the photograph to me. If I only had the photograph, I couldn't know anything about the couple. Thanks to your explanation, the couple becomes real to me and I can love them.

That is the good fortune we have with the Gospels. We think that they provide photographs of Jesus, but in fact they give us something much better: those who knew Jesus, his disciples, tell us who he was, how they gradually discovered his mystery; what changed their lives. A newspaper account of Jesus would not tell us much about him, and would give only a superficial impression. The witness of the disciples shows Jesus at a deeper level.

'Yes, but if we had a recording of his words, we would know precisely what he meant.' Is that really the case? We have all had the following kind of experience. A friend says something to us which we take in automatically, without paying too much attention to it. Some months afterwards, we say to ourselves, 'So that's what he really meant. . .' Now if you're repeating the phrase in question, do you try to reproduce exactly what this friend said at the time? I suspect that instead you will give an interpretation of it, showing what the person 'meant to' say, what you discovered at a much later stage. The phrase which you repeat will not be exact, but it will be much truer, since it will express what the person really meant to say.

Here again, it's our good fortune that we have the Gospels. They were not written immediately after the event, bringing us words with an enigmatic sense. They are the testimony of disciples who, some years afterwards, tell us what they have understood of the mystery of Jesus, and how their lives enabled them to discover his meaning.

Mosaics

To put it another way, we do not have photographs of Jesus, but rather paintings or mosaics. What we have are the words and actions of Jesus interpreted by authentic witnesses.

And the life of Jesus remains open. If he had left us a collection of rules, dictated sayings, we would only have had to reproduce them; we would be condemned to repetition. Since the disciples understood Jesus in the light of their lives, it follows that the life of our communities today is always the starting point from which we are better able to understand Jesus.

However, that is always on condition that we respect these witnesses. If we had four mosaics giving different representations of the same scene, it would not occur to us to say: 'These mosaics are so beautiful that I do not want to lose any of them; I shall demolish them and use the enormous pile of stones I get to make a single mosaic which combines all four of them . . .' That would be monstrous! The four Gospels are different, so we must study each one for itself, without dreaming of demolishing them and using the débris to construct a life of Jesus made up of the 'four Gospels in one'. If we compare them, and read them in a synopsis, we do so in order to have a better view of the details and the nuances peculiar to each of them, to have a better understanding of the features of Jesus which impressed the particular evangelist.

Faith and the Spirit

'That's all very well,' you might say, 'but all the same, I would feel much happier if I had photographs and recordings of Jesus. I can see the importance of the kind of testimony that you've been describing, but how can I be sure that the disciples were not mistaken in interpreting their memories?'

We would like to have proof, and that is only natural, because we are dealing with events on which the believer stakes his life. However, on the one hand we can be certain (and we shall return to this point at the end of our study) that the historian who studies the Gospels, whether or not he is a believer, will find enough solid evidence to demonstrate their historicity, and will often wish that he had as much evidence for other figures from antiquity. On the other hand, we might ask whether by looking for proof, the believer is not in fact seeking to do the work of the Holy Spirit and of faith.

We know that we can find proof for physical things, that such and such an object exists, but there is no proof for personal relationships. What proof do I have that I love and that I am loved? I must have confidence; I must have faith. Following Jesus Christ is always a matter of having confidence, having faith. We believe that when these disciples interpreted the words and the actions of Jesus, they were inspired by the Spirit: 'I will send you the Spirit,' Jesus said to them on the night of the Last Supper, 'and he will recall to you all that I have told you, and he will guide you into all the truth' (John 16.13).

Tracing paper

When we have a complicated diagram to reproduce (an industrial design, the anatomy of the human body), we may sometimes build up a series of sheets of tracing paper. The first will contain a framework (perhaps the human skeleton), and on top of that we shall put other drawings made to the same scale on tracing paper, representing the muscles, the various organs, and so on; in this way we can look at each drawing separately or, if we wish, we can put them together and see them superimposed one on top of another.

We can do the same sort of thing with the Gospels. On the portrait of Jesus of Nazareth which they had kept in their memories the disciples superimposed the features of the risen Jesus, as they had begun to discover them after Easter, the glorious countenance of the living Lord who was still in their communities. When we read the Gospels in rather too naive a way, everything might seem clear: Jesus presents himself as Son of God; Peter and the centurion proclaim him; and we are amazed that the Jews never recognized him as such. Everything is clear to us because we are looking at all the drawings together. However, for his contemporaries Jesus was above all one who raised a question and issued a summons. Faith, the light of Easter and the illumination of the Spirit were needed for people to see something of the riches of his mystery.

So as to be able to see this better, in this guide we shall sometimes look at all the drawings together, and sometimes try to distinguish the details of just one of them.

3. Literary Genres in the Gospels

When we are describing a car accident, we do not do so in the same way to both our friends and an insurance company: in each case the 'literary genre' is different. In the latter instance we fit our account into a 'mould': the identity of the people involved, witnesses, conditions and so on; in the former case we have more freedom. And in the former case the 'style' can be different: our account to our insurance company will be a very matter-of-fact affair; we can talk to our friends as though we were describing a national catastrophe.

This distinction between 'mould' and 'style' is completely empirical, but it can help us as we go on to read the Gospels.

Prefabricated moulds

There are, then, a certain number of models or moulds which we may use when we want to get a particular effect. We shall look at them briefly here, and then return to the main ones during our study.

The miracle story usually has five points:

- An introduction which presents the case;
- a request for intervention which shows the faith of the person who asks or the faith of those around him;
- the intervention of the person from whom the miracle is sought;
- the result;
- the reaction of the spectators: fear, admiration

We shall see, for example (p. 66), that Mark describes both the cure of a person possessed and the stilling of the storm in the same way and with the same words.

Parables were used at the time to give teaching that could be easily understood, or even to lead the audience to pass judgment on themselves without being aware of the fact.

The stories of the calling of the disciples by Jesus are usually brief (a glance, sometimes – the call – the response) and are modelled on the stories of callings in the Old Testament: thus Jesus calls with the same sovereignty as God!

One type of discourse, at least, is well known, namely the farewell discourse: an important person knows that he is about to die and gives instructions to his disciples.

The controversy or discussion between scholars was a genre in which the rabbis were trained. We often find the following pattern:
- An action or saying of Jesus provokes amazement, often feigned, on the part of the audience.
- The debate begins: 'Don't you believe. . .?', 'Haven't you read in scripture. . .?'
- At the end, the real point at issue emerges. It is necessary to make a choice, and often the parties differ.

Encapsulated maxims are produced when a saying thought to be important is put into a story which serves as a framework for it. This story, whether miracle, controversy or anecdote, is there only to set off the saying.

Floating sayings, as the scholars like to call them, are sayings of Jesus which people have remembered, though they have forgotten the context in which these sayings were first pronounced. They are given whatever context is possible, in a discourse or a story.

Different 'styles'

Here 'style' denotes a mode of expression intended to produce a certain effect. The important thing is the impression that the speaker wants to produce: to achieve it, he may use certain procedures or certain images which may astonish us. Let's look at some of these styles.

The style of the epiphany or theophany (in Greek, *theos* means God and *phainein* or *epiphainein* means to manifest) sets out to demonstrate the presence of God. People were inspired above all by the theophany on Sinai at which, according to the book of Exodus, there was lightning and fire and the mountain shook, showing that God was there. This brought about fear in the people present.

When people use these images or others similar to them, they do so to show that God is present; we need not necessarily think that the event described happened just like that. When we say 'It makes me sick to see this wretchedness', the expression 'makes me sick' is a way of expressing our compassion; we don't go to a doctor to get a diagnosis or some medicine. In the same way, the tongues of flame at Pentecost, the angel at the Annunciation or at the empty tomb, may perhaps also be images to express the presence of God. And when figures like Mary, the women, those who are listening to Jesus, 'are afraid', we are warned that they feel themselves to be in the presence of God.

The style of apocalyptic is even more disconcerting. We have already come across it with Daniel (*How to Read the Old Testament*, p. 90). Created at an agonizing point in history, in a time of persecution, apocalyptic kept an air of suffering. It endeavours to express a certainty at the heart of this anguish: God is the Lord of history and he will intervene in the end, when evil reaches its climax. The stars fall, the earth quakes, the heavens are rent asunder . . . these are all images meant to show us inner feelings like those we have when we say, 'I felt that everything was going to pieces, that the roof was coming in on me. . .'

The 'narrativization' of ideas is a barbaric expression which simply describes the way that people tell a story instead of expressing an idea in an abstract way. A rather sad story will make this clear. Some years ago a monk living in Palestine went down towards Akabah in a jeep; south of the Dead Sea he ran over a Bedouin and killed him. The court established that the Bedouin was in the wrong, but since he had been killed, according to tradition his tribe had to be paid 'the price of blood'. The parish priest of Kerak was put in charge of the negotiations. He described the accident in his own way to the chiefs of the tribe; the monk paid the price and they parted good friends. When they left, the monk protested to the parish priest of Kerak, 'What did you tell them? You know that it didn't happen like that!' 'Of course it didn't,' said the priest. 'Then why did you say that it did?' 'Listen,' said the priest. 'Was the Bedouin in the wrong?' 'Yes.' 'Well, that's what I told them.' We Westerners would have developed an abstract idea to show that the Bedouin was in the wrong; the priest demonstrated this in a story which he made up. The chiefs present also knew that things hadn't happened like that, but they understood the idea the story was trying to convey. Does that seem strange to us? We're doing the same thing when we tell a friend, 'I've been waiting here for hours.' He doesn't take the phrase literally; he simply understands it to say, 'You're late.'

We must remember this as we read some stories, and ask ourselves: are they historical, or are they meant to help us to understand a particular idea?

The stories of Jesus' birth and childhood belong to another 'style' which we have come across in the Old Testament, that of midrash (see *How to Read the Old Testament*, p. 81). People were engaged in 'research' (that's the meaning of the word midrash) into scripture to see how it concerned them in their day; they attempted to bring it up to date. They were able to discover in it rules for action, or edifying stories. One particular kind of midrash (the *pesher*) tries to show how events or people in the reader's day fulfil the texts of scripture. We shall see that the Christians used this kind of interpretation, but stood it on its head: they did not start from scripture, but from the person of Jesus, and tried to see his place in scripture, in the divine plan.

What should we remember?

That may all seem very complicated to you. Don't worry, because it will be much clearer when we are working with texts and discovering examples.

For the moment, the important thing is to draw your attention to one point: sometimes words mean something different from what they appear to say. In fact we are well aware of this, because we use language in a similar way all the time. If a stranger hears us say, 'the cat's got your tongue', 'my heart's in my mouth', 'he's buttering her up', 'she's got a cast-iron stomach', he might well wonder what strange set-up he had discovered. All these phrases and many others are true, not in what they say but in the meaning that they seek to convey. And we understand them instinctively because they are part of our culture.

The problem with the Bible is that it doesn't belong to our culture.

However, the more you use the Bible the easier you will find it to see what is the imagery and what is the meaning which the imagery conveys.

A tool box

You will find a tool box in *How to Read the Old Testament*, p. 14. This shows you how to strip down a text, i.e., it introduces you to questions which you can ask as you study a text. Read it carefully: it will help you all through this course.

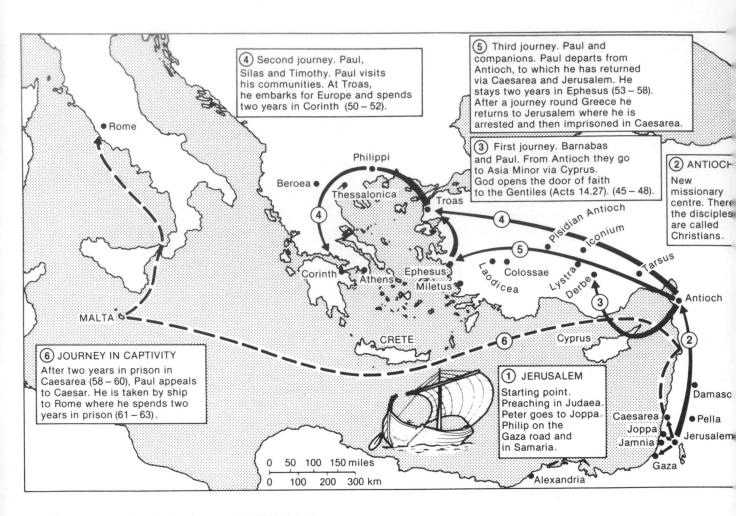

④ Second journey. Paul, Silas and Timothy. Paul visits his communities. At Troas, he embarks for Europe and spends two years in Corinth (50 – 52).

⑤ Third journey. Paul and companions. Paul departs from Antioch, to which he has returned via Caesarea and Jerusalem. He stays two years in Ephesus (53 – 58). After a journey round Greece he returns to Jerusalem where he is arrested and then imprisoned in Caesarea.

③ First journey. Barnabas and Paul. From Antioch they go to Asia Minor via Cyprus. God opens the door of faith to the Gentiles (Acts 14.27). (45 – 48).

② ANTIOCH
New missionary centre. There the disciples are called Christians.

⑥ JOURNEY IN CAPTIVITY
After two years in prison in Caesarea (58 – 60), Paul appeals to Caesar. He is taken by ship to Rome where he spends two years in prison (61 – 63).

① JERUSALEM
Starting point. Preaching in Judaea. Peter goes to Joppa. Philip on the Gaza road and in Samaria.

Rome • MALTA • CRETE • Cyprus • Alexandria • Damascus • Pella • Jerusalem • Caesarea • Joppa • Jamnia • Gaza • Antioch • Tarsus • Iconium • Pisidian Antioch • Derbe • Lystra • Colossae • Laodicea • Miletus • Ephesus • Athens • Corinth • Beroea • Thessalonica • Philippi • Troas

0   50   100   150 miles
0   100   200   300 km

A Roman travelling chariot
Bas-relief found in Carinthia (Austria)

The Roman empire
in the First Century

1 The World of the First Christians

Now we are off on our exploration of the New Testament. At this first stage we shall try to get to know the world of the first Christians. So that we don't get lost, we shall take as our guidebook the Acts of the Apostles. (We shall study its theology later.)

Read the Acts of the Apostles straight through, as though it were the account of a journey. You will come across many new terms, institutions, groups and customs which are unknown to you: try to discover what they signify, with the help of the notes in your Bible, a biblical atlas or a commentary (some books are listed on pp. 122–4). In the following pages we shall go back to them in a rather more systematic way.

To help you read Acts, here is a plan of its contents and some points to note.

A plan of Acts

Acts 1–5 The community in Jerusalem

Acts 6.1–15.35 Missionary activity
  The Hellenists: Stephen and Philip (6–8)
  The calling of Paul at Damascus (9.1–31)
  Peter (9.32–11.18)
  The church at Antioch (11.19–15.4)
  Paul's first mission (13–14)
  The 'Council' of Jerusalem (15)

Acts 15.36–28.31 Paul the missionary
  Second mission in 50–52 (15.36–18.23)
  Third mission in 52–58 (18.24–20.38)
  Prisoner at Caesarea in 58–60 (21–26)
  Taken as a prisoner to Rome in 61–63 (27–28).

Some features of Acts

Places. Palestine in the Roman empire. What are the great cities? What was the population of Jerusalem, Rome, Antioch, Tarsus?

The Roman empire. Look out for allusions to institutions (emperor, prefect, justice), to the means of communication, to the religious and social situation (Roman citizens, slaves) and to the economic situation (jobs, famine, the move of the couple Aquila and Priscilla).

Judaism. The institutions (Temple, Sanhedrin, synagogue), the religious groups (Pharisees, Sadducees). For a long time the Christians continued to remain a sect within Judaism.

The main characters. There are a great many in this lively book! If you have a working Bible, you might underline them in different colours. There are the divine figures: God and the risen Jesus (who is apparently absent, yet is present everywhere) and the Holy Spirit, and also the Word, which sometimes appears as a person (watch the vocabulary: speak, preach, voice). There are the disciples: who are they? What do they do? (Note the role of the laity, of women.) There are the opponents, Jews and Gentiles.

The life of the Christian community. For the moment we need only look at the features of this life in passing; we shall be studying them later in more depth. Preaching: look at the large number of speeches (by whom and to whom? Jews, Gentiles, disciples?). Liturgical life: breaking of the bread (eucharist), baptism, prayer (in what places?). Teaching of the newly baptized. Sharing concerns and sharing possessions.

Jerusalem as depicted on the Madaba mosaic (from near Mount Nebo in Jordan, sixth century AD)

The Roman Empire

In this first stage of our journey we are simply going to set the scene for the story of Jesus and the first Christians. To keep close to the text, I have chosen the Acts of the Apostles as our guidebook. If you have done the work suggested on p. 23 you will already have gathered a good deal of information, supplemented by the aids which you've used.

If you don't have time for that, you can content yourself with a 'guided tour': here you will find the main features you need to know, brought conveniently together. Wherever possible, however, we shall begin with some passages from Acts which you should read first.

Palestine was only a tiny province in the vast Roman empire. The Romans called the Mediterranean, around which their power was spread in the course of a few centuries, *mare nostrum*, our sea. In 63 BC the Roman general Pompey conquered Syria and Palestine; this was the beginning of a military occupation, the climax of which was the capture of Jerusalem by Titus in AD 70 and its destruction in 135. The well-known period of the *pax Romana*, Roman peace, dates from the reign of Augustus (30 BC to AD 14).

Before going any further you should read some texts from Acts which will give you an idea of patterns of life in the Roman empire: 10.12; 13.6–7; 14.12; 16.16–40; 17.6, 16; 18.1–4, 12, 26–28; 19.9, 24; 21.31; 22.25–28; 23.23, 35; 24.22–23; 25.12; 27.1–44; 28.16; Luke 3.1–3. When you read these texts, note the institutions, the titles and the situations in them.

An empire on the way to becoming a society

Rome was at that time organizing its immense empire, rich and unrivalled. After three centuries of conquest, it was trying to unify its subject peoples. Several elements came to its aid.

Latin remained the *language* spoken in the west of the empire (Italy, Gaul, Spain). However, in the east, Greek, the common language (or *Koine*, the Greek word for common), had supplanted the majority of other dialects and was understood throughout the empire. In Syria and Palestine people continued to speak Aramaic, and Hebrew remained the language of the liturgy.

The Gallio inscription, found at Delphi, allows us to date Paul's first mission to Corinth (Acts 18.12)

The empire was divided into *administrative districts* which were more or less closely attached to Rome. Some were governed by a proconsul (like Sergius Paulus or Gallio), and others by a legate (Quirinius); some were entrusted to a prefect or procurator (Pontius Pilate, Felix, Festus); some retained a semblance of autonomy, like Palestine, with Herod the Great and his sons (see the diagram on p. 125).

There was *effective communication*. Roman roads (with their staging posts and their inns), reserved for imperial couriers, the army and a privileged few, made it possible to travel quickly to any destination in the empire. Numerous ships transported goods and passengers on rivers and above all on the Mediterranean, in so far as it was 'open', i.e. navigable (from March to November, see 27.9). There were 276 people on Paul's ship (27.37).

Justice was the same for all citizens. Any of them could appeal to Caesar, in which case all other justice would be put aside and he would be brought to the emperor's tribunal (25.12; 26.32).

Taxes, too, were levied on all inhabitants. There were direct taxes on property and on each individual (cf. Matt. 22.17); indirect taxes, like tolls and city rates, were collected by tax farmers, who paid the total sum and then sought to recover it (and make a profit) through collecting agents, publicans.

The *movement of populations* was common at the time. We have a good instance of this in the married couple Aquila and Priscilla: they came from Asia Minor in the first place, and settled in Rome, from which they were driven out in 49–50 by the edict of the emperor Claudius. Next they settled in Corinth; Paul lodged with them (18.2); three years later he found them back in Ephesus (18.26)!

An empire in the process of forming cities

It is difficult to calculate the population of the empire and of the great cities. The former has been estimated at about fifty million. For the great cities, figures have been produced like one or two million for Rome or Alexandria, half a million for Antioch, Tarsus, Corinth or Ephesus. Jerusalem had a population of only 50,000 (though this tripled or quadrupled at the time of the great festivals).

Not all the inhabitants had the same status. Some of the free men were Roman citizens; they had this much-envied title either by right (in Italy) or by birth (for example, the descendants of Roman colonists), or they bought it at great expense (like Lysias, 22.28). They had protection, and were exempted from certain taxes (16.37–39; 22.25). The other free men were the *peregrini*, that is to say, foreigners in Roman cities; they enjoyed fewer rights. The fate of the extremely numerous slaves (two out of three inhabitants in certain large cities) varied greatly depending on their master's feelings or their situation: this was very harsh in the country, and sometimes more bearable in cities, above all for specialist slaves like craftsmen, cooks, doctors and the like. They could be freed, either by their master, or by purchasing their freedom.

In search of deeper spirituality

In the conquered provinces, people felt that the national gods had failed because they had not been capable of defending their people against Rome. 'Atheism' spread everywhere; people no longer really believed in the gods, even if they practised an official religion which remained a cultural bond. They looked elsewhere for a meaning in life: to philosophical reflection, wisdom (17.16), or to the mystery religions, where they believed that initiation brought salvation.

Small associations of all kinds developed, not only for religious reasons but also to escape the depersonalization brought about by Roman society.

Jews and Christians in the empire

The focal point of Judaism was Jerusalem, centre of the official religion based on the Temple, and extending over the 'land of Israel', Judaea, as it was called at that time (it was only called Palestine, or the land of the Philistines, after 135). There were only about half a million Jews in this area, which was about the size of Belgium or Wales.

In addition, there was the Judaism of the Diaspora, the Dispersion. For a long time Jews had settled outside Judaea; some remained in Babylon after the exile, others were established in Alexandria, where they formed about a fifth of the population. Paul encountered flourishing Jewish communities in all the cities through which he passed (e.g. 13.14; 14.1; 16.13; 17.2; 18.4). It has been estimated that eight to ten per cent of the population of the empire was Jewish, perhaps seven or eight million. Proselytism, the desire to make conversions, was rife (19.13; cf. Matt. 23.15).

The Jews enjoyed a special status in the empire: they were exempt from military service, could observe the sabbath, and could pay an annual tax to the Temple. Thus officially they came under two jurisdictions: that of the emperor, and that of the Sanhedrin in Jerusalem.

To begin with, Christianity was simply a sect which arose within Judaism and enjoyed the same privileges. When it broke away from Judaism it became, under Roman law, an 'illicit religion', a superstition, and could henceforth be persecuted.

0   25 miles

0   50 km

Hermon + 200

Lake Huleh + 68

1208 ▲

Carmel

Tiberias – 212

Galilee

Plain of Jezreel

Jarmuk

Sharon

Tirzah

1247 ▲

Jordan

Samaria

Jabbok

1016 ▲

Jericho

Shephelah

Jerusalem

Qumran

1020 ▲

– 392

Arnon

1075 ▲

NB that some heights on this map are indicated + or – because a good deal of the land is below sea level.

Palestine

Economy

The physical map on p. 25 will enable you to locate the fertile plains (Jezreel, Sharon and the Shephelah), the hill-country of Galilee and Samaria/Judaea, where the stony soil is cultivated, sometimes by constructing terraces, and the Jordan valley with the oasis of fertility centred on Jericho.

The rains, which are quite heavy, fall only between October and March, and water has to be carefully conserved in cisterns.

Agriculture is the chief resource. Wheat, the basic food crop, and barley are cultivated virtually everywhere. Sowing begins after the first rains: barley is harvested before Easter and wheat between Easter and Pentecost.

The olive tree produces abundant oil which is exported to Egypt and Syria; figs are also exported, as far as Rome.

Vines are cultivated above all in Judaea. Wine-presses are built in the vineyards, as is a tower from which a watch is kept to guard against robbers and foxes.

As well as common fruit and vegetables like lentils, chick-peas and salad vegetables, we can also find more exotic produce which even made its way to the Emperor's table: pomegranates and dates from Jericho or Galilee, truffles from Judaea, roses (which were used for the manufacture of a perfumed essence), and above all Judaean balm, which was worth its weight in gold and was the object of a wholesale trade.

At that time, then, the country was very wooded . . . until the goats came along!

Livestock was reared everywhere. Sheep and goats produced meat, milk, leather and wool. The Temple, with its countless sacrifices, consumed a vast number of cattle. Robust little donkeys were also reared; they were extremely useful for agricultural work and for transport. For heavier goods the camel was used. The horse was a rich man's animal.

Industry prospered in several sectors. There was fishing in the rivers and above all in Lake Tiberias, which marketed smoked or dried fish all over the country.

Building did well. From 20 BC to AD 64 a good deal was done to adorn the Temple, and up to 18,000 men were employed in the work. Herod Antipas built Tiberias and fortified Sepphoris and Julias. Agrippa built a wall north of Jerusalem, and Pontius Pilate built a new aqueduct.

Craftsmen met the needs of everyday life: they made clothes (weaving, spinning, dyeing and fulling), vessels (pottery) and jewels.

The Temple was the great 'industrial complex'. Priests and Levites conducted business there; stone-cutters were continually at work; thousands of sheep and cattle were sacrificed there every year; skins (the property of the priests) were tanned, treated and exported. Precious woods and perfume were used there. The influx of pilgrims provided the basis for a good trade in food and also in souvenirs, since pilgrims had to spend a proportion of their annual income, a 'second tithe', in Jerusalem, in addition to the tithe they were obliged to deliver locally in kind.

Domestic trade consisted mainly of barter. Foreign trade was very varied. Imports were chiefly luxury goods: cedar from Lebanon; incense, aromatics, gold, iron and copper from Arabia; spices and fabrics from India. Exports were food (fruit, oil, wine, fish), perfume, skins and bitumen from the Dead Sea. The export trade was largely in the hands of great merchants.

All this meant that Palestine could have been a land 'flowing with milk and honey', had it not been for taxation and the unjust distribution of wealth.

Rich and poor

A minority led what was often a sumptuous life. They included the sovereign and his court, the priestly aristocracy of Jerusalem, the great merchants, the chief tax collectors and the great landowners (mostly from Galilee).

The middle class was made up of craftsmen and country priests; the small farmers, often in debt, were closer to being peasants.

Those who suffered the greatest deprivation were the workers and day-labourers, the unemployed, who often had no alternative to begging, and of course the slaves.

The sick (skin diseases, so-called 'leprosy', seem to have been common) and the infirm lived on alms; almsgiving was an important religious duty.

The robbers and thieves, of whom there were a large number, fall into a special category.

Roman coinage celebrating the conquest of Judaea. One side depicts Titus. On the other, Titus is standing underneath a palm tree; at the foot of the palm, *Judaea captiva*, Judaea captive, is weeping.

Social groups

I shall now introduce you to the various social, religious and political groups. In fact it is impossible to distinguish these groups clearly, since in many cases they overlap.

Alongside the rich, the middle class and the poor, we can isolate a number of special groups.

Read Acts 4.1–17; 5.17–42. Note the groups mentioned: what do they represent?

The clergy

The priestly aristocracy of Jerusalem were worlds apart from the rest of the clergy.

At the top of the hierarchy was the high priest. He was chief authority in the Law and the Temple, and president of the Sanhedrin; he was the only one with power once a year to enter the Holy of Holies, and he was the undisputed leader of the people. At one time he was nominated for life, but the Jewish kings and then the Romans appointed and deposed high priests to suit their ends; the high priest in office therefore sought to please the civil authorities. Besides, the post was enormously profitable: a share of the offerings, the profit on the sale of animals. And since the high priests were drawn from only four families, they had great political and economic power.

The various Temple authorities also made up part of this aristocracy and often came from the same families. All these priests were Sadducees.

There were about 7,000 country priests. They were very close to the common people and shared their life, their work and their poverty. Divided into twenty-four sections or classes, they functioned in the Temple in turn, for one week of the year and at the three pilgrim festivals. Lots were drawn as to who should offer incense, and since a

person could not enter the ballot again until everyone else had had an opportunity, to be successful was the chance of a lifetime (Luke 1.5–9). Some of the more learned were scribes. Many were Pharisees.

The Levites, a kind of inferior clergy who had lost all power, were the Cinderellas among the clergy. There were almost ten thousand of them, also divided into twenty-four sections, and once a year they performed subordinate functions in the Temple: they prepared sacrifices, collected the tithes, provided music and acted as Temple police.

The elders

The elders were a kind of lay aristocracy; the dividing line between them and others is rather blurred. Here again, there was a great difference between the village chiefs and the small group of rich merchants or farmers with seats in the Jerusalem Sanhedrin. They hung on to their power and consequently maintained close links with both the Roman occupying forces and the high priests. They seem to have been Sadducees.

The scribes or doctors of the Law

These were essentially specialists in the Law; they were given official recognition as such at the end of a long course of study, round about the age of forty. They had great influence as official interpreters of the scriptures, providing not only rules for everyday life but also legal judgments for the courts. Some of them were priests, but the majority were lay people and Pharisees. With their mastery in thinking of the people, they often shared the people's poverty. The most famous of them in this period were Hillel and Shammai (before the Christian era), Gamaliel, Paul's teacher (5.34; 22.3), Johanan ben Zakkai, the chief of the school of Jamnia after 70 (see p. 31) and Akiba, who was executed by the Romans in 135.

The scribes surrounded the Law with quite a 'hedge' of prescriptions. They might seem to us to be a yoke of bondage. In effect, however, they served as a means of liberation: by extending to all people the rules of purity which in primitive times were reserved for the priests, they allowed everyone to be close to God.

The publicans

These collectors were not the rich tax farmers, but their auxiliaries. They were Jews who collected taxes on behalf of the Roman occupation forces; for this reason, and because they had a tendency to increase taxation for the benefit of their own pockets, they had a bad reputation and were regarded as public sinners.

THE CLERGY

High Priest

Temple Commander

| *Worship* | *Temple guard* | *Temple finances* |
| Heads of 24 weekly sections | 7 supervisors | 3 treasurers |

| Heads of 156 daily sections | 4 chief Levites about 7200 priests divided into 24 sections about 9600 Levites divided into 24 sections | |

| musicians and singers | Temple guards |

Religious groups

These groups are usually called sects, but clearly in this context the word does not have any pejorative sense. The three main groups came into being in the time of the Maccabees (see *How to Read the Old Testament*, p. 85).

Read 4.1–17; 5.17–42; 18.24–48; 22.2; 23.6–9. Which sects appear? What is their teaching?

The Pharisees

They have had a bad press: that is a pity, and quite unfair. The Pharisees were holy men. They had separated (that is the meaning of the word) from the Hasmonaeans, whom they thought to have broken faith, and they had separated from sin. Above all they were concerned for the holiness of God and meditated faithfully on his Law. Because they knew that it is difficult to live constantly in the presence of the Holy God, they surrounded themselves with a whole network of practices. However, they were not hypocrites: when the Pharisee in Jesus' parable (Luke 18.9–13) says that he fasts twice a week and gives a tenth of his goods to the poor, that is what he does!

The Pharisees are authentic witnesses to the true faith, and Jesus, who was educated by them and taught how to pray to God, felt close to them. Their one fault was to think that they could rely on their holiness in approaching God, that their merits had won them a place in heaven. Perhaps Jesus was so firmly opposed to them because he was disappointed to see them pervert their holiness in this way, and also because they had such an influence on the humble people who admired them. Their influence was due more to their holiness than to their number: there were only about six thousand of them. Some Pharisees had a very open attitude to Jesus and his disciples (John 3: Luke 7.36; 13.31; Acts 5.34; 15.5; 23.9). They proved to be the saviours of Judaism after AD 70.

The Sadducees

These were aristocrats, and above all priestly aristocrats. Their teaching is not well known. They seem to have recognized only the Pentateuch as the Law (and not the Prophets); they did not believe in either the resurrection or angels (23.8). Political opportunists, they collaborated willingly with the Roman occupation forces in order to stay in power. They were very harsh to Jesus and to developing Christianity. They did not have enough religious vitality to survive the disaster of AD 70 and thereafter disappeared from history.

The Essenes

These were a kind of monastic order living as a community on the shore of the Dead Sea. More is known of their teaching since the discovery, in 1947, of the Qumran manuscripts. Under the leadership of a priest whom they called the Teacher of Righteousness, they parted company with the other Jews, whom they thought to be too lukewarm. They lived a life of prayer and meditation on the scriptures, preparing actively for the coming of the kingdom of God. Their monastery was destroyed by the Romans in AD 70.

The baptist movements

Between 150 BC and AD 300 there were many baptist movements, in Palestine and outside it. Their chief characteristics were the importance attached to baptism as an initiation rite or a token of forgiveness, and a hostile attitude to the Temple and to sacrifice. One group rejected any sacrifice which involved blood. The movement led by John the Baptist belongs in this trend, but there is nothing sectarian about it: it was open to all and did not reject any elements of traditional faith. It seems that this movement survived John's death, as there is evidence of a group of his disciples in Ephesus in about 54 (19.1–7).

The 'people of the land'

This is the scornful term used by the Pharisees to describe common people who knew nothing of the Law and were therefore incapable of observing its manifold regulations. This made them impure (cf. John 7.49; Acts 4.13).

The Samaritans

These did not, strictly speaking, form a sect. They were of very mixed origin (see *How to Read the Old Testament*, pp. 45,79), and were separated from official Judaism. They had the Pentateuch in common with the Jews, but built their own temple on Mount Gerizim. Relations between them and the Jews were very tense (cf. Luke 9.52; John 4.9; 8.48). Jesus' attitude towards Samaritans scandalized his contemporaries (John 4.5–40; Luke 10.13; 17.10–17). The Christian mission was first developed in their direction (Acts 1.8; 8.5–25; 9.31; 15.3).

A reconstruction of the altar of burnt offering in the Temple at Jerusalem

Gentile adherents to Judaism

For Judaism, the world was divided into two groups: Jews (who were circumcised), and Gentiles – or the nations (who were not). However, the latter could attach themselves to the former.

The proselytes (the term derives from a Greek verb meaning to draw near) were Gentiles who accepted the whole of the Jewish Law, not only beliefs but also circumcision and so on (2.11; 6.5, 13–43; cf. Matt. 23.15).

The God-fearers accepted Jewish belief but not circumcision, so they remained Gentiles (10.2, 22; 13.16, 26, 43, 50; 16.14; 17.4, 17; 18.7)

Political groups

Confronted with Roman occupation, the Jews became divided into collaborators and members of the resistance.

The rich and the senior clergy collaborated willingly in order to preserve their power. We know little about the Herodians, but these are clearly the supporters of Herod Antipas: they were hostile to Jesus (Matt. 22.16; Mark 3.6; 12.13).

By contrast, 'zeal' for the Law provoked the most religious of the Jews to offer resistance, non-violent on the part of the Pharisees, and violent on the part of those who from 66 onwards were called Zealots (some Zealots were called *sicarii*, after the name of their short sword, the *sica*, which could easily be hidden in clothing). They were mainly responsible for the revolt which culminated in the disaster of AD 70. Before that, there were several abortive rebellions led by people who claimed to be 'Messiah' (5.36; 21.38).

It is important to remember this impassioned situation in order to understand the different attitudes which people adopted to Jesus as messiah (e.g. John 6 15).

1 Holy of Holies
2 Holy place
3 Altar
4 Sanhedrin
5 Beautiful Gate

Courtyards
A of the priests
B of Israel
C of the women
D of the Gentiles

The institutions

Read Acts 3.1–2; 6.1–15; 9.1–2; 13.13–15, 44–52; 16.11–15.

The Temple

Herod restored the Temple to all its former splendour. It stood in the centre of a courtyard measuring about 300 metres by 500 metres. It was the holy place, where God made himself present, though approaches to him had to be strictly regulated. Only the high priest could enter the Holy of Holies once a year, on Yom Kippur, the Day of Atonement. It was an empty room, sealed off by the curtain of the Temple, which at one time contained the ark of the covenant. Around the altar was a first courtyard reserved for the priests. Next came the courtyard of Israel (the males) and the courtyard of the women, which was separated from the courtyard of the Gentiles by a balustrade which no Gentile might cross on penalty of death.

Sacrifices were offered on the great altar, twenty-five metres long and seven and a half metres high. Here, morning and evening. a lamb was consumed as a 'perpetual sacrifice', along with numerous private sacrifices.

At festival times, there were far more sacrifices; priests and Levites bustled about and the crowds surged in.

The paschal lamb had to be sacrificed there before being eaten at the family meal. After the final destruction of the Temple in AD 70, the Jewish Passover was celebrated without a lamb.

The Temple was not only the centre of religion but the political centre (the Sanhedrin met here); because of all the activity it generated it was also the economic centre.

The synagogue and Jewish worship

The word synagogue primarily denotes the congregation of believers. Like our word church, it has come to denote the building in which the community meets. Even more than the Temple, which was a long way off for many people, who could only go there (theoretically) at festival time, the synagogue was the place where the beliefs and religious practices of the people were shaped.

Services, which took place three times a day, had an element of teaching: there was a reading of the Law which was elucidated through the reading of a prophetic text, and then a sermon. Any believer could preach (cf. Luke 4.16f.), but in practice preaching was restricted to scribes and Pharisees, who thus shaped the common faith in accordance with their doctrine. Apart from the recitation of psalms, prayer consisted essentially in the three great benedictions, which provided the framework for the recitation of the Shema, a summary of the faith of Israel (you can find one of these prayers and some information about it on pp. 108–9). It ended with the Eighteen Benedictions, for the wonders of God towards his people.

The festivals

The three great pilgrim festivals were particularly important; they brought the people together around the Temple and strengthened communal faith.

The festival of **Passover** celebrated the liberation of the people at the time of the Exodus (see *How to Read the Old Testament*, pp. 24ff.). About 200,000 pilgrims came to Jerusalem for this occasion. On the afternoon of 14 Nisan, lambs were killed in the Temple, which were then eaten by families after sunset. The festival lasted for eight days. Excitement was so great at Passover time that the Roman authorities feared riots, and the procurator, who usually lived in Caesarea, also came up to Jerusalem.

Pentecost, fifty days later, was originally the harvest festival or the Feast of Weeks (Ex. 23.16; 34.22). At the beginning of the Christian era it had become the celebration of the giving of the Law on Sinai, the festival of the

Restoration of the synagogue at Capernaum (about AD 200)

covenant and the renewal of the covenant (in much the same way as the Christian may 'renew' his or her baptismal vows at the Paschal vigil).

The **Feast of Tabernacles** was the most spectacular. To recall the time in the wilderness, each family built a hut out of branches on the edge of the city (the equivalent of a modern balcony or spare room). Some rituals were very popular, like the procession of priests to the fountain of Siloam, accompanied by people carrying palms (cf. John 7.37ff., and perhaps the 'branches' spread before Jesus on his entry into Jerusalem), together with the lighting of the four candlesticks which illuminated the whole city (cf. John 8.12).

Yom Kippur, or the day of Atonement, was a penitential festival. This was the only time in the year when the high priest entered the Holy of Holies to offer the blood of sacrificial victims in expiation (see the Letter to the Hebrews, p. 54). Rosh ha-Shanah, or the New Year Festival, was the preparation for it. The Feast of Hanukkah, or Dedication, celebrated the purification of the Temple by Judas Maccabaeus in 164 BC (see John 10.22). Purim, or the Feast of Lots, commemorated the salvation gained for the people by Esther; this festival has become the equivalent of a carnival.

The sabbath

Along with circumcision, keeping the sabbath has become the most sacred Jewish practice. Its strict rest, apart from exceptional activities which are laid down in minute detail, was meant to enable people to stop work and to praise God. It could become an insupportable burden (cf. Mark 2.27).

The Sanhedrin

The Great Sanhedrin in Jerusalem (the word comes from a Greek term meaning to sit together) was made up of seventy-one members: elders, high priests (Sadducees) and some scribes (Pharisees). The high priest presided over it. The Sanhedrin was probably inaugurated about a century before Christ; it had sessions in the Temple, twice a week. It had political power: it enacted laws, had its own police, and could pass the death sentence, though in the time of Christ it no longer had the power to carry this sentence out. It was the supreme religious court which fixed doctrine, established the liturgical calendar and regulated religious life. In AD 70 it ceased to exist as a political power; it moved to Jamnia, where it continued to function as a religious power. All over the place there were lesser sanhedrins made up of twenty-three members (cf. Matt. 10.17).

Jamnia – Judaism after AD 70

The Jews rebelled against the Romans in 66. At the end of a bloody war Titus, son of the emperor Vespasian, whom he succeeded, captured Jerusalem in 70. The Temple was destroyed. Thousands of Jews were killed or sold as slaves. Was this to be the end of Judaism?

Some Pharisees, including Johanan ben Zakkai, re-assembled before the final downfall of Jerusalem, at Jamnia (present-day Jabneh, south of Tel Aviv). They succeeded in giving their religion a new lease of life, and modern Judaism is the heir to their efforts. Since the other groups (the Sadducees and the Essenes) had disappeared in the troubles, from now on Judaism was to be Pharisaic. However, for the moment, it had to defend itself on two fronts.

Within Judaism, an end had to be made to the divisions between Jews. One liturgical calendar was established, and synagogue worship was unified; above all, a 'canon of scripture' was established. This was a list of books which were to serve as a rule (Greek *kanon*) of faith. Only those books written in Hebrew were retained, though the Jews of Alexandria recognized others which were written or circulated in Greek (this difference has passed on to our day in the difference between Catholic and Protestant Bibles; see *How to Read the Old Testament*, p. 86).

Externally, Judaism was confronted with Christianity, which was well rooted in Palestine (the Christians left Jerusalem before 70 to settle at Pella, east of the Jordan, and in Galilee), and also in Asia Minor, Greece and Egypt. . . Measures were taken at Jamnia to prohibit Christians from taking part in Jewish prayer; a petition was introduced into the Jewish prayer called the Eighteen Benedictions against 'heretics, apostates and the proud', i.e. Christians. The break was made. Christianity became a Jewish sect rejected by Judaism.

The Christians and Jamnia

The Council of Jamnia is never mentioned in the New Testament. However, some details are best explained by the influence of this revival of Judaism, above all in the Gospel of Matthew, which gathers together the traditions of communities living in Syria-Palestine, i.e. those most closely in contact with the Pharisees of Jamnia. Matthew brings out the similarities and the conflicts.

The conflicts are the most obvious. In Matthew, Jesus is very hard on the Pharisees (Matt. 23); he contrasts Christian prayer with theirs (6.5–6), and the 'yoke' which he proposes is easy compared with the numerous practices which the Pharisees require (11.29–30); the crowds recognize that his authority is not like that of the scribes (7.29). However, in reading Matthew we must always ask who is speaking, the Jesus of the 30s or the risen Lord of the 80s and 90s attacking the Pharisees of Jamnia.

Matthew is also concerned to show his deep agreement with the best of this Pharisaism. The Sermon on the Mount is presented as a great catechism, parallel to the teaching of Jamnia and based on the same three pillars of Judaism: justice, traditional good works and worship. On two occasions in Matthew, and in that Gospel only, Jesus quotes Hos. 6.6 (Matt. 9.13; 12.7); this was in fact a text dear to the heart of Johanan ben Zakkai, the founder of Jamnia. We are told one day one of his disciples was bewailing the destruction of the Temple; it was no longer possible to offer sacrifices to gain forgiveness for sins. 'Do not be troubled, my son,' replied Johanan, 'We have an expiation which is worth just as much: acts of mercy. For according to scripture, I want love, not sacrifices.'

Bas-relief from the triumphal arch of Titus in Rome, depicting the seven-branched candlestick from the Jerusalem Temple

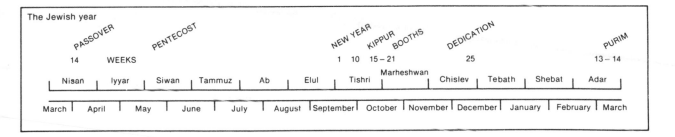

The Jewish year											
PASSOVER	PENTECOST					NEW YEAR	KIPPUR BOOTHS		DEDICATION		PURIM
14	WEEKS					1	10 15 – 21		25		13 – 14
Nisan	Iyyar	Siwan	Tammuz	Ab	Elul	Tishri	Marheshwan	Chislev	Tebath	Shebat	Adar
March	April	May	June	July	August	September	October	November	December	January	February	March

The First Christians

During our journey we shall see who the first Christians were and how they lived. Here we can gather together some details provided by our reading of Acts.

Here are some important texts: 1.13–15; 2.41, 42–46; 3.1; 4.23–31, 32–37; 6.1–15; 9.1–2; 14.27; 15.1–12; 18.24–28; 20.17–38; 21.8–10. . . Try to describe the life of these first Christians.

A rejected Jewish sect

To begin with, and for a long time afterwards, the disciples of Jesus seemed to be no more than a sect within Judaism. They only took the name 'Christians' some years after the resurrection, in Antioch (11.26). Peter and John went to pray in the Temple, Paul preached in the synagogues and went to the Temple to fulfil a vow (21.26). The first followers of Jesus may have had different doctrines from their Jewish contemporaries, but their practices were the same.

Jewish rejection of Christianity began when the Hellenists – Greek-speaking Diaspora Jews who had settled in Jerusalem – questioned these practices (in particular the veneration of the Temple and its sacrifices), and the gulf widened when Gentiles were accepted into the church (at the 'Council' of Jerusalem).

Community life

This church, the assembly of those who had heard the call of God, gathered together in the name of Jesus, Christ and Lord, and was inspired by the Spirit.

According to Luke, it had three main characteristics:
(i) The disciples were constant in passing on the teaching of the apostles. In this catechesis given to the newly baptized, the scriptures were interpreted in the light of the risen Christ; the words and actions of Jesus were recalled and a rule of life was discovered in them. In this way, little by little, the content of the Gospels was brought together.
(ii) The disciples were constant in brotherly communion, a sharing of concerns which was expressed in the sharing of possessions: none of them was in need, because none laid claim to his own personal possessions; they held everything in common.
(iii) The disciples were constant in the breaking of bread, i.e. the eucharist, and in prayer. They prayed in the Temple, in their own homes, or elsewhere (21.5).

The Spirit and the ministers of the church

The Risen Christ had given his Spirit to the community to inspire it. He also gave the community ministers to be at the service of the believers. The various ministries came into being gradually and gradually became distinct.

The Twelve stand apart. As the foundations of the church they were never replaced as such.

In Jerusalem they established elders (or presbyters, the Greek word from which our 'priest' derives), and Paul did the same in his communities. Paul also appointed other authorities, overseers (Greek *episkopos*, which led to our words bishop, episcopacy). The Hellenists were appointed for service or *diakonia*; they were later made the precursors of deacons (though they themselves were not so much deacons as authorities in the church). We can also see the emergence of teachers, prophets and prophetesses (21.9).

However, you must not think that the hierarchy as it was recognized from the second century onwards had yet come into being: that was still in the process of formation.

A missionary community

The disciples felt responsible for passing on what they had discovered to everyone. 'We cannot keep silent,' Peter declared to the Sanhedrin (4.20). Driven by the Spirit, the community in Antioch sent Barnabas and Paul on a missionary journey (13.1–3), and in his enthusiasm for the faith Apollos began to catechize even before he was fully trained (18.24–28).

A community which is one and yet diverse

This one church is also the church of Jerusalem, the church established at Antioch, at Ephesus, and so on. The character of each community was moulded by its experience, its historical and economic situation, and its past; a community made up of Jews who had become Christians did not feel the same way as one which had grown up in a Gentile setting. As we shall see when we study the Gospels, the portraits of Jesus Christ were in turn coloured by the life of these communities.

They make us ask, what portrait of the risen Christ does our particular community reveal in the world today?

Christ the Sun. The earliest known Christian mosaic (Vatican, middle of the third century)

We began our journey through the Old Testament with the Exodus: this event, along with all the reflection to which it gave rise, was in fact the basis of Israelite faith. In the same way, before we read the books of the New Testament, we shall pause at the event which is the foundation of Christian faith, the resurrection of Christ.

This stopping point is important not only for doctrine but also for our learning.

It should allow us to check that Christian faith is based on this event, a mystery so rich that the disciples had to use a variety of images in their attempts to express it.

It will also help us to prepare for the later stages of this book; in fact it will cause us to go quickly through the main stages of the formation of the New Testament. The diagram on pp. 10–11 gave a brief summary of them; here, we shall see in detail how these accounts came to be written.

The stamp test

A magazine once suggested a test to its readers: 'Take a postage stamp and write what you believe on the back of it.' Even if you choose a large stamp and write very small, there is not much room, and you are forced to keep to essentials! What would the first Christians have written on their stamps? That is roughly what we are going to try to discover. In other words, we are going to see what was the good news, the essential message that they proclaimed when they were presenting their faith to a new audience.

Scholars call this essential message, proclamation, news, the kerygma, a Greek word which denotes the cry of a herald or the proclamation that the town crier used to make in former times.

Our course

We shall move on in three stages:

1. The disciples proclaim their faith: the kerygma. On the basis of some speeches from Acts we shall try to see what was the cry, the kerygma, which the disciples used to proclaim their faith to non-believers.

2. The disciples celebrate their faith: creed and hymns. By studying a creed and a hymn quoted by Paul, we shall see that when Christians assembled, they proclaimed or sang the same essential faith.

3. The disciples tell of their faith: narratives. We shall then be able to touch on the latest texts, the Gospel accounts of the appearances of the risen Jesus and his ascension. We shall see that they do not say any more than the kerygma, the creeds and the hymns, but that they say it in a different way, in the form of history.

Before you begin this part of the study, here is a little exercise which you can try (if you want to):

- When you hear the word 'resurrection', what words or images, what comparisons (e.g. spring, light) come to mind? Try to reply without thinking too hard.
- When you think of the resurrection of Christ (in meditation, prayer), what texts of scripture do you spontaneously go to?
- What is important to you in life?

Now go on to the studies I've suggested, without thinking any more about your answers: we shall come back to them later.

33

The Disciples Proclaim their Faith: the Kerygma

When reading the book of Acts, you will certainly have noticed that it contains a great many speeches: eight by Peter, nine by Paul and seven by various other people. As we read some of them, we are going to try to discover what was the essential message that the Christians had to proclaim.

Peter's speeches – or Luke's?

Still, one question arises. Whose voice are we hearing? Is it that of Peter or Paul, or is it that of Luke? It's clear that the author of Acts has rewritten these speeches. They are not just notes taken by a listener, or summaries. Luke, like other historians of his time, followed the practice of composing real miniature speeches, with a beginning, a development and a peroration.

However, all scholars recognize that Luke did not invent all these speeches; he took up earlier material. For example, we can see how certain titles given to Jesus (e.g. *pais*, the Greek word for child or servant) were no longer in use in the time of Luke; to speak of Christ as a man attested by God with mighty works and wonders and signs which God did through him is an indication of reflection on the mystery of Jesus which is still in its infancy.

So we can use these speeches to see how the first Christians proclaimed their faith.

Some speeches in Acts are addressed to disciples, for example Paul's farewell to the leaders of the church in Ephesus (Acts 20.17–35), but the majority of them are addressed to Jews or Gentiles, to persuade them to be converted. It is here that we shall try to discover the essential message proclaimed by the Christians, the kerygma.

❦ The kerygma in the speeches in Acts

Let's read some speeches addressed to Jews. Peter makes five speeches: Acts 2.14–41 (the day of Pentecost); 3.12–26 (after the healing of the lame man); 4.9–12; 5.29–32 (before the Sanhedrin); 10.34–43 (before the Roman officer Cornelius), and Paul makes one: 13.16–41 (in the synagogue at Pisidian Antioch). We may add to these the dialogue between Cleopas and Jesus on the road to Emmaus (Luke 24.19–27).

When you read these speeches you will find that there are always three elements:

The event of Jesus. . . The speaker recalls facts from the life of Jesus. Note which facts are selected, which are not mentioned, and which are stressed.

. . .interpreted by the scriptures. . . In many Bibles the quotations from the scriptures are either indented or printed in italics; you should be able to see at a glance how many there are in some speeches. Their aim is to place the life of Jesus in the context of God's plan, in order to make sense of it. Note, too, the names or titles given to Jesus; they usually come from scripture.

. . .challenges us. These speeches are never the simple explanation of a teacher who is imparting new knowledge to his pupils. The preacher is concerned for his proclamation and is aware that what he is saying forces his audience to make a choice.

If you are working in a group, here is an easy way to study the speeches. Draw eight vertical columns on a blackboard or a sheet of paper: one large enough for you to put down what you discover, in abbreviated form, and seven others, with enough space to note references from other speeches. Each member of the group should then take a speech and read it carefully; then the group should meet and one person should write down in the large column what they have discovered (for example, the miracles of Jesus or his teaching); the others will note down in the relevant column the verse from the speech they have read in which the subject is mentioned.

On p. 44 you will find how the diagram should look when it is completed. However, do not look at it now; it is much more instructive to make it for yourselves.

When you have done the work, think about the diagram. Which features of the life of Jesus do you find in all the speeches? Which do not appear in any of them? Which appear only in some? Try to sum up the kerygma, the proclamation of the faith of the first Christians. Compare it with what you wrote on your postage stamp.

Images to express Easter

Even a quick study of the speeches in Acts shows that Easter is at the heart of Christian faith.

But how did the disciples talk about this event, this mystery? We have become accustomed to using only the word resurrection in connection with it. Did they do the same? What complementary images did they use to present its different aspects? We can see from various summaries.

✶ Reread some verses from the speeches in Acts: 2.23–24, 32–33; 3.13, 15; 5.30–31; 10.40.

Here are some summaries taken from other books:

If you confess with your lips that Jesus is Lord and believe in your heart that God raised him from the dead, you will be saved (Rom. 10.9).

Christ died and lived again (Rom. 14.9).

God has highly exalted him and bestowed on him the name which is above every name (Phil. 2.9).

Christ, the firstborn from the dead (Col. 1.18).

Christ, put to death in the flesh but made alive in the spirit (I Peter 3.18).

Why do you seek the living among the dead? (Luke 24.5).

They had certain points of dispute with him about their own superstition and about one Jesus, who was dead, but whom Paul asserted to be alive (Acts 25.19).

What imagery is used? In fact our word resurrection translates two Greek words: to be raised up (from the dead, from the 'hole'), and to be woken up (from the sleep of death). They are just two images; there are many others.

The various images can be grouped together along two main lines. Some indicate above all that we rediscover the life lost in death; afterwards things are as they were before. Others say that there will be more, that things will be better than before. Try to sort these out.

Some of the imagery will certainly remind you of texts or figures from the Old Testament: which are they? How does that help you?

Note the figures who intervene.

Finally, you might like to go back to the imagery that you thought of spontaneously (see p. 33). Does it belong with the two main lines that I mentioned earlier? Or only one of them? If so, which?

Two images

Christians have felt that the whole of the mystery of Easter cannot be expressed in a single image, so they have used a great many. To simplify things, we can put these into two main groups.

Before and after, or a return to life

Those who die are thought of as falling into a great hole (Sheol, or the nether regions); or perhaps they fall asleep. The resurrection is the fact of raising them up or arousing them. After death they come back to the life that they had before. 'Lazarus, arise,' writes St John.

The advantage of this kind of imagery is clear: it has a context in history, it gives a clear indication of continuity: things are as they were before. Those who knew the person before can recognize him again.

The disadvantage is that it says nothing about the nature of the life which is rediscovered: one can just as well say Lazarus was raised (to die again!) as one can say that Jesus was raised.

Below and above, or an entry into glory

Since people instinctively locate God above, in heaven, the one who has died is said to have been brought near to God. He is exalted, glorified; he ascends into heaven. This imagery has certainly been sustained by reflection on the symbol of the Son of man, the symbol of those who remained faithful to God to the point of martyrdom. Daniel introduces this symbol by showing the Son of man brought on the clouds into the presence of God (Dan. 7, see *How to Read the Old Testament*, p. 91).

The advantage of this kind of imagery is that it states clearly that we are not just talking about a restoration to life as it was before; there is more to it than that. We may say that Lazarus was raised, but not that he was exalted or glorified.

The problem, if this image is used in isolation, is that one might imagine that some element of man (his spirit, his soul) ascends to heaven, and that it is not the whole man, body and spirit, that is glorified.

The risen Christ exalted

The disciples felt that they had to use both kinds of imagery: Jesus was risen, so the one who was now alive was the same being whom they had known earlier: his friends recognized him. But he was also exalted, glorified, he had ascended into heaven; so this was not just a matter of rediscovering life as it was before: Jesus was introduced to a new life, the life of God.

The Disciples Celebrate their Faith: Creed and Hymns

Every group wants to make itself known by proclaiming, in brief slogans, the essentials of its beliefs. The disciples proclaimed their faith: the kerygma.

At the same time, however, every group needs to remind itself of its basic principles whenever it meets, whether these may form a party political programme, club rules, or whatever. Similarly, when they met together, the disciples celebrated their faith. They expressed it in their creed, sang it in hymns, or meditated upon it in what they were taught.

A creed. I Cor. 15.1–11

We have the good fortune to possess one of these very ancient creeds; Paul quotes it in his letter to the Corinthians. Begin by reading the text.

Some things about this passage are worth noting. Note, first, a change of style: in the middle of a narrative account we come up against a number of short phrases (and scholars note that this is not Paul's usual style). Besides, Paul tells us explicitly that this is not his own work. He is not using his own words, but reciting someone else's. He indicates this by taking up terms used at that time by the rabbis: the disciple *receives* something from his teachers and then in turn *hands it on* to his own disciples.

Paul was almost certainly writing to the Corinthians round about Easter 57. He reminds them of what he told them when he founded their community, in 51. So twenty years or so after Easter, this creed had already been formulated.

He says that he received it himself. When? Was it perhaps from Ananias at the time of his baptism in Damascus, round about 36 (see Acts 9.10ff.)?

In Greek, the form of the verb indicates above all the aspect of particular actions: the present indicates something that lasts, the aorist (roughly speaking, our simple past tense) indicates what happened once at a given moment; the perfect (roughly speaking, our composite past tense) shows the present result of a past action: an event took place once, but its consequences are still felt. Now we may note that all the verbs in this creed are in the aorist except for one, 'He is risen': thus the resurrection is an event which took place once, in history, but has a lasting result. Christ is alive for ever.

♥ Read this creed again carefully.
Note which events happened at one time.

Try to distinguish between the events which belong in history (those which anyone can verify) and those which can be seen only by the eyes of faith. Is the phrase 'the third day' a piece of historical information or an affirmation of faith?

What imagery is used to express the mystery of Easter (see p. 35 again)?

Compare this creed with the creed we use today. What differences can you see?

The third day according to the scriptures

There is general agreement that the starting point of this phrase is to be found in Hosea 6.1–2. The Israelites, shattered by the prophet's preaching, improvised a penitential liturgy. Read this text. Two days, three days, in this context indicates in a little while.

However, by the time of Christ this phrase had taken on a theological significance. This is how the Targum (see *How to Read the Old Testament*, p. 81), interprets this verse from Hosea:

He will revive us on the day of consolations which must come; on the day when he makes the dead live again, he will raise us up and we shall live before him.

And a rabbinic commentary on Gen. 22.4 declares:

The third day, that is to say the day on which life is restored to the dead, as it is written in Hosea: on the third day he will raise us up and we shall live before him.

So in the time of Christ, when people talked about the third day according to the scriptures, they were not giving an indication of time (the day after tomorrow); they were making a theological statement. It denotes what we call the day of general resurrection at the end of time.

In talking of the resurrection on the third day according to the scriptures, the disciples were not giving a date (it is not known when the event took place; all the texts say is that on Sunday morning the women discovered that the tomb was empty); they were proclaiming their faith. The day of general resurrection (the third day) had already arrived with the resurrection of Jesus (Matt. 27.52–53 tells us so in strip cartoon fashion); our own resurrection lies behind us, and has already been realized in Jesus.

A hymn. Philippians 2.6–11

In the Letters, the Gospels or Revelation we can find hymns composed by the first communities. Paul reminds the Philippians of one when he invites them to practise humility by following the example of Christ.

Read this text in your Bible.

How is the Easter event expressed? Is the imagery of resurrection used? What kind of imagery *is* used? (The name given to Jesus is that of Lord.) So this mystery can be expressed otherwise than in the language of resurrection.

Who are the main characters and what is their role?

The interpretation by scripture was not made explicitly, but it is present in this hymn. In fact the hymn is based on a contrast. Jesus did not act like Adam, who wanted to snatch at equality with God (see Gen. 3.5): on the contrary, he acted like the servant in Isa. 53 (see *How to Read the Old Testament*, p. 67). Compare v. 7, he emptied himself, with Isa. 53.12; v. 9, God highly exalted him, with Isa. 52.13. How do these two texts allow us to locate the destiny of Jesus within God's plan? How, by virtue of these two texts, is our destiny bound up with that of Christ?

Meditation on a psalm. Ephesians 4.7–10

Paul wants to show that God gives to the church what it needs to fulfil its mission, namely, to construct the body of Christ: he makes a gift to believers of the various ministries: apostles, prophets, evangelists, catechists, those who build up the community. In this connection Paul bases his words on Ps. 68.19 as it was interpreted at the time (according to the Targum). First let us compare this verse in

The Hebrew Text	Tho Targum
Thou didst ascend the heights	*Thou didst raise up to heaven Moses, the prophet,*
leading captives into captivity	*leading captives into captivity (that is, thou didst teach the words of the Law);*
and receiving tribute from men,	*thou didst give them to the children of men,*
even from the rebellious	*and even to the rebellious if they turned to thee,*
in order to have a dwelling place,	*the rest of the holy presence of the Lord God.*
O Lord God.	

For the Targum it is no longer God who ascends to heaven to establish himself in his dwelling place; Moses ascends Sinai and there receives the Law, to give it to men.

Paul meditates on this psalm. In it, he no longer sees Moses but Jesus, the new Moses, who ascends to heaven after having come down to earth and even to hell. Thus the whole mystery of Easter is presented by this image of descent and glorification.

(We shall see that Luke uses the same psalm to interpret Pentecost. See p. 84.)

The Disciples Tell of their Faith: Narratives

We have listened to the disciples proclaiming their faith to non-believers (the kerygma) and celebrating it in their communities (the creed, hymns); the centre of this faith is always the fact that God has raised up, glorified, given power to this Jesus who was crucified.

They also expressed the same faith in another literary genre, that of narrative. Here they did not make their affirmations in brief formulas, but told stories and made people see. This literary genre corresponds to the needs of a community which had already been formed and which wanted to know more about the meaning of an event; it was a community that had also had liturgical experience. We shall come back to this, but the fact must be stressed very strongly as we begin our next readings. The narratives do not say more about the event itself than the brief statements of the kerygma; they simply say it differently and develop its meaning.

The four Gospels have handed down to us narratives of this kind. They can be classified into three groups, each meeting a need in the community:

The community celebrates its faith in the very place where the event took place: narratives about the empty tomb (Matthew, Mark, Luke, John).

It shows that the apostles' experience of the risen Jesus made them official witnesses: accounts of appearances to the eleven (Matthew, Luke, John).

It appeals to experience had in the liturgy or within the church: appearances to the disciples on the Emmaus road (Luke) or to Mary Magdalene (John).

We shall look quickly at these three kinds of narrative.

(a) Narratives of celebration by pilgrimage. The empty tomb

When believers make a pilgrimage to the Holy Land, they like to have a celebration at the very sites of the events which took place there: for example, at the Holy Sepulchre they recall the event, meditate and pray.

Scholars, on the basis of their study of the texts, have conjectured that the accounts of the empty tomb arose in this way: the first Christians made a pilgrimage to the tomb of Jesus, an empty tomb, and celebrated their faith there.

This gave rise to a first narrative which each evangelist took up in his own way to express his theology.

We shall just read Mark's account.

⭐ The empty tomb. Mark 16.1–8

Read this text. Note the indications of time, the places, the main characters, the actions (look back at the 'tool box' in *How to Read the Old Testament*, p. 14). Try to note these different points in two columns, putting conflicting items opposite each other.

What transformation has taken place between the beginning and the end of the account?

The indications of time suggest a transition from darkness to light (morning, sun, light), from old to new, from sacred to religious, Jewish time (the sabbath – and not Saturday – was over) to cosmic, secular time (the first day of the week).

In terms of place, the closed tomb, guarding its dead, is contrasted with a tomb open on life; here Jerusalem, for Mark the symbol of those who are shut up in their own ideas and kill those who differ from them, is contrasted with the Galilee of the Gentiles, gateway to the world.

Of the main characters, one is absent: Jesus. The young man suggests the new way in which Jesus is now present: he is in white (opposed to the darkness of the tomb), seated on the right, like the glorified Christ, and it is he who transforms the women's quest. They come to the tomb to anoint the body of Jesus, that is to say, to preserve a corpse, but he is no longer there. They come to touch a dead body, but they receive a message. They and the apostles 'will see' the risen Lord when they have proclaimed him as far as Galilee, that is, to the end of the world and the end of history (see p. 62).

(b) Stories of appearances to create official witnesses

Matthew, Luke and John end their Gospels with the accounts of one or more appearances of Christ. In this section we shall look at the appearances to the eleven apostles. We shall keep for the next section appearances to other disciples, which are of a different kind.

The Gospel of Mark probably ended with the flight of the women from the tomb; 16.9–20, which was added afterwards, is simply a summary of Matthew and Luke (look at the way in which it is presented in your Bible).

The stories of the appearances to the eleven seek to show that Jesus himself made them his witnesses. We are not going to read all the stories nor study them in depth (though we shall come back to some of them later). What we need to do here is to check that these stories take up, in their imagery, the affirmation made in the kerygma (look again at p. 19 on 'making ideas into narratives').

Adoration of the glorified Christ. Matt. 28.16–20

Begin by reading this text. Remember the two groups of imagery used to present the Easter event: which is taken up here?

Let's look at the text again. The eleven leave, as in a procession, for the mountain where Jesus, the new Moses, had given them his new law (Matt. 5.1). They prostrate themselves before him: this is the word which in the Greek Orthodox liturgy still denotes the gesture of adoration. 'Come to them' is surprising, since the disciples are lying at his feet. However, in the Bible, He who Comes is sometimes a divine title. By quoting the phrase from Daniel 7 (see *How to Read the Old Testament*, p. 91), Jesus presents himself as the Son of Man who comes into the presence of God on the clouds of heaven. So he is already exalted and glorified. Because of this he can send his disciples on their mission into the world.

So this text takes up in narrative form one of the ways in which Christians tried to present Easter in the kerygma: here is the pattern of exaltation, from below upwards. The only feature belonging to the other pattern (resurrection) is the mention of doubt (v. 17); however, it does not fit very well and could have been added afterwards.

Coin of Agrippa II. On one side, Vespasian crowned; on the other, a goddess carrying an ear of corn and a cornucopia.

The recognition of the risen Lord. Luke 24.36–53

Read vv. 36–43: on what pattern is this account constructed? Then vv. 50–53: what is the pattern here?

It is clear that Luke is using the imagery of resurrection. Jesus takes the initiative in making himself visible. There might be doubts that this is a collective illusion, so Jesus shows that he is as he was before: he has a body and he can eat. All this could be said of Lazarus (except, of course, that Jesus is present in the midst of them without having entered).

Luke then develops one of his favourite themes: Jesus can only be known truly through the interpretation of the scriptures, and the scriptures cannot be understood unless the Risen Lord reads them to us himself (vv. 44–49).

Then Luke describes the ascension (on the evening of Easter Day!); this is a way of saying in narrative form that Jesus is exalted, glorified. When we study Luke-Acts we shall see that Luke has another account of the ascension, which is put at least forty days after Easter. The fact that the same author can give two accounts of the same event, placing them at two different points, warns us that he is not concerned with chronology and history, but with theology.

The two sides of a coin

A coin has two sides, but it is difficult to see both of them at once; to do that, you have to cut the coin laterally in half. Similarly, one cannot see two profiles of a face at once: in some of his pictures Picasso projected a human face so that one could see every aspect simultaneously.

This is rather what Luke has done. He is well aware that there are two main ways of expressing Easter: to say that Jesus is risen or to say that he is exalted. These are the two inseparable sides of the same mystery. Because both seemed to him to be essential, he chose to put them side by side: Jesus is risen – he ascended into heaven. Perhaps we have been too quick to suppose that these were two successive events in history (as if one were to believe that there were two coins) when in fact it is a matter of two aspects of the same mystery.

(c) Christian experience. Appearances to disciples

The stories of the appearing of Jesus to Mary Magdalene in John and to the disciples on the Emmaus road in Luke are of a special kind. They do not set out to show that Jesus is risen or exalted or that he provided official witnesses. They simply seek to help us share in the joy of the disciples' rediscovery of their Lord and their renewal of a loving relationship with him; they are meant to teach us that we today can have the same experience.

We are simply going to read the story of the Emmaus road (Luke 24.13–35) and to compare it with another of Luke's accounts, the baptism of an Ethiopian official (Acts 8.26–40). To make things easier you will find the translation of these two texts side by side on the next page.

If you have time, begin by studying it with the help of your 'tool box'; you will see that the questions under the heading 'the text' work very well and help you to understand the texts.

Luke is trying to reply to a question: How do we meet the Lord Jesus today? He shows the role of three essential elements: knowledge of the earthly life of Jesus – scripture – sacraments. Read the texts and look for these three elements and the role they play.

Cleopas and his companion are very familiar with the life of Jesus: they are talking about it to each other (literally, they are engaged in a homily), they recall it, and their speech is as complete and precise as the speeches of Peter. However, for them things no longer make sense. If the life of Jesus is to make sense, it must be interpreted by the scriptures (what we call the Old Testament); however, this interpretation can be made only by the risen Jesus. After that he can be recognized in the sacrament. And the fact that Jesus disappeared the very moment that they recognized him warns us that from now on it is in the eucharist that we encounter the living Christ. By using a past continuous tense in v. 30 instead of the simple past, Luke probably wants to suggest that Jesus continues to give bread all through the history of the church.

The Ethiopian official is in a different situation. A convert to Judaism (a proselyte), he knew the scriptures, but they did not make sense to him. For them to be made comprehensible they had to be illuminated by the life of Jesus. And here again, only the risen Lord could bring this about, through his witnesses. In fact it is clear that Luke presents Philip as he presents Jesus: each of them appears and disappears mysteriously, and interprets the scriptures (compare Luke 24.27 and Acts 8.35). From now on in the church it is no longer Jesus himself who acts; or rather, he still acts but does so through the medium of his ministers to the degree that they are inspired by the Spirit (Acts 8.26, 29, 39). And the official, too, has the experience of a personal encounter with Jesus in the sacrament of baptism. (I have put v. 37 in brackets because it is not in all the manuscripts; this is probably a formula from the baptismal liturgy which crept into the text afterwards.)

As you read the text, note too the play on words which cannot be reproduced in English: three verbs with the same root are intertwined (you can identify them by the superior figures which mark them): *ginoskein*[1], to know/understand, *epiginoskein*[2], to recognize, and *anaginoskein*[3], to read.

Above all, look at the change in the situation between the beginning and the end. At the beginning, the eyes of the two disciples are kept from recognizing him (v. 16): so it is not that Jesus has changed or disguised himself as a beggar; his disciples have changed. They are so wrapped up in their disappointed hope that they have made themselves incapable of recognizing that this hope has been realized in Jesus, though in a different way from their expectations. Similarly, in the Gospel of John, Mary Magdalene thinks in such a way of Jesus – the Jesus of whom she dreams – that she prevents herself from recognizing him when he introduces himself to her. At the breaking of the bread their eyes were opened: this change of heart which allows them to recognize their Risen Lord does not come from man; their eyes are opened as Jesus opens up the scriptures to them.

When Peter goes to the tomb (v. 24), he does not see Jesus; however, at the end it is said that Jesus has made himself visible to Peter (v. 33). Similarly, the disciples do not recognize Jesus on the road: they recognize him in the breaking of bread (v. 31) and they declare that he made himself known to them (v. 35). Jesus always takes the initiative.

Mosaic from Ostia (Italy)

Luke 24.13–35 The disciples on the Emmaus Road

¹³That very day two of them were going to a village named Emmaus, about seven miles from Jerusalem, ¹⁴and talking with each other about all these things that had happened. ¹⁵While they were talking and discussing together, Jesus himself drew near and went with them. ¹⁶But their eyes were kept from recognizing² him.

¹⁷And he said to them, 'What is this conversation which you are holding with each other as you walk?' And they stood still, looking sad. ¹⁸Then one of them, named Cleopas, answered him, 'Are you the only visitor to Jerusalem who does not know¹ the things that have happened here in these days?' ¹⁹And he said to them, 'What things?' And they said to him, 'Concerning Jesus of Nazareth, who was a prophet mighty in deed and word before God and all the people, ²⁰and how our chief priests and rulers delivered him up to be condemned to death, and crucified him. ²¹But we had hoped that he was the one to redeem Israel. Yes, and besides all this, it is now the third day since this happened. ²²Moreover, some women of our company amazed us. They were at the tomb early in the morning ²³and did not find his body; and they came back saying that they had even seen a vision of angels, who said that he was alive. ²⁴Some of those who were with us went to the tomb, and found it just as the woman had said; but him they did not see.'

²⁵And he said to them, 'O foolish men, and slow of heart to believe all that the prophets have spoken! ²⁶Was it not necessary that the Christ should suffer these things and enter into his glory?' ²⁷And beginning with Moses and all the prophets, he interpreted to them in all the scriptures the things concerning himself.

²⁸So they drew near to the village to which they were going. He appeared to be going further, ²⁹but they constrained him, saying, 'Stay with us, for it is toward evening and the day is now far spent.' So he went in to stay with them. ⁰⁰When he was at table with them, he took the bread and blessed, and broke it, and gave it to them. ⁴¹And their eyes were opened and they recognized² him; and he vanished out of their sight. ³²They said to each other, 'Did not our hearts burn within us while he talked to us on the road, while he opened to us the scriptures?' ³³And they rose that same hour and returned to Jerusalem; and they found the eleven gathered together and those who were with them, ³⁴who said, 'The Lord has risen indeed, and has appeared (made himself visible) to Simon.' ³⁵Then they told what had happened on the road, and how he was known to them in the breaking of the bread.

Acts 8.26–40 The Ethiopian official

²⁶But an angel of the Lord said to Philip, 'Rise and go toward the south, to the road that goes down from Jerusalem to Gaza.' This is a desert road. ²⁷And he rose and went.

And behold, an Ethiopian, a eunuch, a minister of Candace the queen of the Ethiopians, in charge of all her treasure, had come to Jerusalem to worship ²⁸and was returning; seated in his chariot, he was reading³ the prophet Isaiah. ²⁹And the Spirit said to Philip, 'Go up and join this chariot.' ³⁰So Philip ran up to him, and heard him reading³ Isaiah the prophet, and asked, 'Do you understand¹ what you are reading³?' ³¹And he said, 'How can I, unless someone guides me?' And he invited Philip to come up and sit with him. ³²Now the passage of the scripture which he was reading³ was this:

As a sheep led to the slaughter
or a lamb before its shearer is dumb,
so he opens not his mouth.
³³In his humiliation justice was denied him.
Who can describe his generation?
For his life is taken up from the earth.

³⁴And the eunuch said to Philip, 'About whom, pray, does the prophet say this, about himself or about someone else?' ³⁵Then Philip opened his mouth, and beginning with this scripture he told him the good news of Jesus.

³⁶And as they went along the road they came to some water, and the eunuch said, 'See, here is water! What is to prevent my being baptized?' [³⁷And Philip said, 'If you believe with all your heart, you may.' And he replied, 'I believe that Jesus Christ is the Son of God.'] ³⁸And he commanded the chariot to stop, and they both went down into the water, Philip and the eunuch, and he baptized him. ³⁹And when they came up out of the water, the Spirit of the Lord caught up Philip; and the eunuch saw him no more, and went on his way rejoicing. ⁴⁰But Philip was found at Azotus, and passing on he preached the gospel to all the towns till he came to Caesarea.

And Now. . .?

We began this stage with two main aims in view: to check that the resurrection of Christ is the centre of Christian faith and to discover more fully how the writings of the New Testament took shape.

However, it is probable that on the way another focal point has emerged: how did the resurrection of Christ take place? How will ours take place? Obviously these are important questions, but they go beyond the scope of this course; all I can do is to give you some indications of where you may find help, by referring you to other books (see p. 123).

★ It would be a good thing if, either by yourself, or better in a group, you tried to sum things up.

How did the first Christians talk about Easter? Why is it important that they used several different images?

How is this faith expressed in the various literary genres: proclamation to non-believers, celebration, stories? Do the stories in fact say more about the mystery than the kerygma, or not?

★ I also suggested that you might try a little exercise (p. 33). It's worth going back to that now.

We use imagery to talk about the resurrection. What? Does it above all (or exclusively) express the resurrection aspect, a return to life as it was before? Does it also express the extra element which the imagery of exaltation and glorification seeks to evoke?

We have favourite texts from scripture, and that is fine. But we have seen that each text gives us only one aspect of the event. What aspect is expressed by our favourite texts? Should we consider adding to them?

You may have been surprised by the question 'What is important to you in life?' But if belief in the resurrection is basic, it cannot be disconnected with what is important for us. Go back to your answers: what connection does your faith in the resurrection have with them?

Some strong points

First, let's bring together some firm conclusions that have emerged in the course of our work.

No one ever says that they saw Jesus in process of being raised (unlike a great many paintings which, from this perspective, are dangerous). The disciples say that they saw the risen Jesus. They stressed one aspect or another depending on the circumstances, and sometimes two different ones at the same time. They recognized Jesus, so he was the person they had known before his death; however, this was not just a return to life but an entry into definitive life: he is exalted, glorified, he has ascended to heaven, is seated at the right hand of God, made Lord.

This event can only be perceived in faith. We do not see the Risen Lord when we want to, as we might see a friend today; he makes himself visible when he wants, where he wants and to whom he wants. So the witnesses had a very real experience (which they expressed, for example, by saying that Jesus was capable of eating, see Luke 24), even if they were the only ones to do so. Thus Paul's companions saw that something had happened to him, but they did not see the Christ. The use of this expression 'made himself visible' may point to an experience which was real but completely inward.

Our faith rests finally on the affirmation that God works in us. The Gospel of Mark did not have any account of an appearance of Jesus. The young man (i.e. God) asserts that Jesus is risen: that is to be enough to bring about faith.

The scriptures (for us, the Old Testament) are basic to any belief in and understanding of this mystery. We have seen this in connection with the stories of the Emmaus road and the Ethiopian official; we could have read it also in the episode where John shows Peter and the other disciples coming to the tomb (John 20.3–9): the other disciple also went in, and he saw and believed; for as yet they did not know the scripture, that he must rise from the dead (vv. 8f.); if they had understood the scripture,

42

they would not in fact have needed to see the empty tomb (with their physical eyes) in order to believe; they would have believed and seen the Risen Lord (with the eyes of faith: John 20.29).

The scriptures make sense of the earthly life of Jesus, and this life makes sense of the scriptures.

However, only the Risen Lord, either by himself (Luke 24.27, 45) or through his disciples (Acts 8.35), can make sense of the scriptures.

The episodes of the Emmaus road and Ethiopian official, like many others, show us that the believer of 82 or 1982 is not at a disadvantage in comparison to the first disciples: they too can have and must have the same experience of meeting the Risen Lord, since he is always also present in reality in the unknown brother whom one meets on the way, and in the sacraments, above all the eucharist.

That may present us with a question: is the experience of the Christian today fundamentally different from that of Thomas and the other apostles? Obviously, this question can be answered in different ways. Here is one of them. This experience is basically the same: if a non-believer, utterly ignorant of Christianity, went into a place where Christians were worshipping, he would see from their attitude that something was happening; if he asked them what it was, they would reply, 'The Lord Jesus is present among us, he invites us to his table, we eat with him, we listen to him and speak to him. . .' and this reply is remarkably like the accounts in the Gospels.

However, there is one difference: in these accounts it is said that the disciples recognize Jesus. They had known him in his earthly life, and so they could verify that their experience of the Risen Lord now corresponded to the experience of the earthly Jesus which they had had before. And for us that is impossible. To verify the authenticity of our experience we have to compare it with that of the apostles. Certainly the experience itself is not fundamentally different, but the reference to the past which authenticates it is different: for the apostles it was the life of Jesus; for us it is the experience of the apostles.

An observation

We have seen that the first Christians used two main kinds of imagery to evoke the mystery of Easter: that of resurrection and that of exaltation. We have seen the advantages and disadvantages of each type when it is taken by itself (see p. 35).

We might ask — though this is only a hypothesis — whether some of our difficulties do not derive from the fact that we have separated these two types of imagery.

In the case of Jesus, we have virtually limited ourselves to the language of resurrection. And that has led us to ask questions about how it took place: what kind of body did he have? could he eat? The language of exaltation should remind us that while indeed he is a real man, and therefore has a body, he is exalted, and therefore different. Now, to take up a phrase of Paul's, he has a spiritual body.

For ourselves, often without being aware of it, we keep only the imagery of exaltation: when we die, our bodies will turn to dust but some part of us, our soul, will go up to heaven; so we see no need to get our bodies back again. The language of resurrection should remind us that we can exist only as corporeal beings.

A certainty

It is useless and impossible to imagine how the resurrection took place. The only certainty the believer can have is to hold on to two things: Jesus is risen and glorified and we shall be with him. When we read Paul as the next stage, we shall be able to look at the words which he used or invented with the help of the preposition *with*: suffer with, die with, rise with, be glorified with, live with. . . We shall be for ever with him.

The event of Jesus. . .	Acts 2.14–41 Pentecost	3.12–26 Lame man	4.9–12 Before	5.29–32 Sanhedrin	10.34–43 Cornelius	13.16–41 Paul	Luke 24.19–27	Other texts from Luke
Earthly ministry								
preaching of John the Baptist						24–25		Luke 3.15–16
Jesus of Nazareth	22		10		38		19	
his baptism by John					37–38			*He stirs up the people, teaching*
teaching					(36)		19	*throughout all Judaea, from Galilee*
miracles	22				38			*even to this place, Luke 23.5*
Death								
condemned by Jewish leaders	23, 36	13,15,17	10	30	39	27	20	Luke 23.2, 4, 5, 20, 22, 23, 25, 51; Acts 7.52
executed by Gentiles	23, 36	13, 14				28		
through God's plan	23, 36	18	28			27	25–27	Luke 18.31 *Everything . . . will be accomplished*
innocent		13				28		Luke 23.4, 14, 15, 32
buried						29		
Easter								
God raised him up	24, 32					33		
God raised him		15	10	30	40	30, 37	34	
We are witnesses	32	15		32	39, 41	31	48	Acts 1.8–22; Luke 24.48; Acts 1.3–4
exalted to God's right hand	33	13.21		31				Luke 24.51; Acts 1.9–11
he gives the Spirit	33							

. . .interpreted by the scriptures. . .

Titles

Before: Child, servant		13.26	27, 30					
Holy, righteous	(27)	14						
After: Lord of life, saviour		15		31				
judge of living and dead								
Before and after: Lord	36				36			
Christ	31, 36	18, 20						

Scripture. In general

Scripture announces								
his day		24			(43)	(27–40)		
his suffering		18					26–27, 46	
his last coming	20	20						
The Jews chief heirs	39	25				26–33		**Quotations in other texts**
through them, Gentile salvation	39	25						

Particular texts

Ps. 16.10 *Your holy one to see corruption*	25–31					35–37		
Ps. 2.7 *You are my son*	30					33, 20		Acts 9.20; Heb. 1.5; 5.5; Mark 1.11; Luke 3.22
Ps. 110.1 *Sit at my right hand*	34							Matt. 12.36; Heb. 1.13; Mark 14.62; Acts 7.55; Rom. 8.34; Eph. 1.20; Col. 3.1; I Peter 3.22; Heb. 1.3; 8.1; 10.12; 12.2
Ps. 118.22 *Stone rejected/exalted*			11	31				Mark 12.10; I Peter 2.7
Isa. 55.3 *Realities promised to David*						34		
Joel 3 *Gift of Spirit*	17, 21, 39							
Deut. 18 *Prophet like Moses*		22						Acts 7.37; John 6.14
Hag. 1.5						41		

. . .challenges us

salvation by faith					43	38		
salvation only in name of Jesus	(21, 39)		12		43			
be converted	38	19		31				
baptism for sin	38	19, 26		31	43	38		
gift of the Spirit	38							

Παυλος αποστολος χρυ ιηυ δια θελημματος
θυ και τειμοθεος ο αδελφος τοις εν Κολασσαις
αγιοις και πιστοις αδελφοις εν χρω χαρις υμιν
και ειρηνη απο θυ πατρος ημων Ευχαριστουμεν

The beginning of the Letter to the Colossians. A papyrus from about 230.

3 Paul and his Letters

Paul has the reputation of being a difficult author. That's true. But he is so engaging! All through his letters he reveals himself for what he is, a saint with countless failings. He talks about himself all the time; he is emotional, and needs to have faithful friends by him. When he was a Jew he was an integralist; now that he has become a Christian he remains in character and his colleagues and congregations learn this to their cost: Peter ('I opposed him to his face because he stood condemned', Gal. 2.11); Barnabas, who wanted to take his young cousin John Mark on the mission, against Paul's wishes ('There arose a sharp contention, so that they separated from each other,' writes Luke in Acts 15.39); the Corinthians whom Paul proposes to visit again, so as to thrash them into behaving themselves (I Cor. 4.21; see 11.16). At the same time he is someone who is utterly caught up in his mission; all that counts for him is love for his Lord and the service of his communities, his dear children for whom he feels as emotionally and as physically as a mother.

Many passages in his letters seem obscure to us (they already did so to the author of II Peter 3.16!). We shall not spend time on them here; you can go back to them later. Above all we shall try to discover the main outlines of his theology and read some of those marvellous passages in which we discover Christian faith in the first flush of youth, when we can see, also through Paul, what the grace of God can achieve in the heart of man.

Paul's life can be divided into two almost equal parts: for thirty years he was a Pharisee (he was perhaps born about AD 5 and had his experience on the Damascus road about 36); then for thirty years, as a Christian (he died as a martyr in Rome, probably in AD 67), he was the tireless missionary who founded communities throughout the Mediterranean basin and wrote to his Christians.

Paul the Pharisee

Born in Tarsus, the capital of Cilicia in Asia Minor, a university city with perhaps more than 300,000 inhabitants, Paul was at the crossroads of two civilizations.

As a Jew, a Pharisee, he studied in Jerusalem under one of the greatest rabbis of the time, Gamaliel (see Acts 22.3; 5.37). He was back in Tarsus during the time of Jesus' activity, of which he seems to have been unaware. Perhaps in his parents' home, he had learned to weave the rough material, made of goats' hair, which in French, *cilice*, takes its name from the province of Cilicia. He was almost certainly a rabbi, and therefore married.

At the same time, however, he received from his parents the status of Roman citizen, and on occasion he would use his privileges with pride (Acts 22.25–28). He probably went to the university, and used its learned approach to literature; at times he also quotes poetry (Acts 17.28). His double name, Saul(Jewish)/Paul(Greek) indicates that he belonged to two civilizations.

As a sincere Pharisee, Paul had only one passion: to serve God by scrupulous observance of the Law. He could even say that the Law was his life. When he returned to Jerusalem in about 36, he was appalled at the preaching of Peter and others. Because he was a theologian, he probably saw better than Peter that the message of the apostles ran the risk of overturning Judaism: they put this Jesus, rightly condemned by the authorities as a blasphemer, on the same level as God. An intransigent Pharisee when it came to the purity of faith, Paul decided to fight against this new sect. He approved the death of Stephen and left for Damascus to pursue disciples of Stephen who had taken refuge there.

A coin from Tarsus

On the Damascus road

The glorified Lord who appeared to Paul was the one who had died an accursed death on the cross: the whole of Paul's theology is contained in this reversal. Jesus had been condemned by the Law of whom the religious authorities were the guardians; he was accursed of God, who had done nothing to deliver him, as it is written: 'Cursed (by God) is the man who is hanged on the tree' (Deut. 21.23; cf. Gal. 3.13). Now God had glorified this 'accursed' man! That meant that God had taken his side. So the Law which had condemned him was itself condemned by God. The Law had come to an end. For Paul, his very life was falling apart. . . So we can understand how he remained in Damascus for three days, blind, prostrate, trying to make sense of things. And in that tormenting, vast abyss, Jesus took his place. From that time on Paul was to say, 'My life is Christ.'

All his theology can be found here in embryo, like an intuition which it took him all his life to explore. I shall try to bring out some of its main features here.

Justification by faith. As a Pharisee, Paul believed himself to be justified by his faithful observance of the Law; he thought that everything he did, his efforts, his 'works', as he called them, made him righteous before God. Now he discovered that only Christ could make him righteous. So it was not a matter of achieving his salvation but of receiving it freely, from God's hands, in faith. By believing in God, by holding fast to Christ with all one's being, by having complete confidence in him, one was saved, made righteous. Of course that did not mean that it was enough to believe and then to act in any old way. Those who believe, those who love, try to live accordingly; however, what they then do is not done in order to compel the love of another; it is because they know that they are loved.

The grace of God became a key word in Paul's theology. He discovered that he was loved by God, freely and mercifully. God does not love us because we are good, but in order that we may become good. The source of Paul's joy and security and that of the believer is that they do not rely on what they do or what they are (which can often be demoralizing), but on the love of God, who is faithful.

Jesus Christ crucified. The accursed man hanging on the cross is glorified. Paul tries to understand what this means. If God glorifies him, it is because this death forms part of his plan. So Paul has to reread the scriptures. In particular, the Servant Songs in Second Isaiah give him an answer (see *How to Read the Old Testament*, p. 67). Jesus has not been condemned because of his own sins; 'he was wounded for our transgressions, he was bruised for our iniquities, and with his stripes we are healed' (Isa. 53.4–5). From now on, the cross, always illuminated by the resurrection, will be at the heart of Paul's theology.

It is there, at the feet of the crucified Jesus, that he discovers himself to be a sinner. However, he is a pardoned sinner. Brooding on his sins can only lead to sterile remorse; we see our sins on the faces of others, in the evil that we have done to them. Paul sees this in the tortured figure on the cross. What he sees there above all, however, is forgiveness. From now on, becoming aware of our sin is thanksgiving to God who purifies us from it through Jesus Christ.

The church as the body of Christ. Why are you persecuting me? asks Jesus of the man who is persecuting the Christians. Paul can see the intimate union between Jesus and his disciples: they make up a single body, the church. From now on, this is to be the foundation for Paul's morality: through faith and baptism the Christian puts on Christ, becomes his body, and lives accordingly.

Apostle of Jesus Christ. 'We cannot refrain from speaking,' said the apostles. When someone finds that they are loved with such a love, and it becomes the very meaning of their life, they must want this fact to be known to other people. For Paul, to preach Jesus Christ became a vital necessity (I Cor. 9.16), and to proclaim him to all men, Jews and non-Jews, was a labour of love.

Entry into a tradition. Paul had all the gifts for becoming the leader of a sect: he was intelligent, passionate, chosen directly by God. Yet he was baptized at the hands of Ananias, who does not seem to have been outstanding either for his knowledge or for his courage (Acts 9.13). His call at Damascus, exceptional though it may have been, brought him, humbly, into the tradition of the church. And it was at the moment when he received baptism into this church that his eyes were opened.

It would be wrong to believe that on the Damascus road Paul received a ready-made theology which henceforward he had only to draw on. The Lord had 'made him his own' (Phil. 3.12) or, to take up the imagery I developed earlier (p. 12), had made an impression on him. For this image of the Risen Christ to be revealed fully to Paul, however, he needed the experience of everyday life in contact with different communities, whose questions would force him to deepen his knowledge of Christ. We shall discover that this took place in four main stages. Before we go through them, let's read his letter to the Philippians, in which he opens his heart to us.

Letter to the Philippians

Paul's letters are usually occasional writings; that is, he is replying to questions from a community or dealing with certain doctrinal or moral lapses. His letter to the Philippians, which is perhaps composite, consisting of three different letters, is different. It seems to have been written simply because Paul is very fond of his Philippians, the only church from which he was willing to receive financial help: he had enough confidence in their disinterested love to know that he would not be tied by this help. In the letter, he opens his heart to them, and tells them of his joy and his sufferings (he was in a Roman prison and was feeling sick and discouraged); he shows them his passionate love for Jesus and the meaning which Jesus has given to his life. He is probably writing from Ephesus round about 57.

Philippians 3

You should begin with this chapter.

Paul is the target for attacks from Jews or rather, from Judaizing Christians, that is, Christians who are reverting to Jewish practices in the belief that there they can find security before God (3.1–3; 18–19). For the difficult expressions, see the notes in your Bible or a commentary.

Paul has reason to be confident in himself (3.4–6); how does he see this (3.7–13)? How could we put verse 9 into contemporary language?

Note the significance of both the Christian's passivity (Christ does all things) and his activity (what he must do): how are these two aspects expressed?

Note, too, the expressions which indicate unity with Christ. What does faith mean to Paul?

The letter as a whole

This letter does not present any great difficulties. A good way of studying it would be to read the text straight through, underlining in different colours the following words (or equivalent expressions): Jesus (note the prepositions associated with his name: for, with, in), gospel – joy – suffering.

This letter glows with a feeling of tenderness towards the Lord Jesus who has made Paul his own (3.12), and whom on this one occasion he calls Jesus my Saviour (3.8). The primitive hymn which we have already read (p. 37) sums up the whole mystery of Jesus.

Christian life is the work of God (1.6; 2.13) and it is a life in Christ. This knowledge (3.8) is an indissoluble communion with the suffering and death of Christ (note the expressions which show this for Paul, for Epaphroditus and for the Christians) and his risen life. The Christian life is the work of Christ; Christ is the one who does everything in the believer. Our works are to no effect (3.4ff.).

However, this Christian life should be shown outwardly in actions: prayer (4.6), the glorification of God in our body (1.20; 3.21), unity between Christians (2.1–4), and by a kind of state that can be summed up in the word joy (note the causes of this joy).

Finally, the joy of the Christian consists in proclaiming the gospel, in words but also in his life, and by putting himself at the service of others. For communion with Jesus creates communion among brothers and sisters: note Paul's passionate love for his fellow Christians.

Four stages

We can divide Paul's letters into four groups, which mark so many stages in his thought.

I and II Thessalonians (51)
Paul takes up the main themes of the kerygma; he lives in the hope of the imminent coming of Christ.

I and II Corinthians, Galatians, Philippians, Romans (56–58)
There is one central question here: how can we become righteous and be saved? We are not justified by what we do (works, observing the law) but by faith in Christ. Paul sees the role of Christ above all in his church.

Colossians, Ephesians, Philemon (61–63)
Because he wrote these letters from prison in Rome, they are often called the Captivity Epistles, or Paul's Letters from Prison. Here Paul discovers the place of Christ in history and in the universe.

Titus, I and II Timothy
These Pastoral Letters were written either by Paul before 67 or by a disciple who took up his spiritual legacy after his death. They have one concern: to organize the churches and to keep pure the deposit of faith.

I and II Thessalonians

These letters, which were sent from Corinth in 50–51, are the earliest writings in the New Testament. They introduce us to a very young church founded in a Gentile setting, a minuscule community in a vast city of perhaps 300,000 inhabitants. In it we discover enthusiasm and a brand-new faith, a somewhat disordered hope, and passionate love, all aroused by the preaching of Jesus Christ.

Here Paul touches on the question of eschatology, or reflection on the end of time. He still thinks that the definitive coming of Christ is very near. Some Thessalonians therefore ask what good it is to go on working. Like other Christians, Paul takes time to accept that the delay before this coming – the time of the church – may be a long one (it is still going on!). It is worth singling out some points from these texts, which are sometimes difficult (see the notes in your Bible). Hope does not make the believer immobile: he has to live as though he had eternity before him, while being aware that the Lord is near. It is no use asking how the end will come: it is enough to know that after our death we shall be for ever with the Lord (I Thess. 4.17). To evoke the coming of Christ Paul draws on imagery which will have been well known to the Thessalonians: the *parousia* (a Greek word meaning entrance) of the emperor as he makes a triumphant entry into his city.

In these letters we also find some first preliminary reflections on the ministry of the apostle. This consists essentially in preaching the word. It calls for assurance and faithfulness; these can be recognized from two signs, authenticity and disinterestedness. Paul takes up these two themes at length in II Corinthians.

♥ The Christian life

We could spend some time on the way in which Paul presents the Christian life. It consists in becoming involved in the plan which God had formed from eternity and which he realized in Jesus Christ: in Jesus we are sanctified by the Spirit in order to form the church.

Here are some points that you might study.

God has a loving purpose. Note the terms which express this calling (Greek *klesis*), this choice or election. What kind of God is involved in this call?

God puts his plan into practice through Jesus Christ. Men are challenged, invited to become involved in it, when the word of God is proclaimed to them. Note the expressions which indicate the dynamism, the power of this word which acts in the believer. What is the content of this word? Compare it with the kerygma. The proclamation of this word compels those who hear it to make a choice: they either reject it (in which case, what is the consequence?), or they accept it.

Acceptance of the word is faith, hope and love. These three virtues have already been brought together: in what way are they qualified (verbs and adjectives)?

Faith is acceptance of the Word (I Thess. 2.13; II Thess. 2.13). What role is played by the Spirit? And by man? Try to describe this faith. It is often accompanied by verbs indicating a journey: it is not a question of 'having' faith, but of making the journey, of progressing in faith. And morality, Christian action, is a consequence of this.

Hope is expectation: of what? Note its two characteristics: patience (constancy) and vigilance. How does it fare when faced with the sleep of death?

Christian life is love or life in Christ. Note the expressions which indicate this union with Christ – whether present or future.

It is the Spirit which consecrates and sanctifies. Note the passages in which the Spirit is mentioned. What is his role?

The church (Greek *ek-klesia*) is the community of those who have responded to the call (*klesis*). It is not a group of like-minded people, but a group of people who are chosen by God and who respond to his call. How is that expressed? What consequences might it have for our communities today?

All this is the work of the grace of God and calls forth thanksgiving from the believer. How is that expressed? How is prayer presented?

Thus Christian life is a personal relationship with each of the persons of the Trinity: what is the relationship of each person with the believer, and vice versa?

The Great Letters: Corinthians, Galatians, Romans

Paul spent three years in Ephesus in the period between 53 and 58; from there he wrote several letters to the Corinthians, the Galatians and almost certainly to the Philippians. From Corinth, where he spent the winter of 57–58, he wrote to the Romans.

One question haunted him at the time. What does it mean to say that we are 'saved by Jesus Christ'? He gained a deeper understanding of the role of Christ in the history of salvation, within the community of believers where he is present through the word, the sacraments, and life lived sacrificially.

Christ in the history of salvation

As a Jew, Paul thought that he could find salvation by observing the Law. Now although the Law was holy, since it had been given by God, it had been condemned in Jesus Christ. In order to try to understand what this meant, Paul reread the history of salvation in his own way.

Well before Moses, God had made a unilateral covenant with Abraham: he was the only one to make promises, without imposing any conditions on mankind (read Gen. 15; see *How to Read the Old Testament*, p. 60). If God is righteous, that is to say, faithful, he must give happiness to Abraham and his descendants no matter how they may behave.

Now the people behaved badly. At that time God gave them the Law of Sinai, a bilateral covenant: he committed himself to bringing happiness to his people on condition that they obeyed his commandments (read Ex. 19–20; see *How to Read the Old Testament*, pp. 51, 60). The Law was given by God because the people had sinned. It was a kind of strait-jacket: since the people had proved incapable of obeying God in love, they had to obey him because of the Law. God acts like a father with his son; there is no contract between them, and the father has trust in his son, who obeys him in love. However, if this love should cease, the father will discipline his son with an iron hand, will impose rules on him until he arrives at a better frame of mind. So the Law was given to keep people in the love of God. It is holy, because it comes from God. However, in fact it increases sin because it tells us what we must do without giving us the strength to perform it, to such a degree that with the Law, people are fully aware of their own sinning. So God finds himself in a dilemma: to be righteous and faithful to his covenant with Abraham, he must bless his people; to be righteous according to the covenant made on Sinai, he must abandon the people to the death which they deserve because of their conduct.

God then had this loving idea. Since death stands at the end of the road marked by the Law, he himself will undergo this death in the person of his son; the death of Christ is also that of all sinners in him; thus God is faithful to the agreement made on Sinai. However, he turns this death into a gateway to life: in the risen Christ all men can achieve life and happiness. God is faithful to his promise to Abraham.

So the important thing is for men to be in Christ: united to him by faith and baptism, the believer shares with him in making this transition from death to life; he finds salvation, not in the works that he can do, but in Jesus.

So for the believer the Law is at an end: the only thing that counts is to be created anew in Jesus Christ and to be inspired by his spirit.

Plan of Paul's letters

Paul writes in the manner of his time (for an example, see p. 50).

Address. Letters began: So and So to So and So, Greetings. Paul names both himself and his fellow workers; he names his correspondents and sends them greetings.
Read all the addresses straight through. What is the Christian pattern of greeting?

Prayer. A short prayer was offered to the gods.
Read all the thanksgivings straight through; for what does Paul bless God?

The body of the letter. Paul's letters usually have two parts.
Teaching: Paul develops an important point of teaching, or one that is not properly understood by his Christians.
Exhortation (or *paraenesis*, as some Bibles call it): Paul draws practical consequences from the teaching of which he had just reminded his readers. Morality, or the Christian way of behaving, is based on this teaching.

Salutations. Paul ends by giving news of his fellow workers and greeting the Christians to whom he is writing. He concludes with a short form of blessing.

I CORINTHIANS

Corinth was a busy port, a cosmopolitan city of about 600,000 inhabitants, two-thirds of whom were slaves. It had quite a reputation: 'To live like the Corinthians' meant to have very loose morals. It was there, with the small Christian community, made up of poor people who had enthusiastically come to Christ, that Paul 'invented' Christian ethics. The letter which he wrote to them tried to show how faith in Christ and baptism put a completely different complexion on the various situations of everyday life. We shall return to this point at more length on pp. 55–56.

You should read at least some texts from the letter: the hymn of love (13); the earliest account that we have of the Last Supper (11.17–34) and the early creed that we have already studied (15.1–11, see p. 36); belief in the resurrection of Christ and in our own resurrection (15).

II CORINTHIANS

Relations between Paul and his community were often turbulent; his authority, and consequently the true faith, had been put in question. In this letter Paul defends him-

---

Here is a letter written by a young Egyptian, serving in a Roman legion, to his father on arrival in Italy (a papyrus from the second century AD).

(Salutation and prayer) *Appion to Epimachus, his father and lord, heartfelt greetings. Above all, I hope that you are well and that all continues to go well with you, and also with my sister, her daughter and my brother.*

I thank the Lord Serapis for having saved me when I was in danger on the sea.

(Content) *As soon as I arrived at Misenum, I received from Caesar my travel allowance: three gold pieces. That was good. I beg you, my lord father, write me a short letter, first about your health, secondly about the health of my brothers, and thirdly so that I can revere your hand, since you brought me up well. That is why I hope for rapid promotion, if the gods are gracious.*

(Final salutation) *Many greetings to Capito, my brothers, Serenilla and my friends. I am sending you my portrait by Euthemon. My military name is Antonius Maximus, a centurion of the Athenonike. I hope that you are well. Serenus, son of Agathos Daimon, greets you, as does Turbo, son of Gallonios.*

The address can be read on the back: *To Philadelphia, for Epimachus from his son Appion. To be sent by the first Apamean cohort of Juluis Antonius, to the secretary, from Appion, to be delivered to Epimachus, his father.*

---

self, and the greater part of it is devoted to the apostolic ministry as Paul sees it (1.11–7.16). He feels the tremendous responsibility that he bears: as he presents the word of God, he knows that he is offering his audience the choice to be for or against Christ (2.14–4.44). The passage in which Paul demonstrates that thanks to Jesus the Christian reads the scriptures in a new way and at last understands their true meaning may seem to you to be rather complicated, but in it you will discover at least one very fine affirmation: the Christian who accepts Christ is transfigured by the glory of God which shone on the face of Jesus, and he is illuminated by it in order to give light to his brothers (3.5–4.6).

In Jesus, who died because of the sin with which he identified himself (5.21), God has reconciled us to himself; in Christ, henceforth we are a new creation.

If you want to see the sufferings which Paul endured and at the same time the grace with which he was blessed, read 11.16–12.10.

Finally, in 13.14 you will recognize a blessing which can still be heard in churches today: it is the first clear attestation of belief in the Trinity.

GALATIANS

These rather foolish Galatians are the first cousins of the Gauls; like the Gauls, they were impulsive, engaging and freedom-loving. They gave Paul's preaching an enthusiastic welcome and committed themselves to Christ. However, other preachers came, and they began to 'Judaize', that is, they added Jewish practices to their Christian faith. Although they were former pagans, they submitted to the yoke of the Jewish Law. No doubt they were well-meaning, but Paul sensed danger: if you have to add anything (in this case, Jewish practices) to Christian faith, it is a sign that faith in Jesus is not enough to save us. Paul launches a passionate counter-attack, drawing on all his theology, and it is rather complicated! Finally, however, he asks his Christians only one question: 'Do you remember what you became through your commitment to Jesus Christ? Are you faithful to your baptismal promises?'

After a very lively introduction, Paul defends the gospel that he preaches, in three stages.

Where does his gospel come from? He received it directly from Christ, on the Damascus road (1.11–2.21).

What is the content of his gospel? Rereading the history of the people of God, he shows that the Law was merely an escort to lead us to Christ. Now that we have come to him, we no longer need it (3–4). As you read these passages you will find some very fine statements: on faith in Christ (2.16, 20), on Abraham (3.6–14), on the equality of all men in Christ Jesus (3.26–29), and on the spirit of sonship (4.6–7).

Where does his gospel lead to? To freedom (5–6). For a Christian there are no more commandments; only this inner law, the Holy Spirit, which is in the heart of every believer and tells him what he must do. 'In Christ you are a new creation; live as free men' (5)!

The letter to the Galatians is a polemical letter. It has a great many obscure passages, but Paul's passion gives it an extraordinary feel. Read it without bothering too much about the difficult phrases; they will make more sense later – perhaps!

Some months later, Paul took up the same ideas in a longer piece of writing which remains one of the high points of his thought: the letter to the Romans.

ROMANS

There have been many different analyses of the letter to the Romans. This one may help.

In the doctrinal part (1–11), Paul develops the same idea in four different ways.

As a statistician, he makes an observation: all men, whether or not they are Jews, are sinners; they all need to be saved by Jesus Christ (1.18–5.11).

As a believer, he begins his reflections by noting what we became at baptism: baptism united us with Jesus, who died and rose again and is the new Adam, the second first man. In him we are a new creation (5.12–7.6). (For original sin see *How to Read the Old Testament*, p. 41).

As a psychologist, he shows us that man is torn inwardly between the good which he wants to do but cannot, and the evil which he does not want to do and yet does (7.7–25). The spirit unifies the believer again by reconciling him with God, whom he can call 'Abba, Father', with others and with the whole universe (8).

Finally, as a historian he rereads the history of Israel: he shows the tragedy of Israel's refusal to recognize the Christ; he proclaims that Israel will be saved when all the people do recognize Christ as Messiah (9–11).

In the moral section (12–15), he draws the consequences of this faith for everyday life (see p. 54).

You should read at least Rom. 6–8, pausing over certain passages.

☙ Baptism. Rom. 6.1–7.6

Paul wants to reply to an objection which might arise from

what has gone before: he shows that the Christian need no longer sin. As usual, he bases this ethical statement on doctrine.

Look for some of the important words which colour this text (unfortunately they are now translated in any old way in our Bibles): baptize (in Greek, the word means dip into); serve, servant (or slave, 6.6, 19; read I Thess. 1.9; for the transition from servitude to service see *How to Read the Old Testament*, p. 31); offer oneself – in the Greek Bible, this word often expresses the offering of oneself to God in worship, e.g. Deut. 10.8; 17.12; 18.5, 7; 21.5, and in Rom. 6.13 (twice); 6.16, 19; 12.1; obey, 6.12, 16 (three times), 19; this verb sometimes defines the Christian: Rom. 10.16; I Peter 1.2, 14, 22.

Note the contrasts: formerly/now; new/old (6.4; 7.6); death/life; wages/free gift (do we 'deserve' heaven?).

Note the comparisons between the destiny of Christ and that of the believer; in particular see the expressions which mark the similarity: as, with, like. . . By whom is Christ raised (see 6.14; 8.11; Col. 2.12)?

Look again at the tenses of the verbs. What is in the past? What is in the future?

Given all these observations, what meaning is attached to baptism in this passage?

If you have time, you might like to look at other images of baptism in Paul:
bathe, be washed: I Cor. 6.11; Eph. 5.26; Titus 3.5.
be buried with Christ: Gal. 3.27; Col. 3.9.
be sealed, as a mark of ownership: II Cor. 1.21f.; Eph. 1.13; 4.30.
illumination: Eph. 5.14.

☙ Life in the Spirit. Romans 8

Romans 7 showed us man divided: even if some passages are obscure (with their reference to earthly paradise and to the Law) we can easily recognize ourselves in this tragic description. Is there any hope? (Be careful about the word 'flesh' in Paul: it does not denote sexuality, as we might say 'the sins of the flesh', but the whole of man as he rejects God; the old man, or the sinful ego.)

Romans 8 shows how the Spirit unifies the believer again. Note how it brings him into communion with God, with himself, with others, indeed with the universe.

You should study the hymn to the love of God which ends this part (Rom. 8.31–39).

Note the context of a trial that we find here. On whom can we rely in order to win? On ourselves? On God?

What is the ultimate assurance of the believer?

The Letters from Prison: Colossians, Ephesians, Philemon

Between 58 and 63, Paul spent four years in prison, first in Caesarea and then in Rome. He had time to meditate. An opportunity to think more deeply about the mystery of Christ was presented to him by the Colossians, who were tempted to locate Christ among the various heavenly powers whom some believed to exist between God and men. Paul succeeded in bringing together his thought by placing Christ at the heart of the universe and of the church. He expresses this in his letter to the Colossians (and also in his letter to the Ephesians, which in some respects is similar and may even have been written by a disciple) and his note to Philemon.

The note to Philemon is the most personal of Paul's letters; in it he comes fully to life. Here we can guess at the nature of life in a church which has grown up in the Gentile world. People have been amazed that Paul does not call for the abolition of slavery. However, he does something better than that: by establishing the equality and even the brotherhood of all men, masters and slaves, he overthrows this institution from within.

In his letter to the Colossians, thanks above all to what he discovered in scripture about the Wisdom of God (see *How to Read the Old Testament*, pp. 92–93), Paul succeeds in placing Christ in relationship to God – he is the Son in whom the fullness of the deity dwells – and in relationship to the world – he is the one by whom and for whom all things were made. This gives our human life new meaning: since nothing escapes the influence of Christ, when we construct the earthly city we are also, mysteriously, building the kingdom of God. From now on we should live as though we were already risen with Christ (3.1–4).

❧ The Lord of the world. Col. 1.15–20

Here two strophes are hinged on a central verse: 16d–17a sum up the first strophe, 17b–18a the second.

Begin by looking for corresponding expressions: the prepositions used (in, by, for), the titles given to Christ. Some come from the Old Testament. What do they mean? (For 'image', see *How to Read the Old Testament*, p. 93.)

The first strophe presents the place and role of Christ in the universe: what are they? The second presents the place and role of Christ in mankind reconciled with God, in the church: what are they?

The letter to the Ephesians offers a harmonious synthesis of Paul's thought. It does not present any great difficulties. As you read it, you will find some very fine passages. Let me single out some of them: the majestic hymn on God's plan of bringing all things together in his Son (1.3–14); the reconciliation of all beings in Jesus Christ (2); a fine prayer that we should be rooted in the love of Christ (3.14–21); the organization of the church (4.1–16, a text that we have already studied, p. 37); an old hymn quoted in 5.14: the church as bride of Christ, and marriage (5.21–33).

Two images of the church

Paul uses two complementary images to present the church; both are necessary.

The church is the body of which Christ is the head, receiving from him its vital impulses. The advantage of this image is that it shows the unity between the church and Christ.

The church is the bride of Christ. The advantage of this image is that it shows that Christ and the church remain two entities: the church is not holy as Christ is, but its love is constantly called forth by his own.

The temple of Artemis at Ephesus, depicted on a Roman coin (third century AD)

The Pastoral Epistles: Timothy, Titus

Whether they were written by Paul, or by a disciple after his death, these letters clearly show his preoccupations at the end of his life: to keep intact the faith in Jesus Christ received from the apostles. Here the church already seems to have a structure, with different ministries, notably the episcopate and the diaconate. They also allow us to share in the praise of the early church, thanks to the hymns which they quote: I Tim. 2.5–6; 3.16; 6.15–16; II Tim. 2.8–13.

Hebrews and the Catholic Epistles

JAMES

It was Saturday evening in a country church: a woman from the parish read the epistle, splendidly, a passage from James on riches. Our breath was taken away by the relevance of these words. 'Do you believe?' asks the author (writing between AD 60 and 80). 'That remains to be seen. Show me the practical consequences of your faith, and first of all your regard and your love for the poor. Otherwise, your faith is not true. . .'

HEBREWS

This is not a letter so much as the sermon which a pupil of Paul's addresses, round about AD 70, to some disoriented Christians. They are Jews who committed themselves to Christ enthusiastically; now, however, they have become disillusioned and miss the fine ceremonies of Judaism. They have suffered for their faith as Christians, and now new difficulties are imminent. The author tells them off: 'You suffer too much in comparison with what you believe; give up the "milk and water" of the children's catechism; you must deepen your faith. Are you bewildered by what is happening now, by your difficulties? Fix your gaze on the leader of the faith, Christ our high priest.'

In a constant mixture of teaching and exhortation, the author meditates on Pss. 2 and 110 and refers to the ceremony of Yom Kippur, the Day of Atonement, which was well known to his readers. This was the only day in the year when the high priest could go into the holiest part of the Temple, where God dwelt; he took blood there to obtain forgiveness for sins.

This is an image: if we are truly to be able to enter God's presence, it is necessary that Christ, the high priest, should have appeared there with his own blood, i.e. the offering of his life. The Jewish priest had to perform the same ritual all over again every year, but Christ entered once for all into the presence of God, thus definitively giving us access to him. Now, with our eyes fixed on Christ, we must go towards the promised land in faith and hope, without flagging.

You should read at least some passages: 5.1–10 on the humanity of Christ; 7.20–28 on Jesus the only priest; 9–10, the new covenant; 11, the journey in faith.

I PETER

This letter almost certainly comes from Rome and was written round about AD 64. It is not read often, which is a pity, because apart from some pieces of out-of-date teaching, it fits our present situation very well. Peter is addressing the exiles of the dispersion (Greek Diaspora); these do not form a racial or national group, but are a great brotherhood spread over the world (5.9), united in the same faith and the same pattern of moral and social conduct, which has to stand out clearly from that of their contemporaries.

The doctrinal part (1.1–2.10) develops some great themes of scripture which make it possible to live like this: the Exodus; the Suffering Servant of Isaiah who offers himself for the salvation of all; the stone rejected by the builders which God has made the foundation stone; the image of Jesus rejected by his people but exalted by God, on whom Christians, as living stones, build up a spiritual edifice.

The second part of this baptismal catechism draws some practical conclusions from this: they can be summed up in the need to conduct oneself well among non-believers (see p. 54). And Peter gives a magnificent definition of witness (3.15).

This new people of God has come into being in dispersion; it is called from amidst the nations, where it lives without ever ceasing to belong to them. A people in exodus, its purpose is to proclaim by its praise and its conduct the mighty acts of the one who has called it from darkness to his wonderful light (2.9).

JUDE

This letter is sometimes disconcerting, and makes use of some contemporary Jewish texts. It was written in 80 or 90 to put Christians on their guard against false teachings.

II PETER

Although this letter is attributed to Peter, it was written at the beginning of the second century. It calls on Christians to remain faithful to their vocation, despite false preaching, even if the coming of Christ is delayed. At least look at its interpretation of the Transfiguration (1.16–18) and its definition of the inspiration of scripture (1.20–21).

Paul's Christ

At each stage I shall try to present Paul's Christ, Mark's Christ, Luke's Christ and so on.

That's a risk, since such brief portraits are inevitably subjective. But at least they will help us to see that the New Testament does not give us a single picture of Christ: his personality is too rich to be capable of representation in a single picture, and everyone develops his own perspective from what he is and what he has experienced. Every Christian, every community today, offers the world a different face of Christ. All these different aspects enable us to get nearer to the one who remains invisible to us.

In Paul's life there is a before and an after: Damascus is a threshhold. Before, Paul was a Pharisee and, because of his faith, was against Jesus, whose disciples he persecuted. Afterwards, he was utterly devoted to the one who had seized hold of him on the road. Peter, John and the first disciples slowly discovered the personality of their master, and it was only after Easter and Pentecost that they began to feel that their friend was Son of God. They resemble those Christians of today, baptized from birth, who have to discover from within the nature of the faith which they have received. Paul is akin to the converts whose life is turned upside down, in a moment.

Unlike the evangelists, Paul did not write a book in which we can find his thought in final form: he wrote letters, very much governed by circumstances, and in them we can see the development of his discovery of Christ.

The one who was accursed is glorified

The one whom Paul thought to be accursed by God, since he had been condemned by the religious authorities and by the Law, now appeared to him in the glory of God: as we have seen, this is the source of Paul's thinking. He puts this appearance on the same level as the appearances of the Risen Lord to his disciples; because of it, he is an apostle in just the same way as they are (see the various forms of address in which he declares himself to be 'called to be an apostle', and I Cor. 15.9; 9.1; Gal. 1.1).

Paul certainly did not know Jesus during his earthly life; right from the start, he encountered him as the risen and glorified Lord.

The Lord who comes

Paul presents his experience on the Damascus road as a 'revelation' (Gal. 1.16). The first stage of his Christian life was marked by the astonished enthusiasm of the convert who has been seized by Christ. He was so fully aware of the life of Christ in him and the new world to which he had been introduced by baptism that he had only one desire, that the day of the Lord, the Parousia, should come quickly and put an end to history. Paul began his ministry living, and making his fellow Christians live, in imminent expectation of the Lord who was to come.

The crucified one who brings salvation

However, the parousia delayed. People had to hang on. Above all, Paul made a fuller discovery of Greek thought and its concern for human wisdom (I Cor. 1–2). Without doubt his failure at Athens left a mark on him (Acts 17). He puts more and more stress on the theology of the cross, which to begin with he had left rather in the shade: I decided to know nothing among you but Jesus Christ and him crucified (II Cor. 2.2). Paul becomes more acutely aware of the weakness of the Law: the justice which comes from the Law and from all that we do is of no account; we are saved by grace, by unconditional commitment to Christ by faith and baptism. The new Adam is the second 'first man' of a new world.

All through his letters to the Corinthians, the Philippians, the Galatians, the Romans, he shows in concrete terms what must be the nature of everyday life with Christ, *in Christ*, the significance of being saved by the cross.

The Lord of the world and of history

Paul's reflection through his four years in prison, his meditation on the scriptures, and in particular the wisdom texts, and the crisis with the Colossians, led him to accord Christ his true place in the universe. Christ is not just the saviour of his community, he is the Lord of history, the image of the invisible God, the firstborn of all creation, the creator of the universe, by whom and for whom all things were made. He is the one in whom God seeks to bring all together. He is Lord to the glory of the Father.

Christian Action or Christian Morality

The Christian way of life, what we call morality, does not appear in the New Testament in the form of commandments and prohibitions. Throughout the Epistles and the Gospels we can see a common teaching: united to Jesus by faith and baptism, we become a new being; from now on, therefore, we must live like new beings. We must imitate the Father, whose children we have become, and his Son, and allow ourselves to be guided by the Spirit. It is by living our everyday existence in this way that we offer spiritual worship to God.

A baptismal catechism

At a very early stage baptism seems to have been accompanied by a catechism, instructions which developed the consequences of baptism for everyday life. In fact we find the same pattern, taking up the same themes, in different writings, but all in the context of baptism. Here's one example.

If you have time, read I Peter 2.1–10. The author presents baptism as a new birth (v. 2); the newly born, built on Christ as a living stone, become a community. From now on they can offer their spiritual worship to Christ (v. 5). The author then develops some aspects of this worship, which consists in behaving well in the midst of pagans (v. 11); he describes how people should behave before the authorities (2.13–17), how servants should behave to their masters (2.18–25), wives to their husbands and husbands to their wives (3.1–7), and how Christians should behave in the community (3.8–12).

James sums up the same teaching: new birth (James 1.17–18); the consequences for daily life (1.26–27).

Paul reminds the Colossians that baptism is dying and living with Christ (Col. 2.20; 3.1) and he continues: live accordingly (3.5). He first says this in general terms (3.5–17), and then takes up this teaching to apply it to each category of the faithful (3.18–4.1).

After reminding the Ephesians of their baptism (5.14), the author talks about how they should live (5.15) and develops the same themes (5.21–6.9).

If you don't have much time, you could read just I Peter 2.1–5 and Rom. 12.1–2. In Rom. 6, Paul has recalled his teaching on baptism, and then, in Rom. 7–8, has shown how the Christian lives inspired by the Spirit. In Rom. 12 he develops the practical consequences: the true worship that we must offer to God is the offering of our very persons, daily life lived in a certain way in a certain spirit. The rest of ch. 12 traces out the main lines of authentic Christian behaviour.

Norms for Christian action

For a Christian, the Law no longer holds. He must be guided only by the Spirit; he must live as one who is united with Christ and who imitates the Father.

The Spirit as the 'law' of the Christian. Jeremiah had announced that God would remake his covenant and put the law in the heart of every believer (Jer. 31.31–34), and Ezekiel had given its name to this 'law': the Spirit (Ezek. 36.26–27). Paul takes up this teaching and develops it, in particular in his letter to the Galatians: Christ has freed you, so allow yourselves to be led by the Spirit (see Gal. 5, especially 5.1, 13, 18, 22–25).

Life in Christ. Christian morality consists in living our lives as the new beings we have become once faith and baptism have united us with Christ. Become what you are is a good summary of the thought which Paul takes up in so many ways. You can see this from a great many texts. To keep things simple, we shall limit ourselves to I Corinthians.

One might say that in writing to his Corinthians, Paul invented Christian morality. These Gentiles had committed themselves to Christ with enthusiasm. However, one cannot change overnight from one kind of life (for Corinth read Soho or 42nd Street, New York, to get some idea of the atmosphere) to life in Christ. So Paul tried to work out with the Corinthians how this new life should change their behaviour. He did not say to them, 'You must . . . that's forbidden. . .' He asked them, 'What did you become through your faith? What is its consequence?' So his letter is a succession of specific instances.

⭐ As you read some texts, see what the particular issue is and what Paul appeals to as the basis of his morality.

Petty squabbles (I Cor. 1.10–4.21). The Christians adopt rival leaders (1.11–12). To what does Paul refer in an attempt to restore unity? See 1.13; 3.16–17.

A disreputable Christian who is living with his stepmother (5). How does Paul deal with this? See 5.7–8.

Christians who go to law (6.1–11). How does Paul deal with this? See 6.11.

Christians who set themselves above morality (6.12–20)! What does Paul refer to, to remind them of the Christian understanding of the body? See 6.15, 19–20.

Is the Christian condemned to the ghetto (8–10)? Underlying this strange problem of meat sacrificed to idols is a very topical question: what is the status of the Christian in the world? In Paul's day, meat offered to idols in the temples and not consumed was sold in the market; every Christian ran the risk of buying some. If he was to be certain of not doing this, was he to give up meat, or have a Christian butcher? Are Christians condemned to living in a ghetto, to creating their own Christian institutions (from trade unions to schools)? For Paul, the only principle was love (8.1–3). All that God has created is good, provided that one accepts it with thanksgiving (I Tim. 4.4–5). So Christians are free to eat meat and to resort to civic institutions. However, love counts above their rights: if by doing this one risks causing offence, it is better to refrain (I Cor. 8.9–13).

Like the Father. Since faith and baptism unite us to Jesus, and the Spirit makes us sons of God (Rom. 8.15–16), the only rule is to be holy as the Father is holy. Matthew stresses this in the great catechism which he puts on the lips of Jesus in the Sermon on the Mount.

⭐ You might read the Sermon on the Mount (Matthew 5–7), underlining all the mentions of the Father. What significance does this give to all these 'laws'?

Read the parable of the merciless servant (Matt. 18.23–25). How should the disciple behave in imitating the Father (God)? He should forgive because he knows himself to be forgiven: that is the basic attitude of the Christian.

Under grace

You are no longer under the Law but under grace, Paul says yet again (Rom. 6.14). 'Should you not have had pity on your fellow servant, as I had pity on you?' asks the master (Matt. 18.33). This was the foundation of morality for the first Christians.

It is not a matter of *doing* something, of earning one's salvation, but of *receiving* it in thanksgiving (see p. 46 again: 'Justified by faith'). Because we know that we are loved freely, by grace; because we know that we are forgiven, we feel the need to love God in return and to love others, to pardon them, to hand on to them what we ourselves have received. We do not practise morality because we are Christian but because we are human; we do not perform works in order to obtain salvation, but because it has been freely given to us. What we do, our 'works', are not like a bunch of flowers which a child gives to its mother in order to be allowed to go to play with a friend, but like the bunch of flowers the child gives on Mothering Sunday, because it knows that it is loved and wants to express the fact. The Christian aspect of morality does not lie primarily in what we do but in the sense that we give it: the wife who irons her husband's shirt does not do it better or less well than the laundry worker, but for her the shirt is her husband's.

Amazed at being so loved, at being freely pardoned, the Christian, in Jesus, inspired by the Spirit, wants to be like his heavenly Father and to hand on to all the joy which Christians receive from him.

4 The Gospel according to Mark

Mark and the lion. Keystone of the rood-loft at Chartres (thirteenth century)

Mark is generally given the honour of having invented the new literary genre of the Gospel. Jesus proclaimed the gospel, that is, the good news that, through him, the kingdom of God had come. Mark wrote a book presenting the good news about Jesus. The one who proclaimed, Jesus, became the subject of the proclamation: it was now his words and his actions which were proclaimed as the good news, the gospel. And the title given to this kind of book from the second century onwards is significant: the Gospel *according to* Mark, the Gospel *according to* Luke, and so on. Jesus proclaimed a single gospel; the evangelists present the life of Jesus as they saw it, in accordance with what they had discovered; they give their testimony.

Of course Mark did not make it all up himself. Words and actions of Jesus had been brought together before him, first orally and then in writing. Several collections already existed: a collection of sayings (or logia), an account of the passion from the arrest of Jesus to his burial, and doubtless other sequences (see p. 15). As the first to write a book which brought them all together, Mark imposed a geographical and chronological framework on the life of Jesus, a framework which Matthew and Luke were to take up after him (but not John). This framework is useful but, as we shall see, it is more theological than historical: Mark does not claim to represent events as they actually happened. He offers a certain view of the ministry of Jesus as seen by him and the community whose spokesman he was.

Mark's community

It is generally accepted that the first Gospel was written in Rome, about AD 70, and takes up the preaching of Peter. Round about 110, the bishop Papias was already writing: 'Mark was an interpreter of Peter and wrote down carefully what he remembered – though not in order – what was said or done by the Lord. He had in fact neither heard the Lord nor followed him, but later on, as I said, he followed Peter. The latter formulated his teachings as was needed, though without making an ordered composition of the oracles of the Lord.'

The indications that we can note in his work fit this tradition very well. His community was made up of former Gentiles: Mark is obliged to translate Aramaic words and to explain certain Jewish customs. We can understand the importance attached to the evangelization of Gentiles, and it is no chance that the finest confession of faith occurs on the lips of the Roman centurion at the foot of the cross.

This community was threatened with persecutions. The faith which Mark presents is not a quiet faith: it comes up against opposition and is forced to take risks. That fits in very well with what we know of the church of Rome under Nero. Peter suffered martyrdom in AD 64.

So this is a community 'dispersed among the Gentiles', as Peter wrote in his letter.

The author

The author of the Gospel was almost certainly the young John Mark mentioned in Acts (12.12). He left on a missionary journey with his uncle Barnabas and Paul, but he left them when they embarked for Asia Minor and preferred to return home to his mother (Acts 13.5, 13)! Paul refused to take him on his second mission; this will have been the cause of his parting from Barnabas (Acts 15.36f.). However, they were later reconciled, since we find Mark at Paul's side again during his imprisonment by the Romans (Col. 4.10), and Peter indicates in his letter that Mark, his son, is with him in Rome (I Peter 5.13).

A millstone closing the entrance to a tomb

The Gospel as a Whole

All too often we know only separate bits of the Gospels. So first of all, you are invited to take a guided tour (for Mark, this will take about an hour). You will certainly be amazed at how interesting you will find it.

If you have time, take the Gospel of Mark and read it purely for pleasure. At the end, take stock of your impressions: see what has delighted you, what has astonished you, what you have discovered. If one particular feature has caught your eye (the titles given to Jesus, the way people look at him), you can read the Gospel again and take special notice of this theme.

If you have less time, and want to take a guided tour straight away, here are some points of interest.

Geography

Mark has given a very simple framework to the life of Jesus. After his baptism in the Jordan (1.1–13), Jesus preaches in Galilee (1.14–9.50), goes up to Jerusalem (10), preaches and dies in Jerusalem (11.1–16.8); the angel of the resurrection announces that the disciples are to gather together again in Galilee.

However, the Gospels are not Ordnance Survey maps; their geography is primarily theological. If you compare the maps in the margin, you will see to what extent they differ among themselves.

In Mark, Galilee is opposed to Jerusalem.

Galilee of the nations, or Galilee of the Gentiles, as it was called at that time, had experienced many invasions, and in the eyes of the religious authorities belief there was not very pure. Nothing good could come out of Galilee, far less a prophet (cf. John 1.46; 7.52). However, Isaiah (8.23) had announced that one day God would manifest himself there to the Gentiles, so Galilee was also a symbol of hope and opportunity. Now it was there that Jesus was born, lived and preached, and the crowds gave him an enthusiastic welcome. This region was opened up; from there Jesus went to the Gentiles in Tyre and Sidon (7.24, 31).

By contrast, Jerusalem seems to be a city shut in on itself, a refuge for the godfearing, certain of their truth and not allowing any contradiction. From the beginning of the ministry of Jesus, in Galilee onwards, the fiercest attacks on him came from Jerusalem (3.22).

The two shores of the lake

Lake Tiberias is no longer neutral: the west bank is Jewish and the east bank is Gentile. Constantly, and despite the storm, Jesus draws his disciples towards the Gentile shore, in this way preparing them for a mission which they will find it difficult to understand.

The mystery of Jesus

From his very first words, Mark lets his readers into the secret: the Gospel of Jesus, Christ, Son of God. Two titles appear beside his name, Jesus, which identifies him as a man: Christ/Messiah and Son of God. John the Baptist claims to be the forerunner of the Messiah, and the Father proclaims to Jesus that he is his Son (1.1–13). So the reader knows what is going on. However, from this point on he is invited to share with the disciples their slow discovery of the mystery of Jesus. This takes place in two stages.

In the first stage (1.14–8.26), Jesus proclaims the imminent coming of the kingdom of God, and gives signs of its coming, miracles. However, he refuses to say who he is and forbids the demons to divulge it: there is a secret, what has been called the 'messianic secret'. The only title which Jesus applies to himself is the mysterious title Son of man.

The second part (8.27–16.8) begins with Peter's proclamation, 'You are the Messiah.' We have the impression that Jesus breathes a sigh of relief; one step has been taken: his disciples have seen one part of his mystery. At the same time, however, he is disturbed: there is a risk that they, too, will get the wrong idea about the Messiah, will see in him the liberator who will establish the kingdom of Israel by force of arms. He forbids Peter to communicate his discovery, and at the same time leads his disciples towards the second stage: the Son of man will suffer and be put to death!

In a series of controversies at Jerusalem (11–13), Jesus introduces another title, Son of David. That, too, is dangerous, and only heightens the opposition from the religious authorities. Here we are at the heart of the drama. These authorities were looking for the Messiah, and one would expect that they were most qualified to recognize him when he appeared. However, they had a very precise idea of him, *their* idea. Now Jesus presented himself as the Messiah, but he did not correspond to their ideal. Opposition between these two conceptions became so strong that someone had to die: either the authorities had to die to the notions they had previously entertained and accept this disconcerting Messiah, or they would persevere with their ideas and Jesus had to die. Because he knows that he is already condemned, and that there is therefore no danger that he will be taken to be a temporal Messiah, in the dramatic scene of the judgment before the Sanhedrin Jesus clearly declares himself to be Christ. And he is condemned to death.

However, at the foot of the cross a Gentile takes over and finally recognizes Jesus as Son of God. Jesus, condemned by the Sanhedrin, and the centurion, over the corpse of a crucified man, tell us the journey that has to be made for the confession of Christian faith to be true.

And by means of this drama, Mark continues to make us ask questions. Jesus is disconcerting! Are you ready to die to the idea you have of him, in order to accept him as he is?

🔖 During your reading you might underline in different colours the titles given to Jesus, the people who recognize him, etc.

A human drama

Jesus did not leave anyone indifferent. As soon as he appeared, groups formed and there were questioners, friendly or hostile. Right at the beginning, Jesus chose disciples, particularly the Twelve, to be with him. This was the first group, which was often under strain because of the disciples' failure to understand. The family of Jesus rarely appears, and when it does, it tends to be hostile. There is always a crowd; Jesus loves the people and makes his disciples serve them. However, this crowd is fickle. Jesus' enemies come from Jerusalem; they appear right at the beginning and are unrelenting.

🔖 You could assign a colour to each group and by marking your Bible, see how they come up against one another and clash, and also how people can change sides.

As you go through the Gospel, you can distinguish six stages.

1.14–3.6. Each of the groups establishes its position.

3.7–6.6. The break between Jesus on the one hand and his enemies and kinsfolk on the other is complete. Taken out of the crowd, the disciples are given private teaching (parables and miracles).

6.6–8.26. A rift develops between Jesus and his disciples: they do not understand his mission or their own. Jesus sends them out on a mission and shows them that his table is open to all (the feeding of the multitudes); he makes them serve the crowd and draws them towards the Gentile side of the lake. They remain deaf and blind; this is represented by two miracles.

8.27–10.52. The disciples do not understand the course of suffering on which Jesus is leading them (see 10.32).

11.1–13.37. In Jerusalem, Jesus confronts his adversaries (the parable of the vineyard); the story of the withered fig tree symbolizes their situation.

14.1–16.8. Jesus prepares his disciples for the drama, but in vain. He dies alone. However, the angel of the resurrection puts the disciples on their way; only when they get to 'Galilee', i.e. to the end of the world and the end of history, to which Jesus has gone before them, will they 'see' the Risen Lord. The conclusion (16.9–20, as your Bible will indicate) was added later.

Some features of Mark

Mark is written in a popular style; he deliberately substitutes 'and' or 'immediately' for other conjunctions, and some of his phrases aren't quite right. For example, he writes: 'The blind man beginning to see said, "I see people, it is as if they were trees which I see walking" ' (8.24). He uses words which were considered vulgar at the time (2.11 might be translated 'pick up your sack'), and is not afraid of repetitions.

Mark is a marvellous storyteller. He does not have many speeches. His narratives are always specific and lively, sprinkled with touches from real life. The verbs are often in the present tense, which makes his accounts so vivid, but he also mixes tenses. The use of the word 'for' on numerous occasions appeals to a logic which disconcerts us ('. . . for she was twelve years old', at the end of the story of the raising of Jairus' daughter, 5.42).

He makes an emotional impact, less by his appeal to our feelings than by his blunt account of the facts: this is particularly evident in the account of the passion.

Mark's Gospel has been called the Gospel of before Easter; it shows us Jesus through the eyes of Peter as he follows his master on the roads of Palestine. But Mark is also a profound theologian, and he retells the life of Jesus in the light of Easter.

Some Texts from Mark

We have now read Mark straight through. Next, we shall be reading some texts from the Gospel in more detail. You won't be able to study them all, so choose!

Title. 1.1

Mark proclaims Christian faith in a terse phrase. He also announces the stages through which the disciples had to go (and still have to go) to arrive at it. This title, like the prologue to the Gospel of John and the infancy narratives in Matthew and Luke, shows the theological profundity which Christians had achieved forty years after Easter.

Beginning. The ministry of Jesus ushers in something new in history, a new creation ('beginning' is the first word of Genesis). This is a beginning which opens up all the period of our history. There is a task to be performed!

Gospel. This word, 'good news', takes us back to the announcement made by Second Isaiah (see *How to Read the Old Testament*, p. 67). Compare this gospel of Mark with that of Jesus (Mark 1.14–15); the difference I pointed out on p. 57 leaps out at us: Jesus proclaimed the good news of the coming of the kingdom of God; Mark proclaims the good news about Jesus. The one who proclaims has become the subject of the proclamation! From now on the arrival of the kingdom of God is embodied in the person of Jesus.

Jesus. This simple name evokes the human aspect of the 'carpenter, the son of Mary and brother of James, Joses, Jude and Simon', whose sisters are also known (Mark 6.3). He is a man, but also someone quite different.

Christ. Jesus is the Messiah announced by scripture, the one whom God was to anoint in order to invest him with his mission and establish his kingdom. We have seen how Mark's Jesus rejects this title and forbids anyone to attribute it to him ('the messianic secret'); Peter proclaims it at Caesarea Philippi, but Jesus compels him to keep quiet, and foretells his sufferings (8.29–30). He only accepted the title when he was condemned (14.61–62).

Son of God. In the time of Jesus this title was virtually equivalent to Son of David. After Easter it gradually took on the stronger significance which we now attach to it. The Gentile at the foot of the cross was charged with proclaiming it.

The baptism of Jesus. 1.9–11

The baptism is indicated by one word (Matthew and Luke mention it in a subordinate clause and John doesn't mention it at all). The essential feature is the theophany (or manifestation of God) in action and in word.

The heavens opening is a theme from apocalyptic. The heavens are 'closed' because there are no longer any prophets; the spirit does not come down to guide the people any more; history has therefore come to an impasse. However, people waited for the end of time, when the heavens would open (see the box below). By using a term which should be translated 'rent' here, Mark is clearly seeing the event as a response to the anguished appeal of Isa. 63–64; read that text, and especially 63.10–13, 19. How does it illuminate this scene?

The symbolism of the dove remains obscure. Hosea 11.11 and IV Esdras (a Jewish writing which appeared for a while in the Latin Bible) compare the people to a dove. That would signify that the coming of the Spirit on Jesus is to constitute the new people of God.

The voice brings together several texts. 'My son' comes from Ps. 2, 'beloved' from Gen. 22.2, 12, 16 (the sacrifice of Isaac); this is the only time when the phrase 'beloved son' occurs in the Old Testament. To be well pleased with: Isa. 62.4; 42.1 (quoted by Matt. 12.17). What meaning does the saying take on in the light of this?

What we have here seems to be a private experience of Jesus: it is his investiture as Messiah, perhaps the Messiah destined for sacrifice, as Isaac was.

'The heavens shall be opened, and from the temple of glory shall come upon him sanctification, with the Father's voice as from Abraham to Isaac. And the glory of the Most High shall be uttered over him, and the spirit of understanding and sanctification shall rest upon him' (Testament of Levi 18.6–8).

'And a man shall arise from my seed, like the sun of righteousness, walking with the sons of men in meekness and righteousness; and no sin shall be found in him. And the heavens shall be opened unto him, to pour out the spirit, the blessing of the Holy Father. And he shall pour out the spirit of grace upon you, and you will be to him sons in truth' (Testament of Judah 24.1–6).

The Testament of Levi and the Testament of Judah belongs to a collection of apocalypses known under the name of the Testaments of the Twelve Patriarchs. They are certainly pre-Christian, but they may have been retouched by Christians.

Five controversies. 2.1–3.6

This group of five discussions between Jesus and his adversaries introduces us to the literary genre of controversy (see p. 20). We shall study two of them.

The healing of a paralysed man. 2.1–12

Look at the main characters: what are they doing? What are they saying? Note the contrasts: lying, sitting, standing.

This is a strange story: The paralysed man does not expect to hear that particular saying (v. 5). The story is formed by the combination of a miracle story and a controversy: try to distinguish them both.

The miracle (3.5a and 11–12). Look for the different elements (see p. 20). Jesus turns a bed-ridden invalid, who needs assistance, into a man on his feet who can look after himself. How can that signify the coming of the kingdom of God? What is the crowd's reaction? In Greek, the verb 'arise' is the same as that used for resurrection: for a Christian, to put others on their feet can be experienced as a way of realizing the resurrection of Jesus today.

The controversy (5b–10). The scribes are seated, in their official position (see pp. 58–59). They are already thinking to themselves what they will later shout aloud at the time of Jesus' trial: this man is blaspheming! For a Jew, the phrase 'Your sins are forgiven' must mean that they are forgiven by God; however, at the very least Jesus shows that God's forgiveness is bound up with his action in Jesus. He presents himself as the Son of man to be found in Daniel 7, to whom God has entrusted all power and, according to Jewish tradition, judgment over men.

The combination. How do these two healings, of body and soul, help to illuminate each other? What do they teach us about the salvation brought by Jesus? Is this not the word spoken by him (v. 2)?

The call of Levi. 2.13–17

Mark notes that Jesus taught the crowds. However, here again, this teaching is given above all through actions.

The starting point of the controversy is the story of a call, of a kind that can often be found in the Gospel. This kind of story usually has three elements: Jesus' glance – the words 'Follow me' – and an obedient response.

Levi is a tax collector, and therefore considered to be a sinner. To celebrate his call, he gives a party: this is the starting point of the controversy, since Jesus is sitting at table with sinners.

Fasting and the Bridegroom. 2.18–22

As often, this controversy has been supplemented by two short parables, for the purposes of teaching. Mark presents Jesus as the Bridegroom, the divine partner in the covenant (see *How to Read the Old Testament*, pp. 47, 61). Fasting gives place to the wine of the wedding feast.

The Lord of the sabbath. 2.23–28

In this classic controversy, Jesus puts forward a revolutionary principle by referring to scripture: the sabbath, and therefore every institution, whether religious or human, is at the service of men.

Healing on a sabbath. 3.1–6

1. *Again he entered the synagogue*
   and a man was there who had a withered hand.
2. *And they watched him, to see whether he would heal*
      him on the sabbath,
      that they might accuse him.
3. *And he said to the man who had the withered hand,*
      'Come here.'
4. *And he said to them, 'Is it lawful on the sabbath*
         to do good or to do harm,
         to save life or to kill?'
      But they were silent.
5. *And he looked around them with anger,*
      grieved at their hardness of heart,
      and said to the man, 'Stretch out your hand.'
   He stretched it out, and his hand was restored.
6. *The Pharisees went out, and immediately held counsel*
   with the Herodians against him, how to destroy him.

Look for the main characters: Jesus and his adversaries; the sick man only serves as an occasion for the controversy. Note the parallels brought out by the way in which the text has been printed. The synagogue is the place of the Law; the religious authorities are at home there. At the beginning, Jesus enters; at the end, they go out.

This head-on clash is over the significance of the Law. Jesus' opponents are caught up in their ideals (the disciples are reproached for this hardness of heart: 6.52; 8.17). For Jesus, the most important thing is not the practice of a law, but man. In this confrontation, who comes out on top? However, 'how to destroy him' creates a sense of suspense which is only resolved by the passion (for 'accuse' see 15.3–4). By raising up Jesus (evoking the 'resurrection'), God shows that he is Lord over the Law.

What significance might this text have today?

❧ The blind man of Jericho. 10.46–52

Who are the main characters? What do they do? What do they say? Note the transformation brought about between the beginning and the end: a blind man – sitting – at the side – of the road/he saw – he followed him – on – the road. What is this transformation (is it the same 'road'?), and how is it brought about?

Look for the usual features of a miracle story (see p. 20); the plea for intervention (vv. 47–50) here is of disproportionate length; there is no final reaction. This story must have been used as more than a simple miracle story.

See the passage which leads up to it: in 10.32–34 the disciples are going up to Jerusalem: what road are they taking? Can the disciples see it? In 10.35–45 are not James and John blind? Note the link between this story and the one which follows (the same question appears in verses 36 and 51).

Look at what happens next. In 11.11ff. they arrive in Jerusalem: Jesus is hailed as Son of David (v. 10). But can the crowd see the significance of this title, which will be discussed in Mark 11–13?

What meaning does this story seem to have by itself? In the context of Mark's Gospel?

Here we arrive at a turning point in the Gospel of Mark. Jesus knows where his journey to Jerusalem is taking him. He warns the disciples three times (8.31–33; 9.30–32; 10.32–34). However, they are frightened and blind. The inability of James and John to understand is obvious: they have the wrong idea of the Messiah. According to Mark, this miracle is an attempt by Jesus to open the eyes of his disciples. Bartimaeus becomes the model of the true believer. He 'sees', not only with his physical eyes; he follows Jesus on this 'road' which is more theological than geographical, the ascent to the cross. When he asks, 'Let me see', Jesus does not reply 'See', as he does in Luke (18.42), but 'Go'. The blind man's faith enables him to follow Jesus.

Here he has done something for which the rich man did not have the courage (10.17–31). He has left everything. While he was still blind (physically), he threw off his mantle, all that he had, sprang up, and came to Jesus (v. 50).

For the people, Jesus was only the man from Nazareth (v. 47): for the blind man he is the Son of David, not the figure dreamed of still by James and John, but as Jesus will himself present him: the suffering Messiah.

❧ The empty tomb. 16.1–8

This is the conclusion of the Gospel; verses 9–20 were added later.

Try to put into two columns the contrasts which are either implicit or explicit. The time: the sabbath (religious time) is past/the first day of the week (secular time); darkness/light, morning. . . The places: closed/open; here (Jerusalem)/Galilee. . . The actions: anoint a corpse/hear a message. . . The main characters: corpse, in the dark, lying, naked/young man in white, sitting on the right, clothed. What do these contrasts suggest to you? What transformation has taken place between the beginning and the end? How is it achieved?

Mark's Gospel ends with this story. So to believe in the resurrection of Jesus it is not necessary to have 'seen' it: it is enough to believe in God who affirms it.

The women come to anoint a corpse; they go away with a message. They wanted to seal up Jesus in death; they have to announce that he is alive. Jesus is no longer a body that can be touched; he has become a word that must be proclaimed. One of the ways in which he remains mysteriously present in history is in preaching. Now he is seated at the right hand of God, as is suggested by the attitude of the young man. And it is only when the disciples arrive in Galilee (to which he has preceded them), i.e. to the end of the world and the conclusion of history (see the geography, p. 58), that they will 'see' him. Matthew will tell us that the resurrection of Jesus is the end of time: everything has been accomplished! Mark stresses the other aspect: everything has still be be done!

If you have put the contrasts in two columns, you will have seen that everything that belongs to the old world (darkness, the corpse, the sabbath and Jewish time, the tomb with its dead sealed inside) is now past. A new world has begun: it is the beginning of a new creation (cf. Mark 1.1).

The Passion according to Mark

An account of the passion of Jesus from his arrest to his burial must have existed from a very early stage. The four Gospels take it up, but each gives it a particular tone.

Mark is addressing non-believers or those whose faith is weak, and he wants to lead them to join the Gentile at the foot of the cross in proclaiming that Jesus is truly the Son of God.

By narrating the facts without embellishing them, he is trying almost to upset us. With him we can see better how disconcerting the realization of God's plan is for men. The cross is scandalous. However, it is there that the Son of God reveals himself.

The silence of Jesus during his passion is impressive. Jesus knows that people are 'hardened' when it comes to penetrating his mystery, that there is a risk that they will understand him wrongly. Throughout his ministry, too, he always refuses to say who he is. Now that he is condemned, there is no longer any danger of interpreting his titles as a concern for power, so he agrees to lift the veil somewhat. From his arrest on, despite the questions pressed on him, Jesus opens his mouth only three times: before the High Priest he declares that he is Messiah/Christ and Son of Man; before Pilate he acknowledges that he is king of the Jews; on the cross, he takes up the complaint of the Suffering Servant in Isaiah, bringing upon himself all the suffering and anguish of the world, 'My God, why have you forsaken me?'

In Mark, Jesus' solitude stands out in all its harshness: he goes forward alone, abandoned by all, denied by Peter, into the dark night of the cross. It is by accepting the call to follow him so far that his disciples can proclaim him Son of God.

The conflict between Jesus and the high priests comes to a head with the conspiracy against Jesus (14.1–2): from this point on, Jesus is doomed. He knows it. During a meal with Simon (14.3–9), a woman pours perfume over his head: Jesus sees this as the celebration of his burial. So he goes to meet his passion in full awareness.

The story of his farewell meal (14.22–25) is framed by the intimation of Judas' betrayal (14.17–21) and Peter's denial (14.26–31). So Jesus knows what is to come; he is the one who directs his passion (14.10–16). At the last supper, he offers his body and his blood in total destitution, knowing that he can expect neither recognition nor fidelity from men. The account of the institution, which comes very close to that of Mark, takes up the liturgical text of celebrations in the Palestinian churches.

The Christ of Perpignan (fourteenth century)

In Gethsemane, Jesus is in anguish, prostrate (14.32–42). Fully man, he is afraid of death. The name which he uses in his cry to God, 'Abba, Father', sheds momentary light on this tragic scene. When he is arrested, all forsake him (14.43–52), even the young man who tries to follow him but flees, naked. This word, which brings the story to an end, sets its tone. Jesus drives himself, naked, into his passion. And the disciple who plunged naked into the pool at the time of his baptism would know that this was the course he too was to follow.

At the trial before the Jews (14.53–64), Jesus for the only time in Mark proclaims who he is: Messiah, the glorified Son of man. However, everyone seems to go wild at this affirmation: the guards mock him (14.65), Peter denies him (14.66–72). Jesus keeps silent.

At the Roman trial (15.1–15) Jesus claims to be king of the Jews and the high priests call for his death. . . Their king is crowned with thorns (15.16–20)!

The scene on Calvary (15.21–41) takes up the theme of the two trials: the title King of the Jews is recalled between two mentions of the crucifixion (vv. 25, 27), and the high priests mock his claim to be the Christ. However, it is by dying abandoned by all, apparently even by the Father, by taking upon himself all human suffering as the Suffering Servant, that Jesus reveals how he is both Christ and King. The Gentile calls on us to recognize him as Son of God. And by marking out his narrative with the hours of Christian prayer (terce, sext, none, vv. 25, 33, 34), Mark invites us to celebrate him in faith.

In Mark the account of the burial is peaceful (15.42–47). The last honours are paid to Jesus. And the night of the burial becomes a night of expectation.

Mark's Jesus

A man

Mark presents us with the everyday Jesus, a man like ourselves. We get the impression that we are discovering him, from day to day, through Peter's eyes. During the two years of their life together, Peter had watched Jesus on the roads of Palestine, had welcomed him into his home at Capernaum, had watched him eat and sleep, talk and pray. He had seen him angry at the synagogue or in the Temple, irritated towards a leper or towards his disciples, full of pity when confronted with the crowd, amazed that people in Nazareth would not believe in him. He had watched the harassed life of Jesus as a wandering preacher, which at times did not even allow him a chance to eat; he had seen Jesus asleep, exhausted at the height of a great storm.

Peter had been impressed by the way Jesus looked, his anger, his questioning, his love; he had been intrigued by the mystery of Jesus, as on the first night that Jesus spent at his home or when he saw him get up before dawn to go to pray alone in a desert place (1.35).

Mark does not hesitate to report certain features which must have stunned his audience, accustomed to seeing Jesus as the Son of God: Jesus did not know everything; he did not know what his disciples were talking about and had to ask them (9.16, 33); he did not know when the end of time would come (14.33); he was afraid of death (14.33) and died in despair (15.34). He was so disconcerting that even his parents did not believe in him: 'He's lost his head' (3.21).

A 'man with' – a man by himself

Mark's Jesus is above all Jesus-with-his-disciples. His first act is to call them, and then to choose twelve to be with him. His opponents try to break up this team by attacking Jesus in the disciples' presence and the disciples in his (2.18–27). Jesus prepares these disciples for their future ministry by making them serve the crowd, a service which comes before rest or food (6.31f.), and by directing them towards the Gentiles.

Against this background, the solitude of Jesus appears all the more dramatic. He is alone, because he cannot make his companions realize his mystery; they are hardened (6.52; 8.17), doubt, abandon him the moment he is arrested, and deny him.

The teacher

Straight after his baptism, Jesus preaches that 'The kingdom of God is at hand.' For Mark, Jesus is the one who teaches the crowd (about twenty times). When he sees the crowds who have followed him into the desert and have nothing to eat, Jesus takes pity on them, and begins to teach them, guessing that this is their most important hunger (6.34).

Now the paradoxical fact is that there are very few discourses in Mark. Did he perhaps want to convey that Jesus taught above all by the way in which he acted? Proportionately, the miracles occupy a major part of Mark's Gospel: they show by actions that the kingdom of God is at hand, that Jesus is stronger than evil (3.27).

The crucified Messiah

Jesus refuses to have himself proclaimed Messiah or Christ, and he imposes silence on those who discover who he is, whether these are people whom he has healed or the demons: this is what is referred to as the 'messianic secret'. Many people expected that the Messiah would re-establish the earthly kingdom of Israel. Jesus does not want them to get the wrong idea of the Messiah: he is the Messiah, but not in that sense. He gives himself this title only when it is no longer possible to make a mistake, when he has been condemned to death. It is by suffering and death that he will establish a spiritual kingdom. And he tries to lead his disciples along this road (8.34–38).

The Son of Man

The most frequent title Jesus uses in Mark is Son of Man (fourteen times). Perhaps Jesus was fond of it because it unveiled his mystery while at the same time concealing it. In itself, the expression in fact means simply 'man'; however, when there is a reference to the vision in Daniel 7 (see *How to Read the Old Testament*, p. 91), it takes on the strong sense of the heavenly being to whom God entrusts judgment.

The Son of God

This title is rare, but it appears as the climax of the faith to which Mark seeks to bring his reader. He uses the title in his introduction (1.1), and the centurion proclaims it at the foot of the cross (15.39), echoing the voice of the Father at the baptism and the transfiguration.

The Miracles and the Kingdom of God

'The time is fulfilled and the kingdom of God is at hand: repent and believe in the gospel' (Mark 1.15). This cry of Jesus immediately after his baptism is a good indication of the tone of his preaching; with his ministry, the kingdom of God is on its way.

The kingdom of God

At a time when monarchy was the universal political system, it was natural that Israel should use the image of 'king' to evoke the power of its God. For Israel, God is the sole king, and the earthly king is only his representative. This faith developed when the people experienced the failure of the earthly kingdom. During the exile in Babylon, Second Isaiah announced that God would finally show himself as king (see *How to Read the Old Testament*, p. 67).

Messianic beliefs over the course of centuries deepened this expectation. It was thought that God would establish his kingdom by the agency of his messiah. The messiah most often had the features of the son of David, shepherd of Israel (II Sam. 7; Ezek. 34; Zech. 9–14; Ps. 2, see *How to Read the Old Testament*, pp. 42, 66, 86, 103). The apocalypses, with the figure of the son of man in Daniel 7, brought another component: this kingdom is universal and is for the end of time.

Two main functions were attributed to the king, and thus, *a fortiori*, to God the King.

He was to ensure the liberty of his people: he was a warrior chief who destroyed their enemies. At the time of Christ this led some Jewish groups to cherish the hope that by establishing his kingdom God would free Israel from Roman domination (cf. Luke 24.21). It is notable that Jesus never takes up this aspect.

The true king was also to ensure the reign of justice among the people; he was above all the king of the poor, the oppressed, those who had no voice. And Second Isaiah proclaimed this gospel, this good news: 'God will reign! Blessed are the poor, the sick, the oppressed, since henceforth their misery is at an end.' This is also the good news proclaimed by Jesus. He proclaims it by both his actions and his words. In the next section we shall be hearing his words, above all the beatitudes. Here we are going to look at his actions: the miracles.

Jesus proclaims the kingdom of God

You might begin by looking at the good news (Luke 3.18) proclaimed by John the Baptist (Mark 1.2–8; Matt. 3.1–12; Luke 3.1–18) and the way in which the evangelists sum up the preaching of Jesus (Mark 1.14–15; Matt. 4.17; Luke 4.16–21).

John the Baptist's question

John announced the Messiah who would establish the kingdom of God, purify his people, destroy the sinners. And he thought he could recognize him in Jesus. Now Jesus welcomed sinners, refused to judge and allowed his precursor to be put in prison, facing certain death. We can understand John's doubt and his question. Read Luke 7.18–23 (= Matt. 11.2–6).

What does Jesus do before replying (v. 21)? Look also at Luke 7.11–17, which Luke has put just in front of the passage.

Which prophetic oracles does Jesus take up in his reply (see the notes or references in your Bible)?

What significance does that give to Jesus' miracles and to the beatitudes: 'Blessed are the poor'?

That is particularly important in understanding the miracles. For us they are primarily extraordinary facts, and we ask, 'What actually happened? Are they historical?' For Jesus, as for his contemporaries, the miracles are signs: they say something and speak of someone. To shift the question in this way is essential. Let's take a trivial example. A science teacher gives a flower to a pupil: the question is obviously 'What is it?' A boy gives this flower to the same girl: the question then is, 'What does this mean?' In the one instance the interest is in the flower as an entity; in the other, it is in its message, and what it is as an entity becomes purely secondary. That is important, and we shall be coming back to it.

If you have time, you might also look at the expression 'kingdom of God' in the Gospels, or read Matt. 13 and see what the parables are talking about.

We shall be studying one miracle story, the stilling of the storm. That will help you to see how this kind of story is constructed and what it means.

A miracle story: the stilling of the storm

Matt. 8.18–27	Mark 4.35–41	Luke 8.22–25
[18] Now when Jesus saw great crowds around him, he gave orders to go over to the other side.	[35] On that day, when evening had come, he said to them 'Let us go across to the other side.'	[22] One day he got into a boat with his disciples, and he said to them, 'Let us go across to the other side of the lake.'
[19] And a scribe came up and said to him, 'Teacher, I will follow you wherever you go.' [20] And Jesus said to him, 'Foxes have holes, and birds of the air have nests; but the Son of man has nowhere to lay his head.' [21] Another of his disciples said to him, 'Lord, let me first go and bury my father.' [22] Jesus said to him, 'Follow me, and leave the dead to bury their dead.'		(Luke 9.57–58) (Luke 9.59–60)
[23] And when he got into the boat, his disciples followed him.	[36] And leaving the crowd, they took him with them, just as he was, in the boat.	So they set out.
[24] And behold, there arose a great upheaval on the sea so that the boat was being swamped by the waves; but he was asleep.	[37] And a great storm of wind arose and the waves beat into the boat, so that the boat was already filling. [38] But he was in the stern, asleep on the cushion; and they woke him and said to him,	[23] And as they sailed, he fell asleep. And a storm of wind came down on the lake and they were filling with water, and were in danger.
[25] And they went and woke him, saying, 'Save, Lord, we are perishing.'	'Teacher, do you not care if we perish?'	[24] And they went and woke him, saying, 'Master, master, we are perishing!'
[26] And he said to them, 'Why are you afraid, O men of little faith?' Then he rose and rebuked the winds, and the sea, and there was a great calm.	[39] And he awoke and rebuked the wind, and said to the sea, 'Peace, be still' And the wind ceased, and there was a great calm. [40] He said to them, 'Why are you afraid? Have you no faith?'	And he awoke and rebuked the wind and the raging waves; and they ceased, and there was a calm. [25] He said to them, 'Where is your faith?'
[27] And the men marvelled saying, 'What sort of man is this, that even winds and sea obey him?'	[41] And they were filled with awe, and said to one another, 'Who then is this, that even wind and sea obey him?'	And they were afraid, and they marvelled, saying to one another, 'Who then is this, that he commands even wind and water, and they obey him?'

Read these texts carefully and compare them: underline words in different colours (see p. 16). See where one Gospel has more or less than another; note how Mark shifts v. 40; watch the different use of words.

A miracle story usually fitted into a prefabricated 'mould': look for the five points indicated on p. 20. Does Mark's v. 40 fit into this mould?

Read each of the accounts. To put them in context, go back to the synopsis on p. 17.

Mark. Can you find the features picked out on p. 59? Why does Jesus rebuke the storm as though it were a demon? The word for fear used here appears only four times in the New Testament: in John 14.27 as a verb, in II Tim. 1.7 as a noun and in Rev. 21.8 as an adjective. What kind of fear is this? Towards which shore of the lake are they going (look at the geography on p. 58)? What episode follows this story in all three Gospels? Does that explain the fear of the disciples and the rebellion of the demon?

Why does Mark recount this miracle? What is the meaning with v. 40? Without v. 40?

Luke. Which is he interested in, the ship or the disciples (look at the end of v. 23)? Which episode has he put immediately afterwards? The word Luke uses for Master is peculiar to him (5.5; 8.45; 9.33, 49; 17.13). What is its significance?

Matthew. In which direction do the words which he has added shift the sense (follow, vv. 19, 22, 23; disciples, v. 21)? In whom is he interested (see the end of v. 24)? The word upheaval is used once in the Gospels as one of the signs of the end of time (Mark 13.8; Matt. 24.7; Luke 21.11). Matthew uses it again (noun or verb) in 21.10; 27.51, 54; 28.2, 4: what sense does this give to the narrative (see p. 71)? *Kyrie, sozon*, 'Lord, save,' is a liturgical invocation. Matthew has put v. 26 at the centre of his account: the reproach is addressed to disciples who already believe, but not enough. 'The men' (v. 27) in Matthew usually denotes unbelievers (4.19; 5.13; 10.17; 10.32). On the basis of all this, what significance would you attach to this account?

The significance of the miracle

The miracle, as I said earlier, is a sign. But for whom? Let me take a trivial instance: by the roadside I see a triangular metal plate with an X on it; if I didn't know the highway code I might ask, 'What is it?'. If I do know the highway code, the sign says to me, 'Caution, crossroads.' Similarly, reactions of non-believer and believer to an event will differ, and the story which each tells of it will not be the same.

For the non-believer, the extraordinary fact poses a question: 'Who is this man who is capable of. . .?'

For the believer – and only for him – the event is a miracle, that is to say, a message, a fact in which he discovers a word of God addressed to him.

Now it seems that in the primitive community, before the redaction of the Gospel, the story of the stilling of the storm was used in both ways.

Let's take Mark's account. If we read it without v. 40, we have a text which exactly fits the mould of the miracle story. It is addressed to the disciples before Easter who had not yet discovered the mystery of Jesus, and it could be presented to non-believers; it leads them to ask: 'Who is he. . .?'

With v. 40, the account becomes a catechism put forward to believers: they know who Jesus is. So why this fear? Where is their faith?

This use in catechesis could lead to the development of fully-fledged teaching. Thus Matthew is addressed to disciples, to people who follow Jesus in the ship (there is only one). This ship, shaken by an upheaval – the unleashing of evil powers characteristic of the end of time – is in peril of sinking. In the midst of this ship-church, the disciples pray, *Kyrie, sozon*. Jesus reproaches them for their fear, this apostolic fear of sailing out into Gentile territory, and for their little faith: they already have faith, but not enough. And non-believers all down history have asked how this ship-church can stay afloat when evil is unleashed. We can draw several conclusions from this.

The miracle is a sign. What interests the evangelists' contemporaries is not the fact itself – they are a good audience, and at that time they had no difficulty in accepting the possibility of miracle – but its significance: what does it mean? In *whose name* are you doing that? In the name of the prince of the demons, as Jesus' adversaries claim (Matt. 12.24)? 'It is by the spirit that I act,' replies Jesus, 'and that is a sign that the kingdom of God has come upon you' (Matt. 12.28).

So the important question is not to ask 'What happened?' (you can do that, but it's of secondary importance, and if you can't find an answer, it doesn't really matter), but rather to look for the meaning.

The evangelists often developed this meaning with the believers in mind: that is what we must discover above all.

Miracles and modern man

The miracles bother us. At one time people believed because of them; now people believe despite them. However, perhaps that is only because we get the wrong idea about them. Let me go back over one or two points.

A miracle is a sign. The road sign by the side of the road is real (it is made of metal) and has a shape (circular, triangular); the actual signs may differ, but that's not important: the essential thing is the message they convey, indicating a curve, or a crossroads. Similarly, miracles have a historical reality: they are facts so extraordinary that people notice them. But the essential thing is their message. What is it?

A miracle is a sign only for believers. A present exchanged between friends is a present only because they are already friends; an object given to us in the street by an unknown person is not a sign but a question. If we are to recognize a particular fact as a miracle, we must already have faith. The medical bureau at Lourdes, made up of believing and non-believing doctors alike, only affirms that a particular cure cannot be explained by science. The believer can then, if he or she likes, see the cure as a miracle. For that, the event has to fit into a certain context; it has to correspond with other facts, with statements. Lourdes is primarily a place of prayer, and it is in this context that cures can take on meaning. The miracles of Jesus are always bound up with his teaching.

For the non-believer, a miracle is a question, and never a 'proof'. If I don't know the highway code, the strange object by the side of the road raises a question for me. However, it's no use my examining it: I have to go and ask someone who knows what it means. That tells me its significance, and that is what I accept.

Similarly, an unexplained fact can make a non-believer ask the question, 'What is it?' The believer can then give his interpretation: 'That's a sign from my God.' The unbeliever will accept this interpretation by becoming a believer, or he will reject it and look for another explanation. The miracle is not a proof; people are not converted by miracles – it simply raises a question, but does so because of the meaning handed down by believers.

A miracle is a sign relative to its time. Facts can be extraordinary to one period and no longer so to another. The medical bureau at Lourdes declares that a particular cure cannot be explained by the present state of science. It may be explained one day. That doesn't matter much. If a miracle were a proof, it would be dishonest of God to take advantage of our ignorance to grab us, like a missionary proving God by switching on a tape recorder. If it's a sign, the supporting evidence is not so important; we are concerned with doctrine and not with a portent. Perhaps some of Jesus' miracles might seem explicable to us today.

However, to attempt to discover 'what happened' is to take a wrong turning. To take one example. A native who is an animist tells me, 'The gods are angry; they are spitting fire on the mountain.' He gives me his interpretation as a believer. But what is actually happening? If I did not know the country at all I would know that something was going on, but I would be incapable of saying whether it was a volcanic eruption, a forest fire or a storm. At the time of Jesus, miracles were common among Jews, and the famous Greek sanctuaries associated with miracles, like Pergamon and Epidaurus, with their votive offerings and their hospitals, were as important as Lourdes. Jesus would not have been a religious man of his time if he had not done miracles.

The essential thing is not to check the historicity of a particular miracle but to see what, today, might be a miracle for our contemporaries.

And the sphere of the extraordinary has shifted. It is perhaps less in the physical realm – science has taught us that we can (or will be able to) explain everything – than in the spiritual realm: for instance, a miracle could be an act of forgiveness. In a harsh and violent world, in the struggle for life, the free gesture – even more the gesture of forgiveness – becomes extraordinary and can lead the non-believer to ask, 'Why are you doing that?'

The miracle stories in the Bible should lead us less to ask what happened and more to ask, 'How, today, can I be a miracle, a sign posing a question to those among whom I live?'

Between a married couple, everything becomes a sign of love. Going through the Bible should lead the believer to discover that the whole world is miracle, a sign of the tenderness of God.

5 The Gospel according to Matthew

Matthew and the angel. Keystone
of the rood-loft at Chartres
(thirteenth century)

When we change from Mark to Matthew, we get the impression that we are moving into different country, just as we might go through a mountain pass and find another valley spreading out before us. With Mark we may sometimes have the illusion of discovering Jesus of Nazareth through Peter's eyes. With Matthew, we are never quite sure whether we are beside Lake Tiberias in the year 30 or at the celebration of the liturgy in a Christian church of the 80s. Or rather, Matthew puts us in two places at the same time: he deliberately places upon the Jesus of history the tracing paper of the Lord living in the church (see p. 19). Thus the countenance of Jesus of Nazareth is revealed to us through the glorious features of the risen Lord celebrated by the church.

The 'church's Gospel'

That is the title given to this Gospel, which has left its stamp on Western Christianity more than any other. It is the only one to use the word church (16.18; 18.17); it is concerned with the church's organization, with the brotherly life and the catechesis which it presents in the striking form of five great well-constructed discourses.

It introduces us to the heart of a church which celebrates its Lord in the liturgy: it puts the tracing paper of Christians worshipping the Risen Lord, chanting *Kyrie, sozon* (the equivalent of *eleison*), at the height of the storm, over the disciples of Jesus. It is also a church which runs the risk of stifling itself and having only 'little faith' (8.26).

Matthew's church

The situation of the communities among which Matthew was preaching largely influenced his witness. Three main aspects appear as we read the text.

The communities seem to have been composed above all of Christians who had come from Judaism. They knew the scriptures well: more than 130 passages have been noted in which Matthew refers to the Old Testament. For them, the Law remains the rule of life: 'I have not come to abolish the Law but to fulfil it,' to bring it to its culmination, to perfection, declares Jesus (5.17). They are very familiar with the way in which the rabbis interpret scriptures, and some of their questions (about fasting, almsgiving and divorce) are typically Jewish. It is no coincidence that Jesus is presented as the new Moses.

These communities are in conflict with official Judaism as it was reborn at Jamnia (see p. 31). Christians had already been driven out of their synagogues as Matthew writes. And the very harsh attacks made by Jesus on the Pharisees (Matt. 23) are perhaps less those of the Jesus of the 30s than those of the risen Lord, living in his community in the 80s, against the Pharisees of Jamnia.

These communities are open to Gentiles. By Christian conviction, reflecting on the missionary impetus of the first years of the church, these Jews who had become Christians rediscovered in the words of Jesus his concern to send his disciples all over the world.

The author

A second-century tradition which cannot be checked says that Matthew, the customs officer of Capernaum, who became one of the Twelve (9.9), wrote down the words of Jesus in *Aramaic*.

The present author of the Gospel, an unknown figure, was perhaps inspired by him. He wrote, *in Greek*, round about 80 or 90, in the communities of Syria and Palestine, perhaps at Antioch.

Moses and the
Law. Dura-Europos
synagogue (Syria,
before AD 256)

69

The Gospel as a Whole

It would be a good thing to start, as with Mark (p. 58), by reading the Gospel of Matthew straight through. Here are some landmarks for your guided tour.

Matthew's geography

Matthew follows Mark's scheme, but differs from him in not stressing the opposition between Galilee and Jerusalem. Galilee is the important area. It takes on two particular aspects.

During the ministry of Jesus it emerges as a Jewish area, the borders of which he scarcely crosses; while Jesus goes towards Tyre and Sidon, Matthew notes that the Canaanite woman has come out of her territory (15.21). Jesus preaches only to Jews, and forbids his disciples to approach Gentiles and Samaritans (10.5–6).

After the resurrection, Galilee becomes the gateway to the world, as Isaiah proclaimed (Matt. 4.14–16). It is there – and not in Jerusalem – that the glorified Jesus appears to his disciples and sends them out to preach all over the world (28.16–20).

The most Jewish of the Gospels

He refers constantly to the scriptures: more than 130 times, 43 of which are explicit quotations; 11 are introduced by the formula 'This happened that the saying of the Lord by the prophet might be fulfilled. . .' A true rabbi, he sometimes brings together several passages in a subtle way to produce a quotation which suits him; thus he combines Zech. 11.12 and Jer. 18.2 to explain the death of Judas (27.9), or Zech. 9.9 and Isa. 62.11 to give messianic significance to Jesus' entry into Jerusalem (21.1–19).

His manner of expression is Jewish. He talks of the kingdom of heaven rather than of the kingdom of God, because Jews do not pronounce the divine name. He loves repetitions, particularly inclusions, the repetition of the same expression at the beginning and the end of a passage (5.3, 10; 6.25–34). He uses parallelism (16.25; 7.24–27). He is fond of numerical groupings, whether these are symbolic or simply meant as aids to the memory: seven petitions in the Lord's Prayer, seven parables, seven loaves and seven baskets, three temptations, three good works (6.1f.), three tithes (23.23), etc.

Sidon
Tyre
Caesarea Philippi
Capernaum
Nazareth
Jesus as a child reenacts the Exodus
Jerusalem
Jericho
Second return to Galilee 4.14

Infancy:
To Egypt on the route of the Exodus

The kingdom of God and the church

Jesus inaugurates the kingdom of God (see p. 65). The church is not identical with this kingdom, but it is the privileged place where it is manifested in the world. The kingdom of God and the beginnings of its realization in the world form the central theme of Matthew.

How does he develop it? Some characteristic features will enable us to see this.

The infancy narratives (1–2) are in fact the theological prologue to the Gospel.

An identical closing formula (7.28; 11.1; 13.53; 19.1; 26.1) marks out five great discourses constructed by Matthew. They alternate with six narrative sections in the Gospel, accounts of the actions and sayings of Jesus. What is the link between the narrative sections and the discourses? An inclusion, a repetition of the same phrase at the beginning and the end of the first grouping (4.23; 9.35), gives some indication there: in a discourse Jesus presents a theme which he then puts into action. We might assume that this sequence also holds good for the other groupings.

Two passages at the beginning (3–4) and in the middle of the Gospel (16.13–17.27) are also similar, and serve as a transition. An identical formula, which we find only here, introduces two successive phases of the ministry of Jesus: 'From that time Jesus began to preach, saying . . . the kingdom of heaven is at hand' (4.17), or, 'to show his disciples that he must suffer' (16.21). In both cases there is a proclamation of a title of Jesus: Son (the heavenly voice) or Messiah (Peter); in both cases Jesus is tempted by Satan or by Peter described as Satan.

In the light of these observations we might imagine that Matthew develops his theme of the kingdom and the church in this way.

To begin with, Jesus proclaims to everyone the arrival of the kingdom, which he inaugurates with his actions. He prepares his disciples to continue his work by sending them on a mission. In fact, he is the one who goes off to preach! His disciples will only really be ready for their mission after Easter.

Jesus then devotes himself to the training of his disciples. Peter proclaims Jesus as Messiah, but also tempts him. Jesus gives a rule of life to his church. Then he announces the coming of the kingdom, inaugurates it by his death and resurrection, and sends his disciples to preach it in the world.

Prologue. Presentation of the mystery of Jesus (1–2)

Part one. Jesus preaches the kingdom of God to all men and prepares for the church (3–16)

Transition. The Father proclaims his Son, who is tempted by Satan (3–4)

1. The kingdom of God is at hand (5–9)
   Jesus manifests it through
      his words: the Sermon on the Mount (5–7)
      his actions: ten miracles (8–9)
2. Jesus sends his disciples to preach, and he himself departs to proclaim the kingdom (10–12)
   Discourse commissioning the disciples (10)
   Jesus on his mission (11–12)
3. The decisive choice demanded by the proclamation of the kingdom (13.1–16.12)
   Discourse consisting of seven parables (13.1–52)
   Towards Peter's confession (13.53–16.12)

Part two. Jesus prepares the church for its role in the kingdom of God (17–28)

Transition. The church confesses and tempts its Lord (16.13–17.27)

4. The kingdom of God passes from the Jewish people to the church (18–23)
   Discourse: the 'community rule' (18)
   From Galilee to Jerusalem (19–23)
5. The definitive inauguration of the kingdom of God at Easter (24–28)
   Apocalyptic discourse: the definitive coming of the kingdom of God in Jesus (24–25)
   The death and exaltation of Jesus inaugurating the definitive coming of the kingdom (26–28)
   The church sets out to preach in the world.

The end of time

Mark ends his Gospel by saying: everything has still to be done; the Risen Christ will not be seen until the end of history. Matthew declares: With Jesus, everything has been achieved; the end of time has arrived; victory is won; it remains only to occupy the territory! We should pause for one significant detail.

In his apocalyptic discourse Jesus gave a sign of the end of time: there would be 'upheavals' (Mark 13.8; Luke 21.11; Matt. 24.7). This is not a reference to a historical phenomenon (an earthquake) but a symbolic image.

Matthew, and only Matthew, uses the noun or the verb six times elsewhere. At the 'upheaval' of the cross, the dead are raised (27.51) and, confronted with the sight of this 'upheaval' (27.54), Gentiles acknowledge Jesus as Son of God. On Easter morning there is an 'upheaval' and the enemy, 'caught-by-the-upheaval', are as though they were dead (20.2, 4). So the death-and-glorification of Jesus is the sign for the end of time.

The city is in an 'upheaval' when Jesus enters Jerusalem; this is an image of his glorious entry into heaven (21.10).

So one of the signs given to make it possible to recognize the coming of the end of time takes effect at the time of the passion and resurrection. The kingdom of God is definitively inaugurated by this event. But the church, a frail ship battered by the upheaval (8.29: this is the word usually translated as storm, see p. 87), must experience this crisis all through its history.

Some features of Matthew

Matthew is a teacher. He rearranges the words of Jesus into five great speeches, doubtless in order to present him as the new Moses. He stresses the need to understand the word and not just to hear it (13.19–23). He abbreviates the miracle stories, often keeping only two figures, Jesus and the person concerned; the stories lose their vividness but make a greater impact as teaching.

He is a scribe versed in Jewish methods of interpreting the scriptures, knowing how to draw from his treasure things new and old (13.52).

His Christian faith makes him see Jesus of Nazareth as the glorified Lord. At the very beginning, and frequently after that, he proclaims Jesus to be Son of God, whose majesty and authority are transparent.

The whole of the Gospel unfolds in a liturgical atmosphere: the disciples who worship their Lord in the community appear through the disciples who follow Jesus on the roads of Palestine.

This Gospel, which is centred on the kingdom of heaven and its outcome in the church, has been called the Gospel of the church, and it has left a profound mark on Western Christianity.

Some Texts from Matthew

🔖 The temptations of Jesus. 4.1–11

Let us pause over one feature of the Gospel: how Jesus' life and our own make sense thanks to the scriptures.

It is quite probable that Jesus began his ministry with a 'retreat' and that he was tempted during it (read Mark 1.12–13). However, he was tempted all through his life, by his opponents and by Peter (e.g. Matt. 16.23; 27.42; John 6.15). Christians tried to work out the significance of these temptations. One tradition, taken up by Matthew and Luke, seeks to express it.

Read the text of Matthew. What does desert, forty, temptation suggest? See how each of these temptations is constructed.

The devil puts Jesus in one of the situations experienced by the Israelites in the desert (v. 4 = Ex. 16.14; v. 7 = Ex. 17.1–7; v. 10 = Ex. 23.20–30; 34.11–14). So Jesus was repeating the journey made by his people. They had failed to reach their destiny on entering the promised land because they had been unable to cope with these temptations.

Jesus responds with a quotation from Deuteronomy (see *How to Read the Old Testament*, pp. 57, 111). So Jesus undergoes these temptations and responds to them as the people should have done in order to succeed. The history of his people, taken up by Jesus, succeeds through him: from now on it is possible to enter the promised land, and Jesus proclaims, 'The kingdom of God is at hand' (4.17).

So the temptations of Jesus are his own, but at the same time he is taking on the temptations of his people. (By placing here the genealogy from Jesus back to Adam, Luke is doubtless affirming that Jesus is taking on again the temptations of all humanity.)

Paul takes up these same temptations of the people (I Cor. 10.1–11) to show that they are our own. That happened to them as a type of ourselves (vv. 6, 11). The type is not an example or a model, but a mock-up or a pattern (for a dress, for example). This mock-up represents in advance the object that is to be made; it is this object. The temptations of the people of Israel are a mock-up of our own, and these are the ones which Jesus experienced. We do not have so much to imitate Jesus (that might simply be moralism) as to live out our own existence (and our temptations) in him, because he has taken them on and has already overcome them.

🔖 The Sermon on the Mount. 5–7

Here we shall be reading Matthew: we shall compare his text with that of Luke later (p. 77). If you want, you can go on to study the Beatitudes now (p. 78).

Begin by reading through this Sermon carefully. There is a plan on the opposite page to help you.

Who is speaking? To whom? Who: Jesus of course, but how is he presented? What mountain is this? What Old Testament figure is he replacing? To whom: Jesus is teaching the crowds and the disciples. This is not the first proclamation, aimed at conversion (the kerygma), but a kind of catechism for those who have already discovered the pearl of great price and are ready to give up everything in order to possess it. The presence of the disciples indicates that this is possible: some have already made the choice to follow Jesus.

Note the refrains and the expressions which recur. 'You have heard. . .' 'Your Father who sees in secret. . .' Underline the word Father: it occurs twenty-one times in Matthew, twice in Mark and five times in Luke. It also occurs three times in John. There are sixteen occurrences in the Sermon: in which part? What significance does that give to Jesus' teaching?

One feature of the Sermon is impossible to reproduce in English. The Sermon alternates between the second person singular and the second person plural (to show this, the plural use of 'you' is marked with an asterisk* in the table opposite). The plurals (and similarly those phrases which begin 'whoever' or its equivalent) give general rules which apply to everyone everywhere: the singular use gives individual instances; they are meant to help people discover their own way of practising the general law in their particular situation (Jesus himself did not in fact observe the precept given in Matt. 5.39; see John 18.23). In each passage try to work out the general law, to see ways in which it is applied, and to look for examples which would apply today.

You can work out how Jesus fulfils the Law of Moses: he does not destroy it, but, following the line of the prophets, pushes it to extremes. He internalizes it: it is no longer a matter of outward attitudes but of love. He makes it personal: it is a question of living under the Father's gaze, and that is possible from now on because Jesus is the Son and invites us to enter into this filial relationship which he enjoys with the Father.

	Luke	Matthew	Mark
Opening 5.3–16			
5.3–12 The Beatitudes. The good news (originally 3,6,11–12)	**6.20–26**(24–26)		
5.13–16 Christians, the salt and the light of the world	14.34–35		9.50
	8.16; 11.33		4.21

I The new justice is superior to the old   5.17–48
or, what is the significance for everyday behaviour of having experienced the good news?

  The principle

	Luke	Matthew	Mark
5.17 Not to abolish the Law and the Prophets, but to fulfil	21.32–33; 16.17		
5.18–19 Anyone who breaks a single commandment		24.34–35	13.30–31

Five specific applications: 'You* have been told . . . I tell you*', 5.21–48

	Luke	Matthew	Mark
5.21–24 'Do not kill' – not to be angry with one's brother			11.25
5.25–26 Hasten to be reconciled with your adversary	12.57–59		
5.27–28 'Do not commit adultery' – Do not even desire another woman in your* heart			
5.29–30 If your eye is an occasion for sin, pluck it out		18.9,8	9.47,43
5.31–32 Anyone who repudiates his wife	16.18	19.7–9	10.4–12
5.33–37 'Do not perjure yourself' – Do not swear oaths at all			
5.38–42 'An eye for an eye' – Turn the other cheek	**6.29–30**		
5.43–48 'Love your neighbour and hate your enemy' – Love your* enemies	**6.27–28,32–36**		

II The inward character of the new justice   6.1–18
or, in what spirit are we to perform the traditional good works when we are children of the Father?

  The principle

	Luke	Matthew	Mark
6.1 Only be concerned with the Father when you do good works			

The three traditional good works in Judaism

	Luke	Matthew	Mark
6.2–4 Almsgiving in secret. 'Your Father who sees in secret'			
6.5–6 Prayer in secret. 'Your Father who sees in secret. . .'			
6.7–15 'Our Father. . .'	11.2–4		
6.16–18 Fasting in secret. 'Your Father who sees in secret. . .'			
6.19–21,22–23 The true treasure. The eye, the light of the body	12.33f.; 11.34f.		
6.24–34 Choosing between God and money. Trust in the Father	16.13; 12.22–31		

III Three admonitions   7.1–27
or, who is a disciple? How to be one

	Luke	Matthew	Mark
	(38a)	15.14;	
7.1–5 Don't judge. The log and the speck	**6.37–42**		4.24
	(39–40)	10.24	
7.6 Don't desecrate holy things			
7.7–11 The efficacy of prayer	11.9–13		
7.12 The golden rule: Do not do to others	**6.31**		
7.13–14 The narrow gate which leads to life	13.23–24		
7.15–20 The false prophets: they can be recognized by their fruits	**6.43–45**(45)	12.33–35	
7.21–27 The true disciples: Don't say 'Lord', but do the will of the Father	**6.46**		
7.22–23 It is not enough to drive out the demons in his name	13.26–27		
Build your house on the rock	**6.47–49**		

	Luke	Matthew	Mark
The effect on the crowd 7.28–29	7.1; 4.32		4.22
'He teaches as a man who has authority'			

NB The additions made by Matthew are in *italics*. The references to the speech in Luke **6.20–40** are in **bold**.

❖ Recognizing and following Jesus. 16.13–28

These three episodes form a turning point in the Gospel of Matthew (see p. 71).

Compare the response of Peter in Matt. 16.16; Mark 8.29; Luke 9.20; John 6.69. What, then, might have been this response? How does Matthew explain it by putting over it the 'tracing paper' of Christian faith? The importance of Peter's role in the first community was recognized by all Christians. Was this role handed on to successors? Here the Christian traditions differ.

❖ The community rule. 18

Jesus gives two groups of rules which he illustrates by two parables (18.10–14,23–25). What rules (what canon law?) did Jesus in fact leave to his church?

18.20 is very strong. A rabbi who died in 135 declared: 'When two people are sitting talking about the Law, the Shekinah (God's holy presence) is in their midst.' So Matthew puts Jesus in place of the Law and of God!

❖ The infancy narratives. 1–2

These narratives, like those in Luke, are not folklore, but theology, like Mark 1.1 or the hymn in John 1.1–18. Sometimes a film gives the main themes as a background to the credits, and then by a flashback puts the last images of the film at the beginning. Matthew does the same thing here, and puts at the beginning the main figures in the Gospel, telling us who Jesus is, the new Moses, and what his mission is to be.

Read these two chapters carefully: in the light of reading the Gospel as a whole (p. 70), try to see how Matthew immediately anticipates the features of the life of Jesus.

After the genealogy we have a sequence of five episodes, made up of two groups which are enclosed one within the other, each having a quotation from scripture:

1. The announcement to Joseph (1.18–25). Isa. 7.14.
a. *The magi* (2.1–12). Micah 5.1 + II Sam. 5.2.
2. The flight into Egypt (2.13–25). Hos. 11.1.
b. *The killing of the children* (2.16–18). Jer. 31.15.
3. The return to Nazareth (2.19–23). Isa. 42.6; possibly 49.6.

The first group (1, 2, 3), centred on the angel of God and Joseph, uses the same pattern: situation, message of the angel and mission, scripture, fulfilment of the mission. The second group (a, b) contrasts the two kings, Herod and Jesus.

The genealogy tells us who Jesus is: Christ, son of David, the beginning of the new creation (compare 1.1 with Gen. 5.1).

The announcement to Joseph tells us how Jesus is son of David despite the virgin birth. Being a just man, Joseph does not want to pass this miraculous child off as his own; however, God asks Joseph to give the child his name and his social position by making him part of a line.

The episode of the magi is a piece of scriptural research, a midrash *pesher* (see p. 21). Beginning from memories of Herod's bloody acts, Matthew constructs a story based on Isa. 60; 62 and the star in Num. 24.17 (which was seen as a portrayal of the Messiah at that time, see the box below). He did this to show how Jesus would be rejected by the Jewish authorities and the civil power, but recognized by the Gentiles.

The flight into Egypt shows in symbolic fashion how in Jesus the people achieve a successful exodus. The way to the kingdom of God is at last open.

Numbers 24.17

in the Hebrew text	in the Palestinian Targum
A star	*When the mighty king*
issuing from Jacob	*from the house of Jacob*
shall become ruler	*shall reign*
and a sceptre shall arise	*and when the Messiah, the powerful sceptre*
issuing out of Israel	*of Israel shall be anointed. . .*

So Matthew's star is real; it is the Messiah, Jesus, who has just arisen, and to his light the Gentiles, represented by the Magi, come.

Other texts studied elsewhere

The Passion according to Matthew

Matthew writes for Christians who already have faith and want to deepen it. He tries to unveil the significance of the death of Christ.

He is writing for Christians of Jewish origin: he shows how in Jesus God keeps the promise which he made to his people, and how Jesus fulfils the scriptures. Through its leaders, this Jewish people has rejected Jesus, so now the promise passes to a new people, the church. However, the church must stay on the watch: it, too, can refuse to follow Jesus.

In his presentation of events, Matthew seeks above all to show the power and the authority of Jesus.

Jesus is Son of God; he knows what will happen to him. He accepts this; indeed, events take place as they do because he foresees them.

Jesus is Lord over the whole world. The Father has entrusted his own power to Jesus, who could make use of it to escape death. However, that death marks the end of time and ushers in the arrival of the new world, the kingdom of God in which we now have to live.

The account of the conspiracy (26.1–5) seeks to answer two possible difficulties. How could the Son of God have been put to death? By placing the account on the lips of Jesus, Matthew shows that he is the one who directs events, and the leaders carry them out ('Then. . .', v. 3). How could the religious leaders, whose task it was to recognize the Messiah, condemn him? It was because they were those evil ones who, according to Ps. 2, came together against the Messiah (*How to Read the Old Testament*, p. 103). It is clear that from now on this messiah will be enthroned over the whole world as Lord. And Jesus sees his anointing in the house of Simon (26.6–13) as the celebration of his burial.

The account of the farewell meal held by Jesus (26.26–29) is framed by the announcement of Judas' betrayal and Peter's denial; so Jesus is well aware of the hands into which he will be putting his body and his blood. However, in this way he fulfils the scriptures (v. 31).

Up to that point, Jesus has celebrated his passion with the majesty of the celebrant at the altar. The account of the agony in the garden (26.36–46) shows him to be fully

man: three times Matthew adds the expression, with them, with me (vv. 36, 38, 40). Like everyone who suffers, Jesus feels the need of the presence of his friends. Even that is denied him; they are asleep. However, in reciting the Our Father to help himself to accept the Father's will, he rediscovers all his strength; at the time of the arrest (26.47–56), he teaches once again and refuses to use the power which the Father has given him.

The Last Supper
Lambert Rucky

At his trial before the Jews (26.57–68), Jesus proclaims that henceforth, from now on (v. 64), he will be instituted by the Father into the power of the exalted Son of Man, the enthroned Messiah. The accounts of Peter's denial (26.69–75) and the death of Judas (27.3–10) remind us tragically that we can refuse to recognize his humiliated Lord. Above all, Matthew shows that here the oracle of Zechariah is being fulfilled; the people at that time rejected God, and to make mock of him paid him the derisory price of a slave (*How to Read the Old Testament*, p. 86). In Jesus, then, it is God himself who is being sold.

In the scene of the Roman trial (21.11–26), Matthew adds the intervention of Pilate's wife: even the Romans recognize that Jesus is righteous. Pilate washes his hands of him and the people take responsibility for his death: 'His blood be on us'. From now on, in order to be saved, everyone, Jews and Gentiles alike, will have to enter into the covenant sealed with the blood of Jesus.

For Matthew, the death of Jesus (27.32–54) marks the end of the old world and the beginning of the new world. In this way it fulfils the scriptures, which Matthew quotes abundantly.

Jesus dies apparently abandoned by all, even by God. But his death is resurrection: the earthquake, the upheaval, is an image of the end of time; at that moment the saints rise and enter the heavenly Jerusalem and the Gentiles recognize that Jesus is Son of God.

The high priests seal the tomb and set a watch (27.55–61): the power of the Risen Jesus only appears the greater. They themselves remember the forecast of the resurrection. Apparently all is over. Matthew warns us that it is only just beginning, and that the dawn of the resurrection is breaking in the night of the tomb.

Matthew's Jesus

The Lord living in his community

With Mark we discovered primarily the man Jesus; Matthew presents us from the start with the glorified Lord, celebrated in his community. The disciples prostrate themselves in adoration before the Risen Jesus (28.17), as do the Magi (2.2,11), the leper, the centurion, the disciples in the storm, though they should prostrate themselves only before God (4.10).

The fact is that by virtue of his resurrection, Jesus is truly God with us: the name Emmanuel, proclaimed at his birth (1.23), is given to him only on Easter Day; it is even the last saying in the Gospel: 'I am (the equivalent of God in the Old Testament) with you' (28.20).

He is the well-beloved Son of God. Mark does not use this title very much, and makes us see how difficult the disciples found it to recognize him. In Matthew, Jesus presents himself in this way (11.27; 26.63–64) and the disciples proclaim him to be Son of God on several occasions (e.g. 14.33; 16.16).

Matthew's Jesus is also solemn, hieratic. Matthew leaves out Jesus' emotion and his not-knowing (compare Matt. 13.58 with Mark 6.5) and stresses his power (4.23; 8.24; 15.30). Once, however, this Lord shows himself to be very human by looking for some affection from his friends in his agony.

Jesus is the saviour of his community. The miracles show him to be the suffering servant of Isaiah who takes our infirmities upon him (8.17). By schematizing the miracle stories, by effacing the human features of Jesus and presenting Peter's mother-in-law (8.15) or the disciples in the storm (8.25) in the guise of the Christians of his time, Matthew shows that the Lord Jesus is continuing his saving work in the community in Matthew's own day.

Jesus is the Lord of his community. Moses had given the Law to the people; Jesus is the new Moses who gives the new law, in the Sermon on the Mount and on the mountain where he appears at Easter. The concern of this law is that men should be perfect as the Father is perfect. Restoring the ancient Law to its original purity, Jesus looks for mercy and not sacrifice (9.13; 12.7), and again it is mercy and forgiveness that he leaves as a rule for his church (18.21–35). He wants his disciples to have an intelligent faith, to understand, and asks this of them several times (e.g. 13.19,23,51; 15.10).

Jesus is the model for his community. 'It is fitting for us to fulfil all righteousness', he says to John (3.15), and in a text which appears only in his Gospel, he presents the life of Jesus as the only way of arriving at knowledge of the Father (11.27–30).

The Messiah of Israel

For Matthew, Jesus is the Messiah looked for by Israel and announced by scripture. As a true rabbi, Matthew skilfully quotes the scriptures to show that Jesus fulfils them. He frequently gives Jesus official titles like Messiah (Christ), Son of David, King of Israel. Rejecting him or accepting him decides whether a person belongs to the true Israel: the Gentile magi worship him, but Jerusalem rejects him; priests and scribes condemn him, while the Roman centurion and his men proclaim him Son of God. The kingdom, too, will be taken away from the former to be given to others (parable of the murderers in the vineyard, 21–41). The Messiah of Israel becomes the world's Messiah.

The Son of Man

In the tradition of the apocalypses (see Dan. 7), people looked to the coming of the Son of Man at the end of time to give judgment. For Matthew, Jesus is this Son of Man; he declares himself to be Son of Man before the Sanhedrin and proclaims that from now on people will see him (26.64). Easter is truly the parousia of the Son of Man coming on the clouds (26.64) to his prostrate disciples (28.18), having received all power (28.18; cf. Dan. 7.14). Matthew is the only one to speak of this parousia or arrival (24.3,27,37,39) of the Son of Man. In fact for him it denotes the moment when the kingdom of God takes its place in our history. That happens at the time of the resurrection; this parousia also takes place every time one meets the Son of Man mysteriously present in the little ones with whom he identifies himself (25.31–46).

Jesus sends him community

Enthroned as Son of Man, sovereign judge and lord of all the world, Jesus has won the final victory. Now the territory has to be occupied, so he sends his disciples to establish his victory throughout the world. He had prepared them for this mission (10), but at that time he was the one who went out to preach. The real mission begins on Easter Day (28.18–20).

Catechesis. The Discourses

When the audiences had heard the preaching (the kerygma) of the disciples and had themselves become disciples of Jesus Christ through faith and baptism, it still remained to complete their teaching. 'They devoted themselves to the apostles' teaching', writes Luke (Acts 2.42). When we studied Christian action (pages 55–56), we discovered this catechesis through the Epistles. Now we shall look at it through the discourses of Jesus in the Gospels.

Jesus preached; that's quite obvious. Did he talk at length, like the discourses in the Gospels? That's possible. At all events, however, these discourses are for the most part the result of the work of the communities which brought together the words of Jesus to make them into a kind of catechism.

The most obvious instance of this is the Sermon on the Mount in Matthew, and the corresponding Sermon on the Plain in Luke. We have already studied Matthew's text (p. 73). Here we shall compare the two texts.

Place and importance

In Matthew, the sermon is a programmatic discourse of Jesus, the first one which he gives: it contains 107 verses. In Luke there are only 30 verses, and the programmatic discourse is given earlier, in the synagogue at Nazareth (Luke 4.16–30). Mark does not have one at all!

Towards an earlier text

Without claiming to be able to go back to the words of Jesus, we can try to see whether Matthew and Luke were inspired by a text which they found in their source and how they have modified it or enriched it.

Go back to the diagram on p. 73. If you look at the Luke column you will see that the whole of the discourse in Luke 6.20–40 reappears, sometimes in a different order, in that of Matthew, apart from 6.24–26 and four other verses: 38a, 39, 40, 45.

After a very careful study, the French scholar J. Dupont has produced the following hypothesis. Matthew reproduces his source, but adds to it a certain number of teachings (which have been put in italics in the diagram). Luke reproduces the same source, which had already been enlarged by four verses; however, he prunes it, putting certain pieces of teaching elsewhere.

Whatever the exact position may be, this first form of the discourse was already a collection of isolated sayings of Jesus which had been made by the community; some could be the summary of one of his sermons, others a condensation of a long piece of teaching given in the form of questions and answers. By collecting them together in this way, the disciples wanted to present the whole of Christianity (as a kind of catechism) in comparison to the teaching of Judaism which might already have been put forward by the Pharisees of Jamnia (see p. 31).

Matthew's sermon

Matthew takes up this catechism faithfully. He stresses the practical consequences, and gives instances of possible applications.

⚜ In the light of the study made earlier (p. 72), try to distinguish the main outlines of this catechism on the conduct of the perfect disciple.

Luke's discourse

Luke's discourse is much shorter and keeps the character of a gospel, the proclamation of good news (for the Beatitudes see pp. 78–79). Hearing it makes us feel the demands of a different way of life, and Luke focusses his catechism on this love.

⚜ Compare Luke 6.36 and Matt. 5.48: what is the difference? What significance does it give to Christian life?

Compare Luke 6.33–35 and Matt. 5.47; what is the difference? Luke is virtually the only one, along with I Peter, to use the term 'do good' or 'good conduct' (I Peter 2.14,15,20; 3.6,17; 4.19; see pp. 54–55). What vision of the Christian life does Luke give us?

Compare the refrain in Luke 6.32,33,34 and Matt. 5.46. What difference is there? The word translated 'acknowledgment' or 'recognition' (with a risk of suggesting the idea of a *quid pro quo*, if not some recompense) is grace. What we receive as a *quid pro quo* for our love is not a reward, but grace.

Read the discourse again in the light of these observations. Try to identify the main outlines of this catechism about the behaviour of the one who knows himself or herself to be loved freely by God.

The beatitudes

The Sermon on the Mount in Matthew and the Sermon on the Plain in Luke open with the proclamation of the beatitudes. Jesus' message is thus essentially an announcement of good cheer. But for whom, and how?

Sad to say, we must recognize that as a result of a tragic misinterpretation, the beatitudes have often been used as an opiate to soothe the suffering or the rebellion of the poor. They seemed to say, 'You poor are fortunate because you are loved by God, so – stay poor! Accept your lot and one day, in heaven, you will be happy.' Now we shall be seeing that Jesus proclaimed exactly the opposite: 'You poor are fortunate since from now on you will no longer be poor, because the kingdom of God is on its way.'

Begin by comparing these beatitudes: which ones do Matthew and Luke have in common? To whom are they addressed (they – you)? What kind of poverty is it in Luke? In Matthew? Distinguish the two series of beatitudes: the first eight in Matthew (same style, same expression, kingdom of God, at the beginning and the end) and the ninth (a change of style and of those to whom it is addressed).

The beatitudes before Matthew and Luke

Jesus doubtless proclaimed beatitudes at different times. The community made a first collection which a scholar, J. Dupont, has reconstructed with some degree of probability (see the bottom of the opposite page). What might their significance be at this stage? (We shall only be studying the first series.)

To discover this, we have to put the beatitudes back into Jesus' teaching about the kingdom of God. Read again what I said about it on p. 65. Compare the beatitudes common to Matthew and Luke and Jesus' reply to the messengers from John the Baptist. In his reply Jesus quotes the prophets, so he is aware of realizing their proclamations in his actions. Read some texts again: Isa. 49.9; 52.7; 60.6; 61.1; 35.5–6. During the exile, or just afterwards, prophets announced that God would reign, that he would finally manifest himself as the good King that he was. What signs does he give? Are not these the signs which Jesus performs? So Jesus is affirming that the kingdom of God is at hand in his person and that from now on there will no longer be any poor; that is why they are said to be happy.

An objection: if this is the meaning of Jesus' proclamation, he was wrong, because there are always poor and there is always injustice. To raise this question, though, is to note that unfortunately we Christians have not done our work. People were in fact waiting for a Messiah who would establish the kingdom of God single-handed. Jesus came as Messiah, but he inaugurated this kingdom only by entrusting to his disciples the task of realizing it. The first Christians understood this very well: they held their possessions in common, Luke writes, and there were no longer any poor among them (Acts 4.34). One cannot proclaim the beatitudes without doing everything possible to remove poverty in all its forms, sickness and injustice.

The primary meaning of the beatitudes, then, is theological; they speak of God, the God of the poor, who is going to establish his kingdom of justice and love by his Messiah and his disciples. In the Gospels they have become christological: in different ways Matthew and Luke lay stress on the one by whom this kingdom arrives, Christ.

The beatitudes according to Luke

To whom are the beatitudes addressed? The second person plural is directed to the disciples. Jesus tells these Christians who are poor that their wretched situation is only to be expected: it is the result of their faithfulness towards him. However, at their death, God will rectify the situation.

The beatitudes according to Matthew

Matthew does not just address Christians, but everyone. He is the only one to spiritualize these beatitudes and make them attitudes of mind. Jesus asks those who, like the first disciples mentioned in Acts, try to see that there will no longer be any poor, 'With what feelings are you acting?' Paul understood this very well when he wrote, 'though I sell all my goods to feed the poor and have not love, I am worth nothing' (I Cor. 13.3). We have to fight until there are no longer any poor, but we have to do so with a humble heart. Only those who feel like this can help the poor without smothering them with pity. This attitude has its source in Jesus, who is meek and humble in heart (Matt. 11.29). Only when we know that we ourselves have been given abundant grace can we pass on this good news to the poor, to help them emerge from their poverty.

Matthew 5.3–12	Luke 6.20b–23	Luke 6.24–26
3 Blessed are the poor in spirit, for theirs is the kingdom of heaven.	20b Blessed are you poor, for yours is the kingdom of God.	24 But woe to you who are rich, for you have received your consolation.
4 Blessed are those who mourn, for they shall be comforted	(see 21b)	(see 25b)
5 Blessed are the meek, for they shall inherit the earth.		
6 Blessed are those who hunger and thirst for righteousness, for they shall be satisfied	21 Blessed are you who hunger now, for you shall be satisfied. Blessed are you who weep now, for you shall laugh.	25 Woe to you that are full now, for you shall hunger. Woe to you that laugh now, for you shall mourn and weep.
7 Blessed are the merciful, for they shall obtain mercy.		
8 Blessed are the pure in heart, for they shall see God.		
9 Blessed are the peacemakers, for they shall be called sons of God.		
10 Blessed are those who are persecuted for righteousness' sake, for theirs is the kingdom of heaven.		
11 Blessed are you when men revile you and persecute you and utter all kinds of evil against you falsely on my account.	22 Blessed are you when men hate you and when they exclude you and revile you and cast out your name as evil on account of the Son of man!	26 Woe to you when all men speak well of you,
12 Rejoice and be glad, for your reward is great in heaven for so men persecuted the prophets who were before you.	23 Rejoice in that day, and leap for joy, for behold, your reward is great in heaven for so their fathers did to the prophets.	for so their fathers did to the false prophets.

An earlier version of the text has been reconstructed with a high degree of probability.

Blessed are the poor, for the kingdom of heaven is theirs.
Blessed are those who mourn, for they shall be comforted.
Blessed are those who hunger (and thirst), for they shall be satisfied.
Blessed are you when men hate you and exclude you and insult you
and give you an evil name because of the Son of man;
rejoice and be glad, for your reward is great in heaven,
for so men persecuted the prophets (which were) before you.

The good news of the kingdom of God

The essence of the good news, the gospel that Jesus proclaimed, was that the reign, the kingdom of God, was at hand. Through his actions (the miracles, and also his specific attitude towards the poor, the insignificant and the scorned) and his words (the discourses of which the beatitudes bring out the main theme), Jesus shows that this kingdom is at hand. Above all he is the one who proclaims and inaugurates this kingdom.

Now we can see that in the community and in the Gospels, people proclaimed the good news about Jesus. The one who had made the proclamation became the subject of this proclamation. There is a shift of interest, but the meaning remains the same. 'The dead are raised' was one of the staggering signs of the advent of the kingdom. To proclaim that Jesus is risen is to affirm that *in him* the kingdom has come. This man, transfigured by the Spirit, is the symbol of man who has entered the kingdom.

However, in the light of this the disciples understand better that it is also *through Jesus* that the kingdom arrives. To proclaim the risen Jesus is another even clearer way of announcing that the kingdom of God is here.

The beatitudes: a political programme

If Jesus merely inaugurated this kingdom, we can understand that the beatitudes and all the teachings which are developed from them remain for all Christians a programme of action in their specific political, social, economic and family life.

They remind us that the motive behind our action must be the service of others, primarily the poor, so that there are no longer poor among us. The motive can never be money or power.

They also allow the Christian to give a deeper meaning to his human work: a doctor who fights against sickness, a worker who makes life more humane for others by the products that he makes, a teacher who helps young people to discover themselves, anyone who works so that others around him can live happy lives, standing on their own feet, have

the right to suppose that in a modest but effective way they are bringing about the kingdom of God.

Why does Jesus ask so much?

You will have been struck while reading the beatitudes, the Sermon on the Mount, the discourses of Jesus, by the terrible demands that he makes. You must give everything immediately! How is that possible?

You will also have noted Matthew's stress on the heavenly Father. We are to be as perfect as he is. That stress changes everything. Morality, Christian action, is not a law code which has to be applied: it is a loving demand. When we know ourselves loved with such love, we cannot but want to be like the one who loves us. So this demand is infinite, like the love of God. But when it is a loving demand, everything becomes possible.

What Jesus offers is not renunciation but happiness. The word 'blessed' in the beatitudes means 'happy'. The parables of the treasure and the pearl (Matt. 13.44–46) say this clearly: Jesus is addressing people who already have the experience of that love, who have already discovered the marvels of this kingdom and who are therefore ready to give everything in order to gain it. The law of the gospel can be absolute because it invites us to more-than-living, to happiness.

And the witness of those who have already made this choice is an essential element. When Jesus preaches on the mount, he is surrounded by his disciples (Matt. 5.1): those who hear this call of Jesus see that it is possible to respond to it since some men have already made their choice. And it is no coincidence that the beatitudes end with two comparisons: 'You are the salt of the earth. . . You are the light of the world' (Matt. 5.13–16). That is the best-ever definition of the church. The church is not a container for those who are saved ('no salvation outside the church'); it is a signal, a light on a mountain, revealing a meaning to life, serving as a beacon for the way 'to those who walk in darkness' (Isa. 60), a light which does not come from itself but which draws on its source by which it is illuminated.

6 The Work of Luke: The Gospel and Acts

Luke and the ox. Keystone of the rood-loft at Chartres (thirteenth century)

Luke is original in having written a work in two volumes: the Gospel and the Acts of the Apostles. They should be read together. We have already gone through Acts, rather superficially, using it as a tourist guide; we shall go back to it here, along with the Gospel, to discover the plan of Luke's work.

Taking up the comparison on p. 19, one might say that Luke, like the other evangelists, put over the life of Jesus the tracing paper of the life of the church; in Acts, however, he wanted to give us this overlay by itself.

A believing historian

Modestly, Luke does not write a Gospel but 'an account of events', so that the disciple can confirm his faith: he says as much in a prologue characteristic of the historians of his day (1.1–4).

However, the historian Luke is a believer: what he narrates is for him good news which he wants to share. He constantly tells his reader, 'You can't read this in a detached way; you must choose for or against, and you must do so today...' His account therefore never has the cool tones of a description; it is always at the same time an exhortation. The disciple is at the heart of his preoccupations; he is the one who is being addressed and is being persuaded to enter the marvellous world which Luke has discovered.

Luke's community

We do not know anything precisely about the community in which Luke was writing, but we can easily imagine the kind of church in which his message took shape: these were communities which had grown up on Gentile territory; Greek, like the churches of Antioch or Philippi. As we read the work we can pick out several of their features.

These Christians are former Gentiles. Luke, himself a Greek, adapts to their mentality. He stresses the reality of the resurrection (which the Greeks will have found difficulty in accepting), but uses a vocabulary which says more to them: 'Jesus is alive'. He uses the term 'saviour' to explain the title Christ/Messiah, which will have been obscure to his readers. Emperors were called 'Lord', so Luke is careful to say that Jesus is the only Lord. He avoids the word 'transfiguration' (Greek *metamorphosis*), because there were several accounts of the metamorphoses of Greek gods.

These Christians know that they are accepted into God's covenant with Israel by grace and not by birth. They are keen to reread the scriptures, to find in them the loving plan of God.

They have had experience of the Spirit: their churches came into being outside the Jerusalem circle, and were formed through the word of God and the Spirit. They know that faith in Jesus has brought them into a tradition, that of the apostles, which Luke investigates with care, but they know how to live it out in the freedom of the Spirit which drives them towards their fellow Gentiles. Unlike Matthew's communities, those of Luke find no difficulty in universalism.

The author

Traditionally, since the second century Luke has been seen as the 'beloved physician' (Col. 4.14) who accompanied Paul from Troas to Philippi, where he probably lived between 50 and 58. He rejoined Paul at Miletus, followed him to Caesarea and then to Rome (according to the passages in Acts written in the first person). Perhaps he came from Antioch, of Gentile (or Hellenistic) ancestry? An educated man, he handles with some skill the Greek commonly spoken at the time (the *koine*).

A stone discovered at Caesarea bearing the name of Pontius Pilate

The Gospel and Acts as a Whole

As with Mark and Matthew, it would be a good thing to begin by reading the Gospel and Acts straight through, as though it were a novel. It will take time, but you will see that it pays off.

Here are some points to guide you in your reading.

Luke's geography

The Gospel. In the first volume, Jerusalem has a central place. The Gospel begins and ends in the Temple (1.5f.; 24.52–53). The childhood of Jesus, from Nazareth to Bethlehem and back to Nazareth, comes to a climax in the arrival of Jesus at his Father's house, the Temple (2.41f.), and the Risen Lord shows himself only in Jerusalem (this forces Luke to change the saying of the angels at the tomb, 24.6).

Jesus begins his preaching in Galilee, but does so in order to be able to return to Jerusalem: the second part is organized as an ascent to Jerusalem (9.51–19.28). The paschal mystery has to unfold in the holy city, because 'it is not fitting that a prophet should perish outside Jerusalem' (13.33). In fact Jesus fulfils the divine plan announced by scripture with the holy city at its centre. However, Jerusalem rejects Jesus.

Acts. The second volume also shows how the Word spreads from Jerusalem, into Judaea and Samaria, and then to the ends of the earth, whose capital at that time was Rome.

Three periods in the history of salvation

The other evangelists think of two periods in the history of salvation: that of the promise and that of Jesus with his church. By writing two volumes, Luke can distinguish the times in a better way: that of the promise, that of Jesus, and that of the church.

1. The time of the promise

This is the time of the Old Testament. For Luke, it comes to an end only with the 'Today' in the sermon at Nazareth (4.21). John the Baptist is charged with preparing the people of the promise to welcome the prophet, but he himself remains within this time of preparation (7.28). Jesus also forms part of it; he comes to receive John's baptism in the midst of the people (3.21). These people have returned to the desert to reenact the exodus which failed the first time (the story of the temptations); Jesus is even mankind as a whole, the new Adam, at last taking his place in a true relationship with God (the genealogy, which goes back to Adam). From now on the gateway to the kingdom of God is open to the people of the promise and to all men: God's 'Today' can resound in our astonished ears (4.21).

Luke often refers to the scriptures, but in a different way from Matthew. He does not try to cite precise texts; for him scripture is as it were a subterranean water-table which gives life and meaning to events. And Jesus draws on it copiously before opening the minds of his disciples to understand the scriptures on Easter Day (24.45). That explains the numerous occasions on which Jesus uses the word 'must': it is not a question of blind obedience to a programme prepared in advance, but rather of shaping his life in such a way as to put it back into continuity with God's plan (see p. 113).

2. The time of Jesus: the Gospel

Luke uses material which he receives from the tradition: the Gospel of Mark (or an earlier version of its text) and the logia source which he shares with Matthew (look back at p. 15). However, he arranges these skilfully by adding to them traditions peculiar to himself in order to present us with the divine plan as he sees it.

Leaving aside the birth narratives, to which we shall return, and the time of preparation, the itinerary of Jesus consists of three main stages:

In Galilee, Jesus proclaims his paschal mystery (4.14–9.50). The sermon at Nazareth (4.14f.) is the programmatic speech for it. By bringing together two visits, one in which Jesus is well received and the other, much later, in which he is rejected, Luke shows how this proclamation is to be received. In this part he follows Mark closely except for the discourse on the plain (see p. 77) and the section between 7.1 and 8.2, where he presents Jesus as the new Elijah, the prophet who is the friend of sinners.

Jesus goes up to Jerusalem towards his paschal mystery (9.51–19.28). This is the most original part of the Gospel: the ascent to Jerusalem by Isaiah's servant.

In Jerusalem, Jesus fulfils the paschal mystery (19.29–24.53). On Easter day Jesus shows himself alive to his disciples and ascends to heaven.

3. The time of the church: Acts

Luke uses various pieces of material, some very early, which he brings together or rewrites: themes from the preaching of Peter, Paul and Stephen (see p. 34), archives from the communities in Jerusalem or Antioch, reminiscences of the activity of Peter and Paul, no doubt his travel diary when he himself accompanied Paul (the passages in Acts written in the first person).

The plan of the book is presented clearly by Jesus: the disciples are to be his witnesses in Jerusalem, Judaea and Samaria and to the ends of the world (1.8). The main figures in this development are Peter, then the Hellenists, and finally Paul, but above all the Spirit and the Word of God.

The plan of the book might be outlined as follows:

I. From the beginning of the church to the Council of Jerusalem. 1.1–15.35

    The community at Jerusalem. 1.1–5.42

    The church is opened up to Gentiles. 6.1–15.35

Luke presents successively the missionary activity of the Hellenists (8.1–9.31), of Peter (9.32–11.18 and 12.1–23), and of the church at Antioch (11.19–14.28). This culminates in the Council of Jerusalem (15.1–11), followed later by a meeting held by James (15.12–35).

II. From Jerusalem to Rome: Paul. 15.36–28.31

    In the course of his missionary tours Paul founds communities in Asia Minor and Europe. Taken to Rome as a prisoner, he preaches the gospel there with confidence.

Theological prologue. Luke 1–2

What we call the birth narratives or the infancy narratives are in fact a theological prologue to the whole work, both the Gospel and Acts. As with Matt. 1–2 (cf. p. 75), this is a kind of background to the 'credits', as in a film, where Luke presents the most important themes in advance. It might be interesting to look at the main ones in the order in which they appear.

(i) Jerusalem and the Temple: prayer (1.5f.).

(ii) Jesus, Son of David, Son of God, welcomed in faith by Mary, the daughter of Zion. The role of the Spirit (1.26–38).

(iii) The role of women, the Spirit, prayer, the humbling of the rich and the proud and the raising up of the lowly (1.39–56).

(iv) The name John, which means 'God is gracious', and the visit of God to his people (1.57–80).

(v) The good news to the poor (the shepherds): a saviour, Christ the Lord. God's today. The glory which shines out from this child on all men. And the result: joy for the world. This is the essential feature of the plan of Acts as suggested here, along with the role of the missionaries who go into the world: Peter, Paul and ourselves (2.1–21).

(vi) Again the Temple and the Holy Spirit, prayer, light for the Gentiles. There is a dispute over the significance of Jesus, in the face of which a choice has to be made (2.22–39).

(vii) As the culmination of the childhood of Jesus: the Temple and the first of Jesus' sayings to mention the Father. The first ascent to Jerusalem which evokes thoughts of the last: a disappearance for three days, being sought by the women; the Father, 'I must be about my Father's business', that 'the Christ must suffer to enter his glory'.

Some features of Luke

Luke's is the most 'modern' of the Gospels. His Greek education has given the author a concern for clarity. He handles the common Greek language (or *koine*) spoken at that time with a degree of elegance. However, he is also capable of imitating the language of the Greek Bible, very much coloured by Semitic turns of phrase, for example in the infancy narratives.

He deliberately interrupts his account with brief pauses or summaries, in which he sums up either features which he wants the reader to remember or the progress of the action. Thus three summaries present the activity of the community in Jerusalem (Acts 2.42); the growth of the Word of God is mentioned in Acts 6.7; 12.24; 13.49; 19.20; the expression 'we are going up to Jerusalem' maps out the central section of the Gospel.

As a good historian, he is concerned to locate events in history (2.1–3; 3.1–2); however, he has a poor knowledge of Palestine. He does not know about the construction of houses there or about the climate, and often he is content with very vague chronological notes: 'One day'. His interest is primarily theological.

Simply reading the Gospel, one is struck with the delicate way in which he treats Jesus, the poor, women, fishermen. Dante rightly called him 'the evangelist of God's tenderness'.

Some Texts from Luke

✦ Jesus' programme. Luke 4.14–44

With Matthew, it is the Sermon on the Mount followed by the miracles which makes up Jesus' programmatic discourse. For Luke, this function is fulfilled by the discourse at Nazareth.

Begin by reading this text carefully. What are the places: Galilee, Judaea, but also the synagogue (the place of Jewish religion), outside the city? Who are the main figures?

Look for the key words: Spirit, good news, poor, today, Elijah, go his way (or ascend), Word. . .

Put the Isaiah quotation back in its historical context (see *How to Read the Old Testament*, p. 77). In this context, what do words like poor and freedom imply? Where does Luke end the Isaiah quotation? Why?

Look for the 'inclusion' which marks off this section (inclusion is a procedure which consists in repeating the same things at the beginning and the end of a passage to show that it is a unit). Teach or proclaim in the synagogues (vv. 15, 19, 44); all, crowd (vv. 15, 42); announce the good news (vv. 18, 43); sent (vv. 18, 43). How do the three miracle stories with the verb rebuke (vv. 35, 39, 41) become a concrete realization of this programme (see p. 17)?

Note how the account doesn't quite hang together. Why this abrupt change of attitude in v. 22? In Luke, has Jesus already performed miracles at Capernaum (v. 23)? Look at the arrangement indicated on p. 17.

After this study, go back to the text as a whole.

Who is Jesus? Look at his titles (vv. 18, 34, 41; the new Elijah), the authority of his words (vv. 32, 36), glorified (v. 15; elsewhere God is the only one to be glorified).

What is his mission (vv. 18–19)? The liberation is made specific by the three miracles (see Acts 10.38). At whom is this mission directed: the Jews (his own country, synagogue), the Gentiles (the example of Elijah and Elisha)? What will be his welcome by the Jews?

What awareness does Jesus have of this mission? Look at the verb 'go up' or 'go his way' (vv. 30, 42).

What connection can you see with the beatitudes?

✦ The church's programme. Acts 1.12–2.47

Peter's speech (already studied on p. 34), inserted into the account of Pentecost, forms the programmatic discourse for the infant church. Here we shall look at the whole section.

Begin by looking for the inclusion which marks off this section: they, all (the group of 120), continue, prayer (1.14; 2.42); meet, united, together (the same expression, which is rare in Greek: 1.15; 2.44, 47). In this way we move from a group of 120 to a group of '120 to whom God adds 3,000' (2.41, 47). The text shows what the church needs to preach and to grow.

Note the words which recur in Acts 2 (sometimes translated by different words in our Bibles): tongue (vv. 3, 4, 11); dialect (vv. 6, 8); voice (v. 6, translated noise, rumour, v. 14); speak (vv. 4, 5, 7, 11, 31).

Look for the main characters involved. In particular see the role of God, Jesus, the Spirit, the disciples.

Pentecost appears as the fulfilment of the mystery of Christ, a sign that he is exalted – and as the beginning of the mystery of the church. How would you express it?

The Jewish feast of Pentecost at that time celebrated the giving of the Law on Sinai. Can you see connections between the event as it was described at the time (see the box below) and Luke's account? This Jewish feast was a festival of the new covenant (reread Jer. 31.31f.; Ezek. 36.26), and Ps. 68 was read on it (see p. 37). The Spirit is the gift which the exalted Jesus gives to his church.

The voice of God once came from Sinai; now it comes from the church, the voice of God in the world.

Jews meditated on Ex. 20.18: At Sinai the people saw the voices and the thunderings. The Jewish philosopher Philo, a contemporary of Jesus, wrote: Since God does not have a mouth, he decided that by a miracle an invisible sound should be produced in the air, a breath which, articulated into words which turned the air into fire with the form of flames, made a voice resound in such a way that those who were furthest away could hear it as clearly as those who were nearest. . . A voice resounded from the midst of the fire which came down from heaven and became articulate in the native language of the hearers' (*De Decalogo* 9, 11). And Rabbi Johanan, active between AD 90 and 130, declared that the voice of God divided itself into seventy languages. Since for Jews there were seventy Gentile nations in the world, this was a way of saying that the Law was addressed to all men.

The glory of the Son of God. Luke 9.28–36

The account of the transfiguration is also given in Matt. 17.1–9 and Mark 9.2–10, and by John 12.28; II Peter 1.16–18. This text is important and calls for deep study. Here I can only give you a few comments to follow up.

In the life of Jesus. The event is situated towards the end of Jesus' ministry in Galilee: the crowds who had followed him now left him; the Jewish leaders increased their pressure. Jesus was aware that he was causing too much of a disturbance; if he continued, he risked death. And clearly he accepted this fate as a risk which went along with perseverance in his mission. He went up to Jerusalem under no illusions about the fate which awaited him, and he proclaimed it to his disciples.

In this context the transfiguration would seem to be a response from God to the faithfulness of Jesus and the anguish of his disciples. In what was no doubt an inner spiritual experience to which the three disciples were made privy, the Father shows Jesus the conclusion of his going up: beyond death he will find the glory promised at the end of time to the Son of man (see Daniel 10).

In times of doubt when we no longer know what to do, we may return to those moments of light we may have experienced when our vocation, our mission in life, seemed clear, and this will help us to be faithful to that light. Similarly, in this luminous experience, Jesus and the disciples could find the strength to enter on the agony and the passion. And it is no coincidence that these two scenes, the transfiguration and the agony in the garden, have points in common.

After Easter, the disciples knew that Jesus was caught up in the glory of God at his resurrection. So in the accounts as we have them, Jesus and his disciples go up towards death in the light of Easter, perceived in advance. This aspect is kept above all by Matthew and Mark.

Luke has taken up this story in a more personal way. Jesus goes up the mountain to pray (v. 28); it is during his prayer (v. 29), all through the night (v. 32), that he has this experience. By reaching down in this way to the sources of his being, Jesus sees the glory in which he has been invested since his birth, and in an inward conversation with the two great mystics of the Old Testament, Moses and Elijah, he can serenely envisage his exodus (v. 31): his death and exaltation.

By showing the disciples entering the cloud (v. 34) and stressing prayer, Jesus reminds us that we, too, can know something of such an experience; in prayer we can share in this glory of the crucified Lord and live our daily life in the light of this faith.

The servant goes up to Jerusalem. Luke 9.51–62

The central part of the Gospel (9.51–19.28) is arranged as an ascent to Jerusalem. The introduction indicates the significance it has for Jesus and what it implies for the disciples.

Jesus resolutely takes the road to Jerusalem, or literally, he sets his face to go up to Jerusalem. By making this allusion to Isa. 50.7, Luke shows Jesus to be the suffering servant going in full awareness to be taken up, that is, to his death-exaltation (see p. 111).

He is the new Elijah (v. 61, which alludes to I Kings 19.19), utterly dedicated to his mission, carried along by the Spirit, but not the Elijah of one Jewish tradition who pours out the wrath of God on his enemies (v. 55).

Jesus warns his disciples that to follow him requires total dedication, in which the demands of the mission go above everything else (vv. 57–62; Matthew put these verses at the beginning of his account of the stilling of the storm: see p. 66).

Ten lepers. Luke 17.11–19

You could read this text, simply looking in it for the great themes of Luke's work, especially those that he develops in the 'ascent to Jerusalem'.

The verb 'go up' appears at the beginning and the end: as he was going up; arise, get up (vv. 11, 19; see also vv. 9, 51, 53, 57; 10.1; 13.22, 33). What does this tell us about the way in which Jesus envisages his life and that of the disciple?

Jesus, Master, have mercy on us. The faith of the ten lepers is wonderful. They address Jesus by his first name, as does the thief on the cross (23.42); he too is to obtain salvation. Master: Luke is the only one to address Jesus by this title, which suggests power (5.5; 8.24; 9.33, 49). 'Have mercy' appeals to that which is most profound in God, his tenderness and his pity.

How is the leper described? Successively as one of the ten, a Samaritan, a stranger (v. 18). Here we can detect Luke's universalism: the Samaritans (cf. Acts 8) and the Gentiles hear the message better than the Jews.

Jesus Son of God: the leper prostrates himself when he gives thanks (Greek, 'making eucharist'); usually this was a gesture made only towards God.

From now on salvation is open to all, Jews and Gentiles, solely by faith in Jesus.

The theological prologue. Luke 1–2

These chapters, which form the prologue to the whole of Luke's work, both the Gospel and Acts, are very rich. Here are some suggestions for reading them.

Look at the plan. Write the titles of the episodes in two columns; in this way you will get a parallel between the childhood of John the Baptist and that of Jesus, both linked by the visitation.

Study the prayers: the Magnificat, the Benedictus, the Nunc Dimittis. As you look at the references in your Bible, see how Christian prayer draws on the Old Testament, to which it gives new meaning.

Look for the main themes which Luke develops in his work (see p. 83).

Now you can study the account of the annunciation (see p. 112).

✠ The birth of Jesus. Luke 2.1–20

The event (vv. 1–7). Stripped of all the folk lore with which we have decked it out, the birth is marvellous, like all births, but matter-of-fact. Because the main room was not the place in which to give birth, used as it was by all the family, a peasant mother would retire into the only place where it was quiet and warm: the stable.

The invisible aspect of the event (vv. 8–20). Angels and shepherds take it in turns to announce the birth, while the glory of God shines over it all (vv. 9, 14, 20).

The angel announces the good news (evangelizes). This word, which occurs more than a dozen times in Acts, sums up the activity of the Christian missionaries (5.42; 8.4, 12, 25). Compare v. 12 with Acts 2.36; 5.42; 11.20; 13.33–36; Phil. 3.20.

The shepherds. Using the literal translation in the next column, underline the words which recur and where they do so: what the shepherds do, what the two groups who hear them (v. 18 all those who, v. 19 Mary) do, and their attitude.

Say. This verb, which is very common in Acts, denotes the preaching of the Christian missionaries. The shepherds do not come to adore, but to preach a sermon!

Make known. Almost always, this verb expresses the revelation which God or Jesus has made to the disciples and which in turn they hand on to everyone: e.g. John 15.15; I Cor. 15.1; II Cor. 8.1; Eph. 1.9; 3.3, 5; 6.19.

So Luke took the Christian missionaries as his model for the shepherds. They therefore become the model for what every Christian should do in the world.

Two groups of hearers form: here are two attitudes which Jesus and then his disciples will encounter. All (all those who hear the message of Jesus or of the church down the ages) wondered: in Luke this attitude denotes an attitude of welcome which is only transitory, without roots (see 4.22; 8.13). By contrast Mary prefigures those who hear the Word and let it come to fruition in their hearts.

Note the shift in meaning of the term word (*rhema* in Greek): the shepherds heard a word pronounced (v. 17), they come to see a word which has come to pass: a baby (v. 15). The Word has been made flesh!

15. *When the angels went away from them into heaven, the shepherds said one to another, 'Let us go over to Bethlehem and see this word (*rhema*) which has come to pass, which the Lord has made known to us.'*

16. *And they went with haste, and found Mary and Joseph, and the babe lying in a manger.*

17. *And when they saw it they made known the word (*rhema*) which had been told them concerning this child.*

18. *And all who heard it were amazed at what the shepherds had told them.*

19. *But Mary kept all these words (*rhema*), pondering them in her heart.*

Other texts studied elsewhere

The Passion according to Luke

To enter into Luke's account you must not just read it, but meditate on it as the two disciples were doing on the Emmaus road, when the words and the presence of Jesus as he explained the scriptures to them made their hearts burn within them. On this *via dolorosa*, Jesus is going with us, even if our eyes are still prevented from recognizing him.

Luke's whole account is stamped with delicacy and tenderness for his Lord Jesus. He cannot bring himself to report some details which were too distressing: he does not say that Jesus was scourged; Judas does not kiss Jesus, but simply 'draws near' to do so.

However, Luke is aware of the magnitude of the terrible struggle which takes place between Jesus and the powers of evil. The passion is the last decisive combat. Jesus comes out of it as victor through his patience, a word which is not a very good rendering of the Greek *hypomone* (that word suggests the attitude of the believer enduring blows in his trial because he is sustained by God, see Luke 8.16).

The whole of the passion is internalized. The decisive struggle takes place in Gethsemane: it is in this inner struggle, an agony, that the blood of Jesus flows. Comforted by God, as Elijah once was (I Kings 19.5f.), Jesus emerges victor, and now at peace, held in his Father's arms, he can forget his own suffering, to be entirely at the disposal of others. He welcomes Judas gently, heals the servant's ear, gives Peter heart again by his glance (22.61), speaks to the women who lament his fate, forgives his executioners and those who condemn him. Pilate proclaims him to be innocent three times, as do the women, the people, the thief on the cross, the centurion.

Jesus can die at peace. The cry which he utters on the cross is no longer the scream of human suffering confronted with death; it is the evening prayer known to every Jew: 'Into your hands I commend my spirit'. However, Jesus prefaces it with the term which marks his unparalleled intimacy with God: 'Father'.

In this way Luke invites us to enter with Jesus into his passion: with Peter to recognize our weakness and to feel upon us the forgiving gaze of our Lord; to carry his cross behind him, like Simon of Cyrene; and with him to abandon ourselves to the Father's arms.

The Last Supper (22.14–38) is above all the farewell meal in which Jesus expresses his trust in God and gives his last commands to his disciples. It is also the prophetic action by which he expresses the significance of his martyr death: the inauguration of the new covenant.

The agony followed by the arrest (22.39–53) is the decisive moment when Jesus emerges victor over the power of evil. The new Elijah, fortified by God, he goes forward into the night of his passion, at peace, entirely submissive to his Father's will.

The Jewish trial (22.54–71) opens with the account of Peter's denial. In this way Luke tells us, 'If you cannot follow the passion as a saint, you can always follow it as a forgiven sinner. The gaze of Jesus can always bring about a new being in you.'

Luke makes the high priest repeat his question. In this way Jesus proclaims clearly that he is Christ and Son of God.

During the Roman trial (23.1–25) Pilate declares three times that Jesus is innocent. The account of the appearance before Herod doubtless indicates that one cannot simply have a curious interest in Jesus.

At Calvary (23.26–49), Jesus declares his innocence to the women who are lamenting him, and consoles them. He asks the Father to forgive his executioners. He opens up paradise to the thief confident enough to call him by his first name, and dies in peace in the Father's arms.

The burial (23.50–57) is prepared for affectionately by the women. However, with all these spices they are wanting to keep him dead. They do not yet know that the light of the sabbath is already dawning (v. 54), and better still, the light of the resurrection.

You should read one after another the various disciples' passions which Luke has constructed on the same pattern. The passion of Stephen makes present that of Christ (Acts 4.23–31); Stephen is condemned for the same reasons; he dies forgiving his enemies, his eyes fixed on the Risen Jesus (Acts 6.8–15, 54–60). Paul goes up to Jerusalem, like his master, to bear witness there (Acts 20.22; 21.11).

Twelfth-century Christ. Chapelle St-Michel, Le Puy

Luke's Jesus

Luke did not know Jesus personally. So the Jesus whom he discovered is not primarily the itinerant prophet of Galilee but the glorified Lord showing himself to Paul on the Damascus road, the Lord whose face he discerned in a community like that of Philippi, where the loving power of Jesus was so strong that it enabled great ladies like Lydia and dockers in the port to live side by side in the same communion. Luke also finds features of this Jesus in the memories of the witnesses whom he questions.

The Lord Jesus. Luke is the only evangelist to call Jesus 'Lord' when he is talking about him. The glory of Easter is reflected back on his earthly life. This glory surrounds Jesus from his birth onwards (2.9, 32). The transfiguration is less an anticipation of the future glory of Easter (Matthew – Mark) than an emergence of the glory which he possesses from his conception, because he is born of the Spirit (9.32). The glory which he is to show as Son of Man is his own (9.26, compare Matt. 16.27; Mark 8.26). All men glorify him (4.15), though God is the only one who should be glorified.

Jesus is king (that is perhaps clearer to Greek readers); Luke is the only evangelist to say so, and he does it six times (1.32–33; 19.12f., 28f.; 22.28f., 67f.; 23.40f.).

Luke knows that Jesus acted as Lord and Christ only as a result of his resurrection (Acts 2.36); however, that is possible because he is Lord and Christ in his very being, as the infancy narratives affirm. The title Son of God is not a simple recognition of his role (equivalent to Son of David), but an affirmation of his nature (1.35; 22.70).

The Spirit of Jesus. This expression appears only twice in the New Testament (Acts 16.7; Phil. 1.19; spirit of Christ in Rom. 9.2; I Peter 1.11). The Spirit of God has so entered into Jesus that people can talk of *his* Spirit. Jesus is conceived by its power (1.35); it shows itself at his baptism (3.22), leads Jesus into the desert (4.1); Jesus is endowed with the Spirit to be made the bearer of the good news (4.14, 18). It is in the spirit that Jesus trembles for joy (10.21).

Through his glorification Jesus receives the Spirit from the Father, to give it to us (Acts 2.38) if we ask him (Luke 11.13; compare Matt. 7.11). Acts emerges as the Gospel of the Spirit which gives life to the community after Pentecost, as it gave life to Jesus and to the first witnesses of his life (Luke 1.15, 41, 67; 2.25–26).

Jesus is *the prophet* charged with revealing God (7.16, 39; 24.19; Acts 3.22–23), and his death is that of a prophet (13.33; Acts 7.52). Luke deliberately presents him as the new Elijah (see *How to Read the Old Testament*, p. 46).

The aspect of God which he reveals is above all that of the tenderness of the Father for all men. The main passage in which Luke presents Jesus as prophet (7.11–50) ends with the forgiveness of the woman who was a sinner. This love which arouses the Father's compassion (15.20) is shown by Jesus himself (7.13), and the disciple must show it too (10.33).

The coming of Jesus is God's visit. In Luke, the proclamation of judgment as by a prophet becomes the good news of salvation, a year of grace (4.19; cf. 1.68, 78; 7.16; 19.44). By his attitude Jesus makes this love of the Father visible: he is the friend of publicans and sinners (7.34). He is the saviour, the deliverer from Satan who holds men's hearts in thrall, and from evil which tortures their bodies. Jesus is the friend of sinners, because they need God in the same way as the sick person needs the physician (5.31), but even more because God needs them to show his forgiveness (15). Luke has a great attachment to women, often scorned at that time (Mary, Elizabeth, Anne, Mary Magdalene, Martha and Mary, the women who accompany him); some go on to play an important role in the church (Acts 1.14; 12.12; 16.14; 21.9).

Man before God. Jesus is not only Lord and Christ, but also fully man. He lives what he proclaims so perfectly that he is the model of the perfect man, transfigured by the Spirit, living in his Father's arms: his first word, like his last, speaks of the Father (2.49; 23.46). He constantly lives in the Father's presence and his prayer is a demonstration of it: it is while he prays that he receives his great revelations (baptism and the transfiguration); he spends his nights in prayer (5.16; 6.12; 9.28), and his disciples are so impressed that they want to be introduced to the secret of this relationship with God (the Our Father, 11.1).

Thus the very person of Jesus is at the centre of the Gospel. Confronted with him, men must choose. For this being who is so full of tenderness is also terribly demanding: men must make their choice for him today, simply because he is who he is. This total faith which obtains salvation is the source of the joy which irradiates the Gospel and transfigures the disciple.

The Parables

The parable is essentially a comparison developed in the form of a story. Its primary purpose is not so much to teach as to make its audience reflect on their behaviour, to make them pass judgment on themselves and so lead them to change this behaviour. Because we are bad at judging ourselves, the parable leads us to judge ourselves without being aware of the fact. For example, David sinned by seducing the wife of his officer Uriah and making sure that Uriah died in battle. The prophet Nathan had to make him aware of his sin. That was rather a delicate matter! So Nathan told David a feasible story (it had to be feasible, for David to accept it) about a rich land-owner who stole a poor man's only ewe lamb. David cried out, 'That man deserves to die,' thus passing judgment on himself without being aware of it. Nathan could conclude, 'You are that man' (II Sam. 12.1–15).

The parable, then, is a simple comparison. The details of the story are there only to add verisimilitude. So we need to try to sum up a parable in two phrases. 'Just as. . ., so. . .' Just as this man sinned in taking the poor man's ewe-lamb, so you David. . .'

It is important to distinguish parables carefully from another literary genre which resembles them closely: allegory.

Allegory also takes the form of a story, but is aimed at teaching. It is a story constructed expressly to help us understand something, and the details correspond to particular entities. So Jesus says, 'I am the vine, you are the branches. . .'

It is important to make a careful distinction between these two genres and to resist the temptation to interpret the parables as though they were allegories, although this is often done. Thus the parable of the Good Samaritan invites us to a particular kind of behaviour: 'Just as he was a neighbour to the wounded man without being concerned with his religion or his opinions, so you should make every person your neighbour.' The Fathers made the parable into an allegory – very fine, but far from the actual text: the wounded man was humanity attacked by the devil, the Samaritan was Jesus, the inn was the church, and so on.

However, we must not rule out the possibility that Jesus might have slipped allegorical features into a parable. Features which to us might seem trivial spontaneously evoked themes of scripture for Jews; thus, because of Isa. 5, the vine suggested Israel.

Rereading the parables

Jesus told his parables to Jews. In the community, they were now addressed to Christians. This change of audience often led to a change of meaning, which was expressed in a new conclusion.

In the light of Easter, people had a tendency to move from a theological interpretation to a christological interpretation: the parables of Jesus speak of God and his kingdom; the disciples were interested in Jesus, who inaugurated this kingdom.

There was a tendency to bring together parables which originally had a separate existence: the meaning of one of them would have repercussions for the meaning of another.

Sometimes the context given by the evangelists to parables would influence their meaning. This was also the case with the larger collections. Mark and Luke both put the chapter of parables at the beginning of Jesus' preaching in Galilee: they are primarily a simple way of presenting the kingdom of God. Matthew has put them towards the end of this preaching, at the moment when the crowds were already leaving Jesus. They seem primarily to be his last warning towards them: if you reject my message, it will be harvest: time for sorting out! (see p. 17).

Some practical rules

Reduce the parable to a simple composition (Just as. . . so. . .) making sure that it makes sense historically.

Leave aside all historical details that are not taken up again in the conclusion.

Distrust apparent conclusions which do not make sense historically.

The audience: to whom is the parable addressed by Jesus? To whom is it addressed by the disciples? Has the change in audience led to a change in meaning?

Does a change in the context of the parable change its meaning?

Single out possible allegorical features: have they served to give the parable a new interpretation?

Who is the parable talking about? God? Jesus?

The labourers in the vineyard. Matt. 20.1–16

Read this parable and the context in which it is set (19.27–30). With the help of the rules given on p. 89, try to distinguish the various conclusions with which it has been provided: why has it been reread, and in what way?

Read the rest of this page, but only when you have done that.

This text is a good example of the rereading of a parable. Let's look at the three successive conclusions which Matthew provides.

'For many are called, but few are chosen' (v. 16b). This phrase, with its 'for', is clearly a conclusion. It suggests the following comparison: 'Just as the master called many workers, and only a few came, so. . .' Now that does not match the story, since all those who were called actually came! So that's only a pseudo-conclusion. Some translations of the Bible leave it out, because it does not appear in all the manuscripts: it might have been borrowed from Matt. 22.14, where it fits better.

'So the last shall be first and the first last' (v. 16a). Does this conclusion fit the story well? The first workers protest, not because they are paid after the others, but because they are paid the same amount. So this, too, is a pseudo-conclusion.

'. . . because I am good' (v. 15). Here there is no interest in the first and the last; the intermediate categories are there only to add verisimilitude to the story. This phrase leads to the comparison: 'Just as the master is not unjust in giving as much to the last as to the first, because his standard for wages is not the work done but his own goodness, so God is not unjust in opening his kingdom to all, even sinners, because he does not reckon up our merits but does so of his own good will.'

Try to see which successive situations match these various conclusions.

Jesus spoke to Jews and, more precisely, to the religious élite, the Pharisees, who were scandalized at seeing him welcome sinners. They had taken a good deal of trouble to practise the Law, and some found it unjust that they were not to receive a greater reward because of their merits (see the rabbinic parable in the box opposite). Jesus replied to them: rewards are not measured by human merits but by God's goodness.

In the community, the audience for the parable changed: it was no longer addressed to Jews, but to the disciples. The primary sense, which was still valid for Christians, was retained (one need only think of the reactions which are still provoked: 'In that case it's not worth putting oneself out to earn heaven!'). However, by allegorizing one detail in the text it was turned into a piece of teaching. At this period the Gentiles had entered the church before the Jews, who had all rejected it as a people. History became a warning to them. If you reject the message, the Gentiles will enter the kingdom before you.

This threat was heightened by the addition of v. 16b, which takes up 22.14: You have all been called to enter the kingdom, says Jesus, but in fact very few people accept.

Matthew has put the parable after Peter's question (19.27); in this way it seems to be an illustration of Jesus' reply: the Twelve precede the Jewish leaders, though they were called after them.

The Fathers, and preachers after them, have made the parable into an allegory by adding secondary details. Irenaeus saw it as the call which God made to the five ages of humanity: to Adam, Noah, Abraham, Moses and all men through Jesus Christ. For Origen and Gregory, God calls us ceaselessly, at the five ages of life: birth, childhood, adolescence, maturity and old age. That is true, but it's a long way from the parable!

Rabbi Za'era, who lived about AD 300, tells a parable to explain the scandal of the death of a young rabbi.

What does the death of Rabbi Bun remind us of? It reminds us of a king who employed many workers in his service. One of them showed more zeal in his work than the others. Seeing that, what did the king do? He took this worker aside and walked up and down with him. That evening, the workers came to be paid, and the king paid a full day's wage to the one with whom he had walked. Seeing this, the other workers complained, and said, 'We are tired from working all day; that man, who only worked for two hours, has received the same wages as we have.' 'But,' retorted the king, 'he did more in two hours than you did all day.'

Thus Rabbi Bun only studied the law up to the age of twenty-eight; but he knew it better than one who had studied it devotedly to the age of a hundred.

On this page, we shall now go through two parables to illustrate what we saw on p. 89. You can begin by studying them by yourself. If you have a synopsis, use it.

❧ The parable of the feast and the parable of the wedding garment. Matt. 22.1–14; Luke 14.15–24

When we leave secondary details on one side, the parable, which is common to Matthew and Luke, is simple. The Pharisees feel that they have a right to the kingdom because of their merit in practising the Law; the sinners have no rights, so why does Jesus welcome them? Jesus recognizes that the feast was prepared for the righteous, but because they reject the last decisive call he issues, the 'righteous' should not be surprised to see their place given to others.

Luke makes the parable into an exhortation to Christians. Verses 18–20 develop the main reasons (principally concern for temporal matters) which prevent Christians in his community from responding totally to the call of God. Look at the context: 14.1–14. The connection between vv. 21b and 12–14 is illuminating: people are not interested in the merits of those newly invited, but primarily in God's concern not to see his plan brought to nothing.

Matthew has rearranged two parables.

He has added some allegorical features to the parable of the wedding feast, which allow it to be read as the history of Israel: here is a king (as God is king of Israel) who holds a wedding feast, a symbol of the messianic age. The sending of servants and the way in which they are maltreated suggests the fate of the prophets and the burning of the city, the ruin brought on Jerusalem in 70.

The parable of the wedding garment makes sense in isolation, but when attached to the previous parable it seems to make no sense: how can one criticize a tramp for his dress when he has been compelled to come? Here it becomes a warning to Christians: God has brought them into the church without any merit on their part; however, this is not an automatic assurance of being allowed into the feast. They, too, are liable to the divine judgment; the church is the time when the good and the bad (cf. v. 10) are still mixed while waiting for the final sifting (see the parable of the wheat and the tares, Matt. 13.24–30).

❧ The parable of the murderers in the vineyard. Matt. 21.33–44; Mark 12.1–11; Luke 20.9–18

This parable, which is taken up by all three synoptic Gospels, is important; it expresses more clearly than the rest how Jesus felt about himself: directed towards Jerusalem at the time when the conflict between him and the Jewish authorities was coming to a climax, it is the last warning that Jesus gave them.

You should study all three texts carefully in a synopsis. The diagram below will enable you to see how the meaning has developed between the time of Jesus and that of the evangelists, as the parable was handed on through the community. It would be a worthwhile exercise to write down the conclusions to this parable in three columns: Matt. vv. 42–45; Mark vv. 10–12; Luke vv. 16b–19.

Jesus	The community	The evangelists
is interested in the outcome of the kingdom.	is interested in the fate of Jesus.	are interested in the outcome of the kingdom
Parable of judgment, announcing punishment.	Allegory of the destiny of Christ.	and the destiny of Christ.
The history of salvation reaches its goal after numerous prophets have been sent.		
	adds a quotation (or two): Ps. 118: announces Easter: Isa. 28.16: a choice has to be made.	**Mark** ends with the Easter alleluia. **Luke** quotes the announcement of Easter; adds Isa. 28: a choice has to be made.
If Israel (the husbandmen) rejects the son, the kingdom (the vineyard) will be given to others.		**Matt.** takes up the Easter Alleluia; returns to the primitive sense the kingdom given to others (v. 41), i.e. the church (v. 43); ends with the need to choose (v. 44).

Parables of the kingdom. Matt. 13

Most of the parables are about the kingdom of God and how people should behave in the face of its imminent coming. Matthew 13 gathers a number of these together. You could read them with the help of the table below.

Jesus addresses them to the crowd and explains some of them to his disciples. These seven parables are a good summary of the different aspects of the kingdom. Jesus proclaims that this kingdom is inaugurated by his preaching; it will develop, but only if his hearers are good ground (the sower). To those who are amazed at the very modest beginnings of this kingdom, Jesus retorts: against all odds and despite everything, the seed of the kingdom will become a great tree; it is leaven which will make all humanity rise (parables of the mustard seed and the leaven). The kingdom is so marvellous that as soon as one discovers it one is tempted to leave everything for it (the treasure and the pearl). Throughout the time of its growth, which is also the time of the church, good and bad are mixed: it is still a time of waiting and of mercy, but at the end of time, God will sort things out (the wheat and the tares, the net).

This allows us to distinguish three realities.

• The kingdom of God is an eschatological reality, belonging to the end of time, in which only the righteous will share. However, from now on it has been inaugurated and is at work in the world.

• The kingdom of Christ or of the Son of man will extend from the resurrection to the end: it covers the whole world. Saints and sinners are still mixed in it. At the end of time Christ will hand it back to the Father (I Cor. 15.24).

• The church is not identical either with the kingdom of God (which will be realized only at the end of time) or with the kingdom of Christ (which extends to all men, whether or not they are believers). The church is the particular place in the kingdom of God where it exercises its action fully (or should do so). This is normally the place from which Christ radiates his power and extends his kingdom in the world.

The purpose of the parables

If Jesus uses this simple language, well known to his audience, he clearly does so in order to be understood. How can he affirm the opposite (Matt. 13.13–15; Mark 4.12; Luke 8.10)? We must see that for Jesus, as for Isaiah whom he quotes, this is an interpretation: in fact this preaching was not heard and understood, and in fact his audience was not converted. This interpretation, whether it comes from Jesus or from the community, is an attempt to put the refusal in the context of God's plan (see *How to Read the Old Testament*, p. 63, 'God will punish you,' where we have a very similar interpretation).

Parables about behaviour in Luke

More than the other evangelists, Luke uses the parables to show how disciples should behave. They should mistrust money and concern for material things which are likely to stifle their spiritual life (Lazarus, 16, 19–31; the rich man, 12.16–21; the feast, 14.16–24). They must pray assiduously (the importunate friend, 11.5–8; the widow and the judge, 18.1–8; the Pharisee and the publican, 18.9–14). They must be neighbours to everyone without taking account of nationality or religion (the Good Samaritan, 10.30–37). In a word, they must model their conduct on that of the Father who loves freely and delights in forgiving (the lost sheep, the lost coin, the father and his two sons, 15; the two debtors, 7.41–43).

The sower	To the crowd: the kingdom is inaugurated, and will surely come if accepted.
	To the disciples: the aim of the parables for the crowd.
	interpretation of the parable (by the community?)
The wheat and the tares	To the crowd: Good and bad are mixed now, but at the end of time God will separate them.
	To the disciples: the aim of the parables for the crowd.
	interpretation of the parable (by the community?).
The net	To the crowd: the same sense as the parable of the wheat and the tares.
	To the disciples: Jesus does not need to interpret it, since they have understood.

7 The Work of John: The Gospel and the Letters

John and the eagle. Keystone of the rood-loft of Chartres (thirteenth-century)

The Gospel of John is a strange book. The words in it are very simple, everyday words, yet specialists have still not succeeded in plumbing their depths. Children are at ease with it and mystics make it their bedside book. Like the synoptic Gospels, it narrates the life of Jesus, but it does so in a very different way from them.

The spiritual Gospel

The Gospel of John has been called the spiritual Gospel. It is in fact the witness of a man and a community whom the Spirit has brought nearer to all truth (16.13) as a result of long meditations. So we shall first look at some influences which affected that community. The only thing really necessary for it is the presence of the Risen Lord as experienced in worship. The celebration of the sacraments – baptism and the eucharist – often crops up in this Gospel. It is there in the last resort that the words and actions of the earthly Jesus make sense.

John's community

This is generally thought to have been at Ephesus. There it was subjected to various influences.

Greek philosophy. Just as we may be stamped by thinkers of whom we are perhaps unaware, but whose ideas form part of the air we breathe, so the Greeks 'breathed' Hellenism, that culture dependent on philosophers like Socrates, Epictetus and the Stoics.

In Alexandria, Philo tried to make a synthesis between this Greek philosophy and his Jewish faith. John's community lived in this kind of atmosphere, as is clear from some of his themes, or from the fact that he calls Jesus the Logos, the Word.

Gnosticism. This current is difficult to define, because it can take many forms. Its basic element is that those represented by the trend, the Gnostics, think that they can acquire salvation by knowledge (*gnosis* in Greek), which is reserved for those who have been initiated. The Gospel of Thomas, discovered in Egypt in 1946, gives us an example of it. John had to fight against Gnostic tendencies in his community, and it is certainly no coincidence that he presents Christ primarily as the one who reveals God's secrets.

Judaism. John draws primarily upon Jewish faith. He has assimilated the great themes of the prophets and the wise men. The Exodus, the paschal lamb, manna, water, the vine, all contribute towards his presentation of Christ. Jesus is the shepherd, the light, and above all 'I am' (equivalent to Yahweh), images or titles reserved for God.

The Essenes are known better since the discovery of the Qumran manuscripts in 1947. It is worth noting the points of contact between John's doctrine and theirs; the Spirit which guides men into the truth, dualism or opposition between two realities like light and darkness, truth and the lie. However, this shows above all that John and the Essenes draw on the same Old Testament texts.

The author

It is probable that the source of the Gospel is to be found in the personality of the apostle John. However, his work went through several stages before its final redaction about 95 or 100. We might think in terms of a 'Johannine school', a group of disciples meditating on the apostles teachings and making them more profound.

Papyrus from before 150 (see p.8)

93

The Gospel as a Whole

Begin by reading the Gospel of John straight through; you may possibly find these notes helpful.

John's geography

The geography of the synoptic Gospels is simple and, above all, theological. That of John is primarily – geographical! The author knows the country well, and when he differs from the others on a historical point (the chronology of the passion, for example) people nowadays have a tendency to trust him. Archaeology has revealed the exactness of some details like the existence of the pool with five porticoes, north of the Temple.

In the synoptics, Jesus preached in Galilee and then went up to Jerusalem for the Passover: his public life could amount to no more than a few months. For John, it lasts more than two years: Jesus in fact goes up to Jerusalem for at least three Passovers: 2.13; (5.1;?) 6.4; 11.55. John describes regular journeys from Galilee to Judaea where Jesus must have spent a long time, especially in Jerusalem (1.19–51; 2.13–3.36; 5.1–47; 7.14–20.31).

Some themes

We shall begin by looking for a few major themes which may allow us to find the key to the composition of the Gospel as a whole.

The word *hour* recurs often, but on nine occasions it seems to have a special sense: Jesus or John declare that this hour has not yet come (2.4; 7.30; 8.20). By contrast, on Palm Sunday, Jesus is anguished because the hour has come (12.23,27). Chapter 13 begins solemnly: 'Jesus, knowing that the hour had come for him to pass from this world to the Father . . .' (13.1); Christ affirms this to his disciples (16.32), and says so again in his prayer to the Father (17.1).

Thus throughout a section of the Gospel Jesus goes towards his hour, and this comes on the evening of the Last Supper. This hour is that of his return to the Father. That points us towards another theme.

The contrast between above and below. There is a universe above, that of God, which is Spirit, love, freedom, light, and the 'world' below, which is flesh, slavery, hate, darkness.

Jesus has always belonged to the universe above. The Word of God, he has come down into the world to reveal God to us, and to give us true knowledge (or *gnosis*). His passover is the hour of his return to the Father.

The whole of his life is framed by two great hymns: the hymn to the Word descending from heaven to become man (1.1–18), and the priestly prayer of the Word incarnate returning towards his Father (17). However, if the Word came down alone, in his exaltation he takes with him all those who believe in him (14.3).

Belief. At the end, John expresses his purpose clearly. 'These signs have been written that you might believe that Jesus is the Christ, and that believing you might have life in his name' (20.30–31). So John wants to evoke faith: this consists in recognizing Jesus as Messiah and Son of God. This faith, which is a living bond, is another name for love. To believe is to have life from the Son; to refuse to believe is to choose death.

Life, death, love. These three key words (or equivalent expressions) are distributed in a significant way through the Gospel: three-quarters of the use of the theme 'life' are in John 1–6, those of the theme 'death' in 7–12 and those of the theme 'love' in 13–20.

These several features allow us to think, if not of a plan, at least of a progression.

The 'Jews' and the 'world' in John

We need to pay great attention to the meaning of the word 'Jew' in John. Sometimes it has its ordinary meaning, denoting the inhabitants of the country; sometimes it has a quite specific sense, and denotes those who have not accepted the message of Christ. In this sense, John, who is a Jew by race, is not a 'Jew' but a Gentile, who refuses to accept that Jesus could be described as a Jew. Confusion between these two senses has unfortunately helped considerably to favour the antisemitism which John certainly rejects.

Similarly, the word 'world' denotes the humanity which God so loved that he gave his Son (3.6), but often it is a synonym for the enemies of Christ (12.31; 15.18ff.) that the Father has given him to do.

Reconstruction of the pool with five porticoes in Jerusalem

The signs and the hour

The Gospel is divided into two main parts, the book of signs (1–12) and the hour of Jesus (13–20).

John has been fascinated by this 'hour of Jesus', which he presents as a unity: the death of Jesus is at the same time his exaltation. Christ is raised up on the cross as on a throne of glory; from there he pours the Spirit upon the world. This is the manifestation of love.

However, this mystery is too rich, and it passed too quickly. According to John, Jesus is well aware that his disciples are in danger of missing its meaning. In addition, for two years in advance he develops this meaning sacramentally, by signs: his miracles, but also, in a more general sense, his works (words and actions), which show forth the Work.

These works evoke two different reactions from those who witness them: some believe and thus move towards life; others reject them and choose death.

1. The book of signs (1–12)

A. *The signs announce the life that God gives (1–6)*
The disciples give their testimony: the community (1.1–18), John the Baptist (1.19–44), the first disciples (1.35–51).

A series of episodes announces this gift of life: the sign of Cana manifests the glory of Jesus (2.1–12); by driving the merchants out of the Temple, Jesus gives a sign: the true temple is his body (2.13–25); he explains to Nicodemus that faith is birth (3.1–21); and John, the bridegroom's friend, gives his last testimony (3.22–36).

With the Samaritan woman, Jesus begins from the symbol of the water of life (4.1–42).

Then there is a whole section on the Word which gives life (4.43–5.47).

The bread of life is developed at length (6). The conclusion of this text prepares for the two following sections: some disciples refuse to believe and so join up with the opponents whom Jesus will be confronting in the next section. Peter proclaims the faith of the group which remains faithful (the equivalent of the confession at Caesarea Philippi in the synoptic Gospels); this faithful group will now fade into the background, leaving Jesus alone to face his enemies; it reappears above all in the last part.

B. *Jesus and those who seek his death (7–12)*
In this section Jesus is alone, facing his opponents, and John shows us what is at stake in the struggle: they want his death; by rejecting him, they are choosing their own death.

We can see this through the great confrontations at the time of the Feast of Tabernacles, when Jesus declares that he is the light and the source of the Spirit (7.1–8.2). The healing of the man born blind shows the division which has been brought about (9).

Then Jesus affirms that he is the shepherd who gives his life for his sheep (10.1–21), the Son of God (10.22–42), the resurrection and the life (Lazarus, 11.1–45).

The last episodes take us to the threshhold of the hour (11.46–12.50).

The community can then bring this first part to an end: the nature of true faith (12.37–50).

2. Jesus' hour (13–20)

John presents the Last Supper above all as the farewell discourse in which Christ says good-bye to his disciples and leaves them his instructions: their brotherly love will from now on be the way in which Jesus remains present in the world.

The trial is a good demonstration of the dramatic *quid pro quo*. Jesus is condemned to death; in fact it is he who is judging the world. And his death becomes the source of life; from his open side flows the spring of water announced by Ezek. 47.2; Zech. 13.1: the symbol of baptism and the Spirit.

Some features of John

John is fond of great unified constructions; we do not find any rapid accounts of miracles as we do in the synoptics, but broad narratives of seven chosen miracles (four of which are peculiar to John), often accompanied by discourses, which become the occasions for teaching.

His thought progresses in a spiral. We find that the thought in each construction is self-contained, but when we take it with the next section, we are led to look at it on a deeper level.

John deliberately begins from concrete realities: water, bread, birth; but he shows how these can bring us to a higher level. For him these everyday realities are symbolic: they enable us to catch a glimpse of the world of God, or better, they create a bond with him (that is the meaning of the word 'symbol', which etymologically signifies that which unites).

Some Texts from John

 The purpose of the work

The signs are written here that you may believe that Jesus is the Christ, the Son of God, and that believing you may have life in his name (John 20.31).

I write this to you who believe in the name of the Son of God, that you may know that you have eternal life (I John 5.13).

Compare these two conclusions. Underline the themes they have in common. What is the purpose envisaged by each of these works? I John has been called the book of Christian experience. What do you think of it?

Believers

Rather than treat a theme, say faith, in an abstract way, John prefers to show a man or a woman who believes and who thus becomes the type, the model, of the believer. Without going into too many details, you might read a certain number of texts to make up for yourselves a series of portraits of believers.

Faith born out of witness. 1.35–51
See how each person is taken by the hand by someone else in order to be led to Christ.

Knowledge or rebirth? 3.1–21
Nicodemus is a scholar, a rabbi, who can discuss with Jesus on equal terms. What does faith mean to him?

Belief in the Messiah, the saviour of the world. 4.1–42
As you read the account of Jesus' meeting with the Samaritan woman, see how Jesus begins from specific details: the water and the woman's love life. How do they help us to discover his mystery?

Belief in the word of Jesus. 4.43–54
Note the progression between the two occurrences of the verb believe: in v. 50, the centurion believes what Jesus says, and so he is to see the miracle (which is still in the natural realm); in v. 53 he sees the miracle and believes. Note this sequence carefully: seeing (with physical eyes) and believing – believing in order to see (with inner eyes). It often occurs in John.

Those who are truly blind. 9.1–41
There is a contrast here between a blind man who sees the essential thing and people with sight who are blind to it. Try to retrace the steps by which Jesus progressively leads the blind man to discover who he is.

Seeing in order to believe. 20.1–10
Look at the 'other disciple's' pattern of faith: *He saw and believed because they had not yet understood the scripture.* In other words, when the Risen Christ has opened their minds (or ours) to the scriptures, there is no longer any need to see in order to believe. Scripture is enough to show us who Jesus is.

Believing in order to see. 20.24–29
Thomas is presented here as the type of the doubting man. To what faith does Jesus want to lead us (look at Peter's response in 6.69)?

The sign of the bread. 6.1–71

This section, one of the longest in John, is important. Placed at the end of Jesus' preaching in Galilee, it sums up the essential features of his ministry. Chapter 5 showed the unbelief of the Jews of Jerusalem. Chapter 6 shows the unbelief of the crowds in Galilee. Apart from the tiny group of the Twelve (and even one of them will betray him, v. 71), all Israel refuses to believe.

The miracle of the bread (6.1–15) is a parallel to five other accounts which appear in the synoptics. Like them, John sees Jesus' action in giving thanks and distributing the bread as an anticipation of the Last Supper. However, he makes it above all the messianic banquet: this is the feast which the Messiah holds and which was expected at the end of time. John stresses Jesus' initiative (he is the one who does everything, and distributes the bread); the crowd recognizes him as the Prophet and wants to make him king.

The walking on the waters (6.16–21) stresses the person of Jesus. This is a royal progress of 'I am' (God) in all his glory. By showing the divine power of Jesus, the narrative seeks to prepare the disciples for accepting the message of the bread of life.

After the crowd searches for him and the dialogue about the work (6.22–29), Jesus speaks of the bread of life.

♥ The bread of life

Underline the words which keep occurring and the place of the words in the text (our Bibles translate two different Greek words by 'eat'; in vv.54, 56, 57, 58b, the verb used is in fact our 'munch', which is very realistic). See if some expressions make an inclusion.

Note the objections in vv.30,40–41,52: in this way John is deliberately starting an argument.

You will have noticed that the important words in the text all reappear in the quotation in v.31. This discourse is perhaps a homily (furthermore, Jesus is preaching in the synagogue, v.59), built according to the rules of Jewish preaching. The starting-point is a quotation from scripture, generally from the Pentateuch; each of its words is then taken up and applied to the present, to show how they apply to the audience. Usually a second quotation, from the prophets, appeared in the course of the commentary (v.45 here paraphrases Isa.54.13). There is deliberate use of the contrast, 'Not . . . but . . . for', as at vv.32–33; 46–47.

After the quotation in v.31 and the contrast in v.32, an inclusion marks off the first section: vv.35, 48. From v.49, which takes up v.31a, we have a second section. Verse 58 serves as a conclusion to the whole passage.

What bread is Jesus speaking of in 35–48? Note the frequency of the word 'believe' and its equivalent, 'come to'. The theme of the word of God on which one feeds, which one eats in faith, is well known; see, for example, 'Man does not live by bread alone but by every word which comes from the mouth of God' (Deut.8.3), or Wisdom 16.26; Ezek.3.1ff.

What bread is Jesus speaking of in 49–58? Compare 'My flesh for the life of the world' and 'My body given for you' (Luke 22.19).

There has been much argument over the history of the formation of this text. One might think that Jesus was presenting himself only as the Word incarnate that his hearers might 'eat', i.e. receive by faith. After Easter, the disciples understood that on the evening of the Last Supper Jesus also gave himself in another way: his very being (flesh and blood) given for us becomes food. John will then have reread the whole of the discourse in a eucharistic perspective.

How does that help you to see the link between word, eucharist, faith and life?

♥ John's 'Acts of the Apostles'. 13–17

To put it briefly, we might say that John has placed on the lips of Christ, in the discourse after the Last Supper, the essentials of what Luke tells us about the life of the church in Acts. This whole section is in fact composed of two discourses which overlap slightly.

When you read these texts, see what is said about God/the Father and about Jesus, who he has come from the Father and returns to him; he comes to his disciples after his resurrection in a new spiritual presence; he leads them to the Father. And see what is said about the Spirit.

Try to discover the situation and the questions of a specific community – John's community and your own.

First discourse. 13.31–14.31

First look for the joins: the inclusion from 13.33 to 14.28: 'I am going . . . I will come'; from 14.1 to 14.27.

Underline words which recur: believe, and expressions connected with it: know, perform works, produce fruit; love, and the expressions associated with it: observe the commandments, the word, dwell. 14.1–14 is centred on faith, 14.15–24 on love. Watch the numerous prepositions: in, with and so on.

How does this passage express the essential elements of the mystery of the ascension (the glorification of Jesus) and Pentecost (the new presence of Jesus through the Spirit)?

Second discourse. 15–17

You might see how this discourse develops the same themes, and pause over certain texts.

The vine (15.1–17). How is the doctrine of the church as body of Christ expressed under the form of an allegory?

The Spirit and the community over against the world (15.18–16.15) Look at the roles of the Spirit, making known the Father and Jesus, defending the faith of the believer, and showing him that Christ is victor.

The community charged with bringing Christ to birth in the world (16.16–33). To shed some light on vv.21–22, reread Isa.27.17,20; 66.7,14, and a text to which we shall be returning later: Rev.12.4–6. The passion is presented as the suffering of the community bringing Christ into the world all through its history.

The prayer of Christ through his passion, his resurrection, and his life in the church (17).

The prologue. 1.1–18

This magnificent hymn is difficult. In very simple words, it condenses a long theological reflection.

As a first approach, you might try to look for its structure and see how its thought is rooted in the scriptures.

For the structure, begin by looking for words which recur and passages which correspond. This hymn seems to have been constructed concentrically, according to a procedure common at the time, which we find quite often in the Bible.

1–5	The Word with God	16–18
6–8	John the Baptist	15
9–11	comings of the Word	14
	12–13	

So at the centre (vv.12–13) we find the divine sonship offered to believers. The other matching strophes are not simple repetitions. Verses 9–11 seem to present the comings of the Word into the world and among his Jewish people (his own); v.14 celebrates the incarnation. Verses 1–5 locate the Word in eternity and in his creative action; vv.16–18 stress the revelation accomplished through Jesus Christ.

For the biblical roots of the thought of the prologue, see a commentary or the notes or references in your Bible. Here are just a few points.

In the beginning. The opening of the Gospel is the same as that of Genesis. The coming of Jesus is a new beginning for the world (see, similarly, Mark 1.11).

Denoting Christ as Logos (Word) puts him in the biblical tradition: God creates through his Word (Gen.1; Isa.40.26; Ps.33.6) or through his Wisdom (Wisdom 7.22), to whom he gave being before all things and who lives beside him (Prov.8.23–36; Wisd.7.22–30). This Wisdom, that is to say, God as he is wise, has come to dwell among men (Sirach 24.1–22), and is sometimes identified with the Law, the presence of God among his people (see *How to Read the Old Testament*, pp.83,87,92). However, to call Christ Logos also puts him in the context of Stoic thought, for which this Logos is the principle which maintains the cohesion of the world.

He dwelt: literally, he set up his tent among us (cf. Sirach 24.7–8). The Greek word *skene* (tent) seems to contain an allusion to the Shekinah, the real presence of God among his people. Jesus is the true Temple from which the glory of God radiates towards us.

The First Letter of John

The community is undergoing difficulties: there are divisions (4.3), Christians do not love one another (2.9; 4.20), think themselves to be sinless (1.10), or are tempted by Gnosticism; they claim to be able to attain God by knowledge alone, without being concerned with the way they live (2.4); others have left the community and denied Christ (2.19,22).

To respond to this situation, John appeals to a twofold experience:

His experience as a witness (1.1–4). Read these verses. He does not say that he has seen or heard the Word, but that what he has seen of the Word (human words and actions) has allowed him in faith to go to the heart of the mystery of this man, to recognize in him the Son of God.

The experience of Christians (5.13). He appeals to what Christians have received in their baptismal catechesis and to what they experience in their everyday life. In faith they are to discover that they have been inseminated by the Word of God (2.14; 3.19), that they have been imbued with this Word as though with an oil, thanks to the Spirit (2.20,27).

The basic theme which keeps recurring, as though in a symphony, is that 'You are in communion with God'. However, this mystic has his feet on the ground: this communion with God must manifest itself in the fruits which it produces.

It is difficult to find a plan to the letter, but do we need to find one in a meditation? It is more important to see how the letter matches our own personal experience.

In your reading you might pay particular attention to some features.

The main characters: the Father, Jesus, the Spirit, the author and his community, the believers, those who go astray. How are they presented? What is their role? With what themes are they associated?

The main themes. Note the words and expressions which recur; try to regroup those which go together and to note what contributions these relationships make to the basic vocabulary, for example; love, know, communion, abide in, sin, devil, world, spirit of evil, antichrist, light/darkness, life/death, justice, etc.

The Passion according to John

John meditated on the passion a long time after the events, in the light of the Spirit and the life of the church, and particularly the celebration of the sacraments.

In his account, which is very close to that of the synoptics, he chooses the episodes which have the most significance. He presents this passion as the triumphal progress of Jesus towards the Father. Jesus knows that he is going to die; he knows what kind of a death it will be, and he goes to it freely: 'No one takes my life from me, but I lay it down of my own accord' (cf. 10.18). All the details of the passion not only fulfil the scriptures, but also fulfil the announcements of them made by Jesus.

John underlines the majesty of the Son of God who suffers. When he is arrested, Jesus does not refer, as he does in Matthew, to the legions of angels who could save him: it is enough for him to say, 'It is I', or 'I am', for his enemies to fall back. And it is as king that Jesus is crucified: Pilate recognizes this at his judgment seat (19.13), and the inscription on the cross proclaims Jesus king in several languages (19.19–20).

John does not separate death and exaltation. The lifting up of Jesus on the cross is also his ascension into the glory of God, whence he sends the Spirit upon the world (19.30). 'I, when I am lifted up from the earth, will draw all men to me' (12.32). The cross becomes the throne of glory from which Jesus founds the church: from his open side spring water and blood, the two sacraments of baptism and the eucharist.

The arrest in the garden (18.1–12). John does not describe Jesus' agony (but he has taken up its essentials in the episode of Palm Sunday, 12.23,27) nor the flight of the disciples. He simply shows the majesty of Jesus. The 'I am', repeated twice (vv.5,8), was God's own name in scripture.

The Jewish trial (18.13–27). John does not describe the appearance before the Sanhedrin, and he is the only one to report the interrogation before Annas. Jesus presents himself as one who reveals God in his full light: the verb 'I said' occurs five times, and 'I taught' comes once. There is a tragic contrast: while Jesus is giving his last testimony, Peter is denying him. And despite himself, Caiaphas tells us the significance of the passion: Jesus is dying for all the people (v.14).

The Roman trial (18.28–19.16). This is the principal scene in John's passion. The comings and goings of Pilate, from Jesus who is inside to the Jews outside, break up the event into seven matching scenes, with the crowning of Jesus with thorns at their centre. This is the great legal action between Jesus and the Jews. Jesus is accused, but in fact he is the judge. Jesus is king, but he is a sovereign who reigns over those who hear his word. At the centre is the crowning of Jesus with thorns, stripped of all details (spitting, genuflections), which highlights the title king. And the scene ends with an apotheosis: Pilate makes Jesus sit at his tribunal to proclaim him king (v.13).

Calvary (19.17–37). It is again as king that Jesus is crucified: the inscription bears this out. And the Jews again reject him. The seamless garment which Jesus wears is not torn (Greek *schizo*, hence our word schism). John sees this as a symbol of the unity of the church: Jesus dies to gather into one the children of God who are scattered abroad (11.52).

John is the only one to attach any importance to Mary at the foot of the cross. By calling her 'woman' and giving her the disciple as her son, John seems to suggest the special role of Mary in the church.

Jesus hands over the Spirit (v.30). By using this strange phrase, which is odder in Greek than in many English translations, Jesus portrays Jesus as sending out his Spirit into the world.

The final scene, which appears only in John, shows the significance of the death of Christ for us. He is the paschal lamb of the new covenant. Even more, he is God himself being pierced, as Zechariah 12.10f. foretold (see *How to Read the Old Testament*, p.86). Jesus is the true temple in which the deity dwells, this temple whence Ezek 47.1–12 sees flowing from the right side the water which is the symbol of the spirit. And the water and the blood become symbols, in the church, for the two sacraments of baptism and eucharist.

The burial (19.38–42). Jesus is buried by two nobles, Joseph, the timorous disciple (v.38), and Nicodemus, who had come to see Jesus by night. They lay him in a garden – John is the only one to say this, twice – in a place from which life burgeons.

Descent from the Cross. Museum of the Louvre

99

John's Jesus

'That which was from the beginning, which we have heard, which we have seen with our eyes, which we have looked upon and touched with our hands, concerning the word of life . . .' (I John 1.1). This confidence is a good summary of John's experience. In Paul's life there was a time before and a time after: Jesus changed from being an impostor to being Paul's Lord. John did not experience the same break. Over a number of years he had been the friend of a man, a prophet, in whom he gradually came to recognize Christ. After the night of the passion, he discovered to his amazement that his friend was the Son of God, indeed is the Son of God. Here is the paradox of John's Jesus: he is a very human figure whom one can see and touch; but in him, with the eyes of faith, illuminated by the Spirit, one can perceive the amazing mystery of the Word, the Son of God.

A man

John's Jesus is very human: he has our body and our psychology. Tired, he quenches his thirst by a well, and asks for a drink from an unknown woman (4.5ff.); he has a home where people can spend the evening with him (1.38; 3.2); he has a friend, Lazarus, and women friends, Martha and Mary (11–12); he knows distress and weeps for his friend Lazarus (11.33,35); he goes to a wedding (2.1ff.); he is capable of getting angry and overthrows the heavy tables of the merchants (2.15).

A marvellous psychologist, he knows the human heart (2.25). Infinitely respectful of others, he can remind the Samaritan woman of her turbulent sex life without making her feel under judgment, much less condemned, and the same goes for the woman taken in adultery. He is someone capable of revealing to people, even though they are sinners, what is best in themselves.

A man of God

Here is an interesting personality test to try out! Whatever people ask him, Jesus has only one answer: the Father. Where have you come from? The Father. Where are you going? The Father. What are you doing? The work of the Father, his will. What are you saying? Nothing of my own, but what I learned from the Father. Even more than abstract arguments about the Trinity, this text introduces us to the heart of the divine mystery. Jesus is always completely free, completely himself, but at the same time he is totally related to the Father, with the Father (1.1).

The one who reveals God

As one who was always with God, God's Word and Wisdom, Jesus knows his secrets and has come to make them known. Above all, John's Christ is the one who reveals the Father to us.

He does so through his words; and does so perhaps above all through his signs, his miracles, his actions, his way of life: 'Philip, he who sees me sees the Father' (14.9). He reveals him again by giving us the Spirit which flows from his open side (7.38; 19.30,34), the Spirit whose task it is to lead us into all truth (16.13).

The Son of Man

It is amazing, in so mystical a work, to be plunged into the heart of a trial. Legal terms appear constantly: witness, judgment, accuser, convince, paraclete (defender, advocate). This is because Jesus is the Son of Man, the figure from Daniel who was expected to pass judgment at the end of time. Jesus declares to Nicodemus that he is the only one to have come down (3.11–13); he does not want to be the judge who condemns, but only the Son who saves; however, because he is the light, he forces those who speak with him to reveal themselves, to choose: he provokes judgment. Yet he is alongside the believer as his advocate.

This trial will continue until the end of the world, and Jesus will also send another paraclete (14.16), the Spirit, who will defend him in the believer's heart.

The Son of God

Finally, Jesus can reveal God because he himself is Son of God. The formula 'I am', rare in the synoptics, appears frequently on the lips of John's Jesus, and is even used as an absolute on four occasions (8.24,28,58; 13.19). It corresponds to the name Yahweh, God's own name (Ex.3.6,14).

The life of the believer

Jesus came in our flesh simply to serve believers; he is the shepherd who gives his life for his friends; he is light; he is the resurrection and the life.

Worship – Life Lived in the Eucharist

For today's Christian, the word worship is likely to suggest ceremonial. For the first Christians, as for Jews, above all it suggested everyday life. To offer worship or to serve God was simply to live one's daily life, giving it a particular significance. And this significance was expressed in certain actions which were strictly cultic. To take an example: married couples do not work differently from single people, but usually the whole of their life is coloured by their love; the actions by which they show this love are the expression of their whole life, and they contribute towards giving meaning to this life. Similarly, acts of worship, cultic acts, express life lived in the eucharist and make life itself a eucharist.

Read Rom.12.1–2; I Peter 2.5 again (and what I said on p.55): the sacrifice of Christians is their very persons, their existence lived out as obedience of faith (Rom.1.5; 16.26; Phil.2.17; I Peter 1.2,14,22). For 'obedience' see *How to Read the Old Testament*, p.100.

Spiritual worship in the Old Testament

The true worship which the prophets call for is righteousness and justice towards one's neighbour (Amos 5.21; Isa.58); it is love and not sacrifices (Hos.6.6, quoted by Jesus according to Matt. 9.13; 12.7). Reread the magnificent summary in Micah 6.8 (*How to Read the Old Testament*, p.43).

Blessings in Judaism

Blessings form the very fabric of the life of Jews.

The day is interspersed with synagogue prayers: in the morning, at mid-day and in the evening; long prayers of thanksgiving accompanied by readings and psalms.

Every action is sanctified by one of the hundred benedictions, short phrases built on the same model: 'Blessed art thou, king of the universe, who . . .' Thus, on rising, 'thou who givest souls to their mortal body'; on washing, 'thou who sanctifiest us by thy commandments and hast ordained that we should wash our hands'; on dressing, 'who clothest those who are naked'; in going to the toilet, 'who hast formed man with wisdom and hast created channels . . .'

Thus the whole of daily life, even its most basic aspects, is lived as a thanksgiving. This is exactly the point that Paul takes up in reply to Christians who reject certain foods or even marriage: 'For everything created by God is good, and nothing is to be rejected if it is received with thanksgiving; for then it is consecrated by the word of God and prayer' (I Tim.4.4–5).

Meals, especially festive meals, are religious acts. The father of the family or the one who presides says the blessing, takes bread and distributes it. Saying the blessing is not a matter of blessing the bread, but of putting it back into the vital current which comes from God: God is life, and by blessing one draws on this life. The bread thus charged with divine life is shared and distributed to those at the meal who by eating it are themselves drawn into this current of divine life.

The response to this benediction, this blessing, the gift of God's life, is eucharist, man's thanksgiving: he recognizes in joy and wonderment that every gift, beginning with that of life, comes to him from God.

Christian worship

Born within Judaism, Christianity took over this attitude and these practices. It simply gave them a new colouring, because Christians know that everything comes to us from Jesus and that every eucharist goes to the Father through him.

When we read the book of Revelation, we shall see that Christian liturgy takes over Jewish worship (p.108). The Psalms, too, are re-read in the light of Christ: see the fine liturgy described in Rev.4.23–31.

We shall see how Christians also wrote their own prayers, and we shall study the Lord's Prayer.

For the moment, we shall be dwelling on the centre and the climax of the Christian eucharist: the last supper of Jesus. The accounts are too rich to be studied in one page, so we shall keep to one particular aspect. By looking at the two interpretations given by the Gospels, we shall see better how daily life and worship are united; Jesus is present through the offering of his person and the community of Christians who love him.

♥ The institution of the eucharist

The context

One of the first narratives to be composed was that of the passion. It ran from the arrest of Jesus to his burial, and thus described the *outward* course of the passion. Very soon, the disciples felt that they should preface it with two other narratives which would make it possible to grasp the *inner* meaning of the events. The account of the agony in the garden shows how Jesus, fully man, sorrowfully accepts his imminent death and restores meaning to it: he makes an offering out of failure. The account of the last supper shows how Jesus celebrates his passion in advance. The last supper, the agony, the way of the cross: these are three presentations of the passion, each one of which says everything, but does so from a different point of view.

The texts

The synopsis opposite gives the four accounts of the last supper that we have. John is absent, but he too speaks of the eucharist.

Read Mark 14.23–25. Does the account seem to you to be straightforward? Look at the end of v.23 and v.24; does the content of the cup ('this', v.24) denote the same thing as 'the fruit of the vine' (v.25)? Read the text leaving out v.24b ('This . . . for many'): what kind of meal is this? Read the text with v.24b: what kind of a meal is this?

Read Luke 22.15–18 + 21–38, then 22.19–20. Can you see two kinds of meal?

The memory of Jesus' last supper has been interpreted in two ways: as a farewell meal in which Jesus gives his last commands to his disciples, or a liturgical meal in which Jesus, by a prophetic action, holds a liturgical celebration of his death. Here is an example. Two sons are back one evening at the home of their old father; he takes the opportunity of the meal to share his belongings between them; the sons leave, and the father dies soon afterwards. It is possible that each of them might describe the meal in a different way: one would remember above all that it was his last meal with his father; he talked to them and told them to stay together, to love each other; the other, more realistic, simply recalls the sharing of the inheritance.

A Christian symbol: the bread and the fish (Catacomb of Callixtus, Rome, second century AD)

A farewell meal

The farewell discourse is a literary genre which is well known in the Old Testament and Jewish literature (see e.g. Gen.49; I Kings 2; Tobit 4; 14). Someone who knows that his death is near gathers together his children or his disciples: he exhorts them to be virtuous, above all to show brotherly love; he often puts forward his own past life as a model and makes prophecies about the future. Sometimes this takes place at a meal.

Reread Luke 22.15–18 + 21–38; Mark 14.25; Matt.26.29; John 13–17. Here the last supper was recalled as Jesus' farewell meal; he gives his commands: 'By this sign men shall know that you are my disciples: Love one another . . .'; he prophesies his future: he affirms his trust in God. After his death he is certain to enter the kingdom of God; and he announces the future for his community: that his disciples shall stay united until the final coming of this kingdom. The way in which Jesus remains present in the world is through the community formed of those who share his bread and live accordingly.

A liturgical meal or a prophetic action

The prophets have already introduced us to actions which not only give a message but realize in advance what they express (*How to Read the Old Testament*, p.43).

The action of Jesus in breaking bread, giving it, and pouring wine, realizes in advance the gift of his body and his blood. And because this action is a meal, that is, something that one can have again, with food that one can eat, by re-enacting this meal we can assimilate the very person of Jesus, given over to death and risen again.

Matthew, Mark and Luke put the meal in the setting of the Jewish paschal meal (celebrated in that year on the eve of Good Friday), but they saw its meaning differently.

Matthew-Mark. Read Ex.24.4–8. The death of Jesus appears above all as the realization of the cultic sacrifice which implemented the covenant.

Luke-Paul. Read Jer.31.31–34 and Isa.42.6; 49.8; 53.12. The death of Jesus appears primarily as the prophet martyr's gift of himself. Thanks to him, the new covenant will at last be realized.

In the light of this study, what significance can the Last Supper have for us today?

Matt.26.26–29	Mark 14.22–25	Luke 22.15–20	I Cor.11.23–26
		[15]And he said to them, 'I have earnestly desired to eat this passover with you before I suffer; [16]for I tell you that I shall not eat it until it is fulfilled in the kingdom of God.' [17]And he took a cup, and when he had given thanks, he said, 'Take this, and divide it among yourselves; [18]for I tell you that from now on I shall not drink of the fruit of the vine until the kingdom of God comes.'	
[26]Now as they were eating, Jesus took bread	[22]And as they were eating, he took bread	[19]And he took bread, and	[23]The Lord Jesus, on the night when he was betrayed took bread,
and blessed, and broke it and gave it to the disciples and said, 'Take, eat; this is my body.'	and blessed and broke it, and gave it to them and said, 'Take; this is my body.'	when he had given thanks, he broke it and gave it to them saying, 'This is my body which is given for you. Do this in remembrance of me.'	[24]and when he had given thanks he broke it and said, 'This is my body which is broken for you. Do this in remembrance of me.'
[27]And he took a cup, and when he had given thanks he gave it to them saying, 'Drink of it, all of you,'	[23]And he took a cup and when he had given thanks he gave it to them and they all drank of it. [24]And he said to them,	[20]And likewise the cup after supper saying,	[25]In the same way also the cup after supper, saying,
[28]for this is my blood of the covenant which is poured out for many for the forgiveness of sins.	'This is my blood of the covenant which is poured out for many.	'This cup is the new covenant in my blood which is poured out for you.'	'This cup is the new covenant in my blood. Do this, as often as you drink it, in remembrance of me. [26]For as often as you eat this bread and drink this cup, you proclaim the Lord's death until he comes.'
[29]I tell you I shall not drink again of this fruit of the vine until that day when I drink it new with you in my Father's kingdom.'	[25]Truly, I say to you I shall not drink again of the fruit of the vine until that day when I drink it new in the kingdom of God.'		

The Our Father

Christian prayers

Matthew 6.9–13	Joint liturgical translation	Luke 11.2–4
9 *Our Father who art in heaven,* *Hallowed be thy name.*	*Our Father in heaven* *hallowed be your name,*	2 *Father,* *hallowed be thy name.*
10 *Thy kingdom come,* *Thy will be done,* *On earth as it is in heaven.*	*your kingdom come,* *your will be done,* *on earth as in heaven.*	*Thy kingdom come.*
11 *Give us this day our daily bread;*	*Give us today our daily bread.*	3 *Give us each day our daily bread;*
12 *And forgive us our debts,* *As we also have forgiven our debtors.*	*Forgive us our sins* *as we forgive those who sin against us.*	*and forgive us our sins,*
13 *And lead us not into temptation* *But deliver us from evil.*	*Do not bring us to the time of trial* *but deliver us from evil.*	4 *for we ourselves forgive every one* *who is indebted to us;* *and lead us not into temptation.*

The text of this prayer is sometimes difficult: the word translated 'daily' is in fact found only here in Greek literature and there is some dispute as to its exact meaning; the phrase about temptation is obscure. The texts of Matthew and Luke differ: fidelity to the thought of Jesus seemed more important to the disciples than an exact reproduction of his words.

Compare these two texts with each other and with the joint liturgical text. Note the similarities and the differences.

Our Father who art in heaven: what is suggested by this use of the first person plural, the association of proximity (Our Father) with transcendence (in heaven)? The word Father doubtless reproduces the Abba, the intimate term, which characterizes the attitude of Jesus and the first Christians (Mark 14.36; Rom.8.15; Gal.4.6).

How do we 'hallow' God? See Ezek.20.41; 36.20f.

Thy kingdom come: what are we asking? Look again at p.65.

What is God's will? See e.g. Matt.18.14; Eph.1.9–10; I Tim.2.4; John 6.39–40.

What is the general purport of these three petitions (Luke clearly felt that they amounted to just one)?

Bread. For the different possible meanings of the word for 'daily' look at the notes in your Bible or a commentary or word book. What is this bread? Simply earthly food? Or also the bread of the kingdom?

Forgiveness. This is the essential characteristic of both Jew and Christian: because God has pardoned us, we ourselves cannot but pardon others.

Temptation. We are not asking God not to put us to the test, as he tested Abraham (Gen.22.1) or his people (Deut.8.2), but that he will not allow us to enter a temptation which is too strong for us.

Look at the context. Why do Matthew and Luke think Jesus taught this prayer? What is the theme developed next in Matt.6.14–15; Luke 11.5–13?

Other prayers

The New Testament has preserved a large number of prayers. You might read them and study some of them. Here is a list.

Magnificat: Luke 1.46–55
Benedictus: Luke 2.68–79
Nunc dimittis: Luke 2.29–32
The prayer of the community in Acts 4.23–31
Hymns either composed by Paul or collected by him:
    Phil.2.6–11; Col.1.12–20; Eph. 1.3–9; 3.4–21;
    I Tim.4.16; 6.15–16; II Tim.2.8; 2.11–13;
    Heb.13.20–21.
The hymn in I Peter 1.3–9
The various liturgical acclamations in the book of Revelation.

8 The Apocalypse: The Book of Revelation

Christ in majesty. The royal portal of Chartres (thirteenth century)

The Book of Revelation, the Apocalypse, is a book of fire and blood in the image of our world. We find it disconcerting. Here everything seems strange: the style, the imagery, the logic. But confronted with a painting which is not figurative, we should not ask, 'What does that represent?', but rather, 'What impression does that make on me?' That is also true of apocalyptic books. However, we shall find it useful to have some keys which will help us to find a way into them.

An apocalypse

This book and the book of Daniel are the only apocalypses in the Bible, but at the time apocalyptic was a very common genre in Judaism. For its precise characteristics see *How to Read the Old Testament*, pp. 89–90. Here is a summary of the essential features.

In a time of crisis, to maintain the faith and hope of believers, an author tries to unveil the end of history, to remove the veil (Latin *re-velare*, Greek *apo-kaluptein*) which hides the end of time. This revelation is both pessimistic about the present (our world is in the grip of evil, incurably), and optimistic about the future (in the end, God will emerge victorious and recreate this world).

Using the technique of the long jumper, the author goes back and pretends to be an illustrious person from the past: in this way he can 'announce' the immediate future (between the time in which he is supposed to have lived and his present) and the ultimate future, for which he has less information. This forces him to use blurred imagery! Thanks to the run-up which he has given himself, he has the possibility of discovering the way in which God usually directs history, and can derive from it basic laws which he uses when he envisages the future. Or, to use another image, the author carries out a study in trajectory.

The author of Revelation was probably writing about 95–100, and pretends that he is writing about 60.

A prophetic book

Because this is a Christian apocalypse, the literary genre is substantially changed. The Christian recognizes Jesus as the Messiah: so with him the end of history has come. Jesus is the key to interpreting the world. This book, while using the procedures of apocalyptic, is also above all a prophetic book.

The author does not conceal himself under a false name; he calls himself John, and locates himself on Patmos. He presents himself simply as a witness to the living Christ.

He is apparently pessimistic about the present, and looks towards the new creation of our old world at the end of time. However, the Christian cannot but be an optimist: he knows that Christ is the victor and that he is already at work in the world. Like the prophets, therefore, the author tries to interpret present history and discover its hidden meaning.

A liturgy

Worship is the place where from now on one encounters the Lord as he will be at the end. The sacraments henceforth make him present in our daily life. This is the joyful certainty which the liturgy proclaims and celebrates. And we shall see that the author takes up the Jewish liturgy to express his message of hope.

The author

Is this the man who wrote the Fourth Gospel? There are plenty of reasons (style, thought) for answering this question either way. We can keep to the tradition which identifies the two authors, but in the end the question is of only secondary importance.

Sealed letters. Elephantine papyri (Egypt, about 400 BC)

105

The Book of Revelation as a Whole

Why not begin by reading Revelation straight through? Many passages will seem obscure, but that doesn't matter. If you go into the museum in Angers, on the Loire, where there is an exhibition of Lurcat's tapestries, *Le Chant du Monde*, 'The Song of the World', you will be disoriented and astounded: the significance of many of the details may escape you, but you will be 'living' the Apocalypse.

All the same, here are some pointers which may prove useful. Some are fairly certain, for example the division into three main sections. Others are less so, like the title or the organization of the central part. Use them if they are a help, but don't feel obliged to accept them all.

In its present form the book appears as a meditation on the church: the life of the church depends on God who is Lord of history, on Jesus the faithful witness, and the Spirit who prays in it.

1. The incarnate church. 1–3

After some introductory words (1.1–3), John addresses the seven churches of Asia. Seven is a symbolic number expressing totality. So he is addressing the church, but the incarnate church as it is in local congregations, with their faults and their virtues. This is not the ideal church of which one dreams, but the very human church as we know it, made up of our fears, our sins and our weak desire to serve the Lord.

The vision of the Son of man (1.9–20) is a clear indication that the life of the church unfolds in the presence of the glorified Christ (1.20).

These chapters, which are quite easy, are essential: it is partly thanks to them that the others avoid being abstract, and concern us.

2. The committed church. 4–20

This is where the Apocalypse proper begins – and with it our difficulties!

We see the church fighting and struggling with the problems of its time and of all time. These are of two kinds: the church's relationship with Judaism (4–11) and the confrontation between the church and totalitarian political powers (12–20).

(a) The church and Israel. 4–11

What is the relationship between the church which feels itself to be the 'new Israel', the true people of God, and the Judaism which is fighting against it? John replies: the church is indeed the 'small remnant' of Israel, those who are faithful to God while believing in Jesus, but a people which is open to all nations.

The heavenly liturgy. 4–5

This section begins with a grandiose vision of God, the Lord of history, reigning in the centre of the cosmos, and of the Spirit (4). The Lamb, Christ sacrificed but living, has the power to open the seven scrolls of the Old Testament, each one sealed with a seal (5).

Events seen from 'heaven'. 6.1–8.1

The vision of the seven seals gives us the hidden, 'heavenly' meaning of the events which will be narrated later.

You might spend some time on this vision of the people of God at the end of time. It is made up of the elect coming from two different directions.

Some come from Judaism (7.1–8). They are 144,000, that is to say, not a number limited in a ridiculous way, as certain sects think, but on the contrary, a countless multitude. Twelve is the number for Israel (because of the twelve tribes), and the elect are twelve squared (12 × 12) multiplied by 1,000.

The others come from the Gentile world (7.9–17). Here John abandons cipher language to say plainly that they are a vast, innumerable crowd.

The mediaeval 'mysteries'

In the mystery plays which were acted outside mediaeval churches, there were hardly any changes of scene: one saw simultaneously, on one side earthly events, and on the other the heavenly court judging those events.

John already seems to make use of this procedure. In his imagery he presents an event and then the invisible meaning it has for faith. So the events brought about by the opening of the seven seals (6–7) are followed by others brought about by the successive soundings of the seven trumpets (8–11). These are not extra facts, but the two sides of the same events, visible and concealed.

Events experienced on earth. 8.6–11, 19

The sounding of the seven trumpets announcing the disaster which is to come is not an addition to what has gone before: now we see the earthly side of things. This transition from Israel to the church has been marked by the terrible catastrophe of the ruin of Jerusalem in 70: Israel is cast out and trampled under foot by the Gentiles (11.1–2). However, the church, following on from the two élite witnesses of the Old Testament, Moses and Elijah (11.6), and above all from Jesus (11.7–12), takes the message to the ends of the earth.

The episode of the small book which is eaten (10) here anticipates something that will be taken up in ch. 14.

(b) The church and the totalitarian powers. 12–20
The vision of the woman and the dragon (12.1–6) marks a turning point. It presents the essentials of what is to come: the church gives birth to the Messiah on calvary; Jesus is glorified and Satan defeated. He tries to harm the church, but God protects it. The following visions develop this overall view.

The forces involved. 12.7–14.5

Here again, we first see the hidden object of the struggle: in 'heaven', Michael fights against the dragon, i.e. God is victor over evil (12.7–18).

Specifically, on earth this is translated into the struggle between the powers inspired by Satan and those who are faithful to the Lamb. The evil powers are represented by two beasts: the beast from the sea (13.1–10), the symbol of totalitarian empires (at that time Rome), and the beast from the earth who enters its service (13.11–18), the symbol of the ideologies at the service of totalitarian empires. Facing them are the Lamb and those who follow him (14.1–5).

The announcement of judgment. 14.6–19.10
This is made in four stages.
• First, there is a proclamation of the gospel of judgment (14.6–13). This passage takes up ch. 10, presenting the little book, the gospel. This judgment is the ruin of Babylon, i.e. Rome and all the totalitarian empires, and rest for the faithful.
• However, the victory of the faithful lies the other side of the passion: the martyrs are the clusters of grapes trampled in the winepress (14.14–20). But victory is certain and can already be celebrated (15).
• The downfall of the totalitarian empires (16–17), who are represented by Babylon, the great whore.

• Two songs celebrate the result: the lamentation over Babylon (18) and the triumph song of the elect (19.1–10).

The final victory of the Messiah. 19.11–20.15

This is again presented on two levels.
• in 'heaven', Christ appears, his garments red not with the blood of his enemies but with his own blood (see *How to Read the Old Testament*, p. 104, the 'cursing Psalms');
• on earth, we have the 'thousand years' of the history of the church.

3. The transfigured church. 21–22

After these chapters of fire and blood, the finale, like the final chorus to a hymn to joy, introduces us to the peace of paradise, the paradise of Genesis. However, John tells us that this is not nostalgia for a lost golden age, but hope set before us.

The church comes down from heaven. That indicates that it both is the earthly church in which we live and at the same time has been remade entirely by God. Taking up the great vision with which the Bible begins, this church recreated by God really becomes the kingdom of God, the city in which he establishes his dwelling place with the Lamb, the cosmic kingdom in which all peoples will be at home and in which God is all in all.

However, this is still only a 'vision': it is both that which is already dimly experienced in the church of today and that towards which it journeys and which it must bring nearer. The Spirit, too, does not cease to inspire its prayer: 'Oh, yes! Come, Lord Jesus!'

Numerical symbolism

Seven is the perfect figure, symbolizing fullness.
Three and a half (half seven) signifies imperfection, suffering, a time of trial and persecution. Be careful! Three and a half can appear in many forms, but its symbolic value remains the same: so three and a half, or a time, times and half-a-time (perhaps $1 + 2 + \frac{1}{2}$), or three and a half years, have the same significance as three and a half days, or forty-two months, or 1260 days.
Twelve signifies Israel (because of the twelve tribes).
Four signifies the world (the four points of the compass)
A thousand is an incalculable quantity.

Some Texts from Revelation

🔖 Letters to the churches. 1–3

These letters are all constructed along the same lines:

- The address of the letter (the name of the church);

- the Christ who sends it is designated by an image taken from the opening vision (1.9–20);

- an examination drawing up a balance sheet of failings and virtues and calling for conversion;

- a refrain ends each letter: 'Hear what the Spirit says to the churches', and a gift is promised to the one who conquers, a gift which will be taken up again in the final vision (21–22).

When you read these letters, try to find this structure. Then you might study one letter in detail or look at them all, keeping an eye open for two features:

The particular situation of a church is the place in which it lives out its faith. The examination in each letter in fact often alludes to a particular feature of the city (in Laodicea, for example, there was a famous medical school which made eye ointment) or an event which marked it out (for example, Sardis was captured several times by an enemy 'coming like a thief'). Look at the notes in your Bible or in a commentary. So the specific situation is rather like a sign of the times which the community has to decipher.

The coming of Christ in worship. Reread the different gifts given to the conqueror (at the end of each letter). If you put these back in the context of Jewish and Christian writings of the time, you will see that most of them are allusions to the sacraments. The white robes (3.5), the crown (2.10; 3.11) and the new name (2.17) allude to baptism, and the manna (2.17), the fruits of the tree of life (2.7) and the banquet (3.20) allude to the eucharist.

You might also look at the relationship between these gifts and the summary of them at the end, in chapters 21–22. You will see similarities there, but also a difference: the letters envisage regular liturgical celebrations in the communities, while Rev. 22 envisages above all the last Supper, the last Easter, when Christ will finally come as judge and saviour. However, already, in worship we are invited to the table of this Lord where he gives himself to us.

A reconstruction of the altar of Zeus at Pergamum (third century BC). The 'throne of Satan' in Rev. 2.13 may be an allusion to this.

🔖 The great eucharist. 4–5

Read this text carefully; it is one of the finest in the book. Who are the main characters? What are they doing? What is the relationship between them? What places do we find?

References to the Old Testament in your Bible or in a commentary will help you to discover the meaning of certain images. Here are the main ones. The elders (or old men), those who hold authority in the people of God, form a kind of presbytery round God and recall the elders around the bishop in the liturgy. The four living creatures (or animals) represent the created world with its four horizons: they form God's throne. The seven lampstands probably signify the Holy Spirit. The book is the Old Testament, which remains sealed, incomprehensible, until Jesus opens it.

Note the songs of praise. Who are they praising? Why? Note the paradox which expresses the mystery of Christ well: a lion is announced, and what appears is a lamb as though slain (4.5–6).

What is the relationship between heaven and earth? Between God-lamb-spirit and the universe-humanity?

It seems that here we are midway between the Jewish liturgy and our eucharistic prayers.

The morning office in the Jewish liturgy contains three great benedictions which serve as a framework for the recitation of the Shema, which plays the part of our Creed. The first celebrates God as Creator, and the community unites itself with the hymn of the angels, chanting the *Sanctus* (see the extract in the box on the following page). The second thanks God for the love which he has shown to his people by giving them the Law (see the extracts in *How to Read the Old Testament*, p. 100). After the recitation of the Shema (see *How to Read the Old Testament*, p. 57), the third praises God for the redemption once achieved at the time of the Exodus, the pledge of the redemption which he has still to accomplish.

The liturgy in Rev. 4–5 follows the same pattern. Try to discover the elements in it: praise to God the Creator, to Christ who opens the book of the Law that he enables us to understand, to the Lamb of the Exodus accomplishing the definitive exodus and making his people a kingdom of priests who offer up the world's praise.

Look at the eucharistic prayers in use at your church: can you find the same features in them?

🦋 The woman crowned with stars. 12.1–6

Chapter 12 is virtually a summary of the whole book. It is important to get a good idea of the main characters.

- Who is the dragon? See 12.9.
- Who is the child? The quotation in v. 5 will help you. To which event from the life of Jesus is Ps. 2 applied in the New Testament (see *How to Read the Old Testament*, p. 102)?
- Who is the woman? Before answering, think of what you have just discovered about the child. Then reread Isa. 54.1; 66.7; John 16.21,22 (see p. 97, and *How to Read the Old Testament*, p. 90, 'Daughter of Zion').
- What is the fate of this woman (12.13–14)? What does the desert suggest (for numerical symbolism see p. 107)?

It looks as though here we have a summary of the paschal mystery and the situation of the church, involved in an exodus until the end of time. Can you make this more precise? What significance does it give to Christian life?

> *Blessed art thou, O Lord our God, King of the universe, who formest light and createst darkness, who makest peace and createst all things. Who in mercy givest light to the earth and to them that dwell thereon, and in thy goodness renewest the creation every day continually. How manifold are thy works, O Lord! In wisdom thou hast made them all. . . Be thou blessed, O Lord our God, in the heavens above and on earth below. Be thou blessed, our Rock, our King and our Redeemer, Creator of holy beings, Praised be thy name for ever; Creator of ministering spirits, all of whom stand in the heights of the universe, and with awe proclaim in unison aloud the words of the living God and everlasting King. All of them are beloved, pure and mighty; and all of them in dread and awe do the will of their Master; and all of them bless and praise, glorify and reverence. . . the Name of the Divine King. . . in tranquil joy of spirit, with pure speech and holy melody they all respond in unison, and exclaim with awe: 'Holy, holy, holy, is the Lord of hosts: the whole earth is full of his glory.' And the Ophanim and the holy beings, with a noise of great rushing, upraising themselves towards the Seraphim, thus over against them offer praise and say: 'Blessed be the glory of the Lord from his place.'*
>
> Blessing from the Jewish liturgy: the Yozer

🦋 The transfigured church. 21–22

These chapters are magnificent. Why not read them simply for enjoyment, to savour their poetry and religious depth?

To go further, you will have to see how they show that all the expectation of the Old Testament will one day be satisfied, and that it is already in the course of realization. At the end of this course through the Bible, at the same time it might be a good test of what knowledge of the Bible you have acquired! The great mass of references in the margin of your Bible might discourage you, so give priority to certain themes.

The second creation is like the first, but minus the serpent and sin. In reading Gen. 2–3, see what is taken up and what is superseded (Gen. 2.9; 3.9).

It realizes the announcement of a new creation made by the prophets in the exile: see Isa. 65.17–19; 66.22. In this new creation, there is no more death, no more crying, no more tears. The curse from Genesis has been done away with: see Isa. 25.8; 35.10; 40.2; Gen. 3.2. That is also expressed by the disappearance of the sea, the resort of the powers of evil.

This holy city is a continuation of the earthly church (Jerusalem) and the cosmos, but they are completely recreated (coming down from heaven). It is the abode of God among men, hoped for in II Sam. 7.14; Isa. 7.14; Ezek. 37.27; Lev. 26.11–12. It is the bride of Christ radiant with light: Isa. 52.1; 60; 61.10. Isaiah described the ramparts of this city (Isa. 54.11) and Ezekiel reconstructed its Temple (Ezek. 40). But in this city with twelve gates (one for each apostle, the foundations of the church, though its only real foundation is the Christ, I Cor. 3.11), there is no longer a Temple, for God is all in all.

This new paradise, set before us as a task to be performed and a gift to be received from God, is irrigated by the spring of living water flowing from the side of the Lamb who was slain, a spring which has a name: the Holy Spirit. See Ezek. 47.1–12; Zech 13.1–3; John 19.34 (p. 97).

And all this is already present through the prayer of the church and the Spirit, and is already given in the sacraments to those who conquer.

The Christ of the Apocalypse

The background to this page of text is the royal portal of Chartres: the whole of Revelation is there. Stone saints with ecstatic smiles, and vaulting reaching silently upwards, on which angels and elders sing, all lead us towards one central point: Christ in majesty, enthroned on the universe of the four living beings forming the cross for the tympanum. Only the Christ is represented, because he has a human face. The Father and the Spirit are invisibly present.

Someone. . .

When the heavens open, John sees a throne. And on the throne, victorious. . . There is no name. A participle without a subject. For God cannot be named. However, he is the only one who can be enthroned over creation, because he is the Creator. And before him, the universe, stretching to Ezekiel's four horizons, is transformed into Isaiah's seraphim to proclaim his praise. Even more, he is the God of the exoduses; who is and was and is to come (1.4). One would have expected the phrase to end 'and is to be'. 'Is to come' introduces him into history. He is the one who goes with us through all the events of which scripture speaks. And finally, in his Son, he comes to us.

The Christ

The lamb as though slain. . . This is almost Jesus' proper name, which sums up his whole mystery. The lamb is this man, Jesus of Nazareth, still bearing what are now the glorious marks of his struggle on the cross and wearing the garment stained with the blood that he has shed (19.13). But he is standing, as a result of the resurrection, glorified at the very heart of God, whose throne he shares. The Spirit with the seven flames, the radiance of the life of God, has become the light which gives him inner light, and through these seven eyes allows him to see all things in the light of God (5.6). The second person of the Trinity is a man who takes into his glory all humanity, from the elect of Israel to the Gentile world – and the cosmos which reflects his radiance.

He is the paschal lamb whose sacrifice at the time of the Exodus brought about the people's salvation, the lamb whose blood sealed the covenant. Seen through the evocation of the new exodus hymned by Isaiah, this lamb is the suffering servant of Isa. 53, whose death suffered as a sacrifice became a light and a covenant for all people. In him mankind can at last become the priestly people who give significance to the whole world, involving it in the praise of the God who has saved it.

However, paradoxically this lamb becomes the shepherd, Ezekiel's shepherd (34.23), who is none other than God pasturing his flock with loving care (Rev. 7.16–17).

Son of man: that is how Jesus appears to John in his first vision (1.12–20). Here is that mysterious being announced by Dan. 7 and awaited at the end of time: Jesus is at the same time a priest in a white robe and a king with a golden girdle; his white hair suggests his eternal youth, his voice is powerful, and nothing escapes his eyes, burning flames penetrating the depths of men's hearts. In his mouth the word of God is a sharp sword, separating good from evil.

Like God, he is the first and the last, the alpha and the omega. His resurrection is the gateway to true life. From now on this living being possesses the keys of Hades: he has forced the gates of the abode of the dead, and Christian existence becomes a wait for the true life.

Jesus can be the faithful witness as seen by Second Isaiah because he has entered the divine secret. In him we know the invisible God. What cannot be known has taken the countenance of a man, and from now onwards his beauty is reflected on all human faces, for the disciple must bear witness to him in the world after his example. For Second Isaiah, the martyr bears witness even more by his words than by his death.

Jesus is the faithful companion who knocks at our door and invites himself to dine with us, so that he can invite us to sit with him on his throne (3.14, 21).

The Spirit

As a sevenfold flame burning ceaselessly before the image of God, Christ's seven-eyed gaze, the Spirit is above all the one who tells us the words of Christ: every letter sent by the Christ ends with the words 'Hear what the Spirit says' (1–3). Like a mother, the Spirit invites us to rest (14.13). Above all, it keeps the church faithful to Christ; it is the love which murmurs in the bride's heart those words which it needs must say, 'Oh, yes! Come, Lord Jesus!'

'According to the scriptures'

Often in the course of this reading of the New Testament we have referred to the scriptures, to what for us has become the Old Testament. What I said at the end of *How to Read the Old Testament* (it's worth re-reading pp. 109–111 of that book) should now be clearer to you: the scriptures formed the cultural and religious milieu of the first Christians as they did that of the Jews. They enable us to enter to some degree into their world of symbols, to discover what could be suggested to them by expressions which are at first sight trivial, like 'the third day', or everyday people and things, like the shepherd and the vine.

Even more profoundly, the scriptures are and remain the expression of God's promise and man's expectation. For the disciples as for us, Jesus makes sense only in the context of this promise, and as a response to our expectation.

To convince ourselves further of this, if there is any need, we are going to go back to some texts that we have already studied, and look at one more.

Words filled with meaning

We all have words which, because of our education, our reading or certain events, carry a meaning which is important to us but which others who have not undergone the same experience will not always be able to see immediately.

The way in which the Jews and the first disciples were familiar with scripture means that for them some words were pregnant with a meaning which we find difficulty in discovering, especially as our translations do not always succeed in conveying every aspect of the word. Here are two instances.

Luke begins his account of the ascent to Jerusalem like this: 'As the time drew near when Jesus would be taken up into heaven, he made up his mind and set out on his way to Jerusalem' (9.51, Good News Bible). The way in which this translation reads doubtless suggests Jesus' determination and courage, and inclines us towards a psychological translation. That is why translations like this, however lively and attractive on the surface, have their drawbacks. Fortunately the RSV is much more literal and at least enables us to glimpse a further dimension. It replaces 'made up his mind' with 'set his face', a strange expression which in fact occurs in one of Isaiah's Servant poems. Although he is persecuted and

people spit in his face and pull at his beard, the servant sets his face so as not to yield, because the Lord comes to his aid. Thus the prime concern of this passage is not psychological, as the Good News Bible suggests, but theological. Luke is not interested in states of mind, but is rather expressing his conviction that Jesus was the Servant of Isaiah, that he knew that he was responsible for his mission and that he would not weaken, despite suffering, because the Lord came to his aid.

In the introduction to the account of the passion, Matthew makes Jesus himself announce his imminent death. Then he continues: 'Then the chief priests and the elders gathered in the palace of the high priest. . .' (Matt. 26.3). We get the impression that here we have a simple account. However, the Jerusalem Bible gives four references in the margin. The first, John 11.47–53, sends us back to the more detailed account in John. The three others are stranger: Ps. 2.1–2; Acts 4.25–27; Ps. 31.14. In all three we find the same verb, gather. We may also note that the other evangelists do not use it in their accounts of the passion (except for Luke 22.66, where it appears in the singular), but that Matthew uses it again in 26,57; 27.62; 28.12 to describe the gathering of the high priests against Jesus. And we find it again in Acts 4.25–27, where this time there is a quotation of Ps. 2. So we are led to think that in choosing this verb, Matthew too wanted to allude to the same psalm. And if this is correct, the whole meaning of the passion is illuminated.

As he begins his account, Matthew senses a difficulty: he wants to narrate the passion of Christ, but how can his readers follow it? If Jesus was truly the Messiah, how could he have been rejected by the Jewish authorities who were established by God to recognize this Messiah when he came? By saying that they gathered together, just like the enemies in Ps. 2, against God and his Messiah, Matthew declares: if they rejected him, this was because they were the evil one of whom the psalm (and Ps. 31) speaks. So Jesus is the Messiah. And if now he is in process of living out the first strophe of the psalm – the gathering of the enemies against him – we can be certain that the other strophes will also be realized: God will intervene and establish his Messiah, Jesus, as Lord over all the world.

Realities filled with meaning

A person or event from the past can be filled with meaning in order to express something of the reality that we experience today. Of a child, we might say, 'he's the very image of his father', or, in another case, 'That's where she met her Waterloo'.

Similarly, the Jews and the first Christians discovered in their past history people (Moses, David, Elijah) or events (the Exodus, the return from exile) which could give meaning to their everyday life. However, the way in which this came about was more profound and more complex than ours. For us, people and events are instances, simple images. For them, these really did bear a meaning, a hope: in some way they expressed, or lived out in advance, what would only really appear at the end of time or in Jesus Christ. They are more than examples: they are types or mock-ups (see *How to Read the Old Testament*, p. 111). That is why this way of taking up the scriptures is often called typology.

Unfortunately, it is impossible to say more about this extremely important aspect here. We shall have one instance of it as we study the annunciation to Mary: Luke presents Mary as the daughter of Sion and Jesus as Son of David. However, you should note (or remind yourself of) the way in which Jesus is presented as the new Adam (Rom. 5.12ff.; Luke 3.38, see p. 82), the new Moses (see pp. 72, 76), the new Elijah (see p. 88), the stone rejected and made the cornerstone (Ps. 118, see p. 91), the Temple, the Son of Man.

♥ The annunciation to Mary. Luke 1.26–38

The account of an annunciation

Read this text and note the different parts of which it is made up. Then read the annunciation to Zechariah (Luke 1.5–25) and the annunciation to Gideon (Judges 6.11–24). You will find there the same pattern, the same features, the same questions. So Luke is taking up a well-known literary genre here, and that is illuminating: when it was used, it was meant to stress not the virtues or the psychology of the person involved, but the mission entrusted on behalf of the people of God.

If there is a common mould, are the sayings of the angel and Mary perhaps original? Compare them with the texts of the Old Testament which are in boxes alongside: putting them in the mouth of the angel is a way for Luke of saying who Mary and Jesus are in the divine plan.

For Luke, who is Mary?

The daughter of Zion. The angel takes up the oracle from Zephaniah, or others very similar to it like Joel 2.21–27; Zech. 2.14–17; 9.9–10. If he presents Mary as the daughter of Zion, at the end of time, what mission is he assigning to her? How does that concern us personally (see How to *Read the Old Testament*, p. 61)?

The new name given to Mary comes from a verb which only appears one other time in the New Testament, in Eph. 1.6, where it is applied to the church at the end of time. How does that illuminate the role assigned to Mary as a figure of the church?

The mother of Emmanuel: Isa. 7.14.

The first of the believers at the beginning of a new people, just as Abraham was through his faith (Gen. 18.14).

So Luke is primarily interested, not in Mary's psychology or her privileges, but in her mission among the people of God, in the church. Try to be more specific about this mission.

For Luke, who is Jesus?

Son of David or *Son of the Most High*. He is the Emmanuel of Isa. 7.14, and above all the Son of God in the sense of being the Son of David enthroned as king in II Sam. 7 (*How to Read the Old Testament*, p. 42).

Thus Jesus fulfils the expectations of Israel. However, Luke goes on, he does so in a more remarkable way than one might ever imagine. In fact he is:

Son of God. The verb overshadow (Hebrew *shakan*) appears only in a few Old Testament texts and has a very strong sense: God comes to inhabit his temple in person. This verb led to the word Shekinah, which expresses the real presence of God in the midst of his people (see p. 74 on the subject of Matt. 18). The only true temple is therefore from now on the womb of Mary, and the word Son of God (v. 35) has quite a different meaning from Son of the Most High (v. 32).

Try to be more specific, at the end of this study, in showing how his use of scripture allows Luke to express his faith, discovered in the light of Easter, and allows us to know that this adventure concerns us too.

1. Presentation of the scene and the people involved

26 *In the sixth month the angel Gabriel was sent by God to a city of Galilee named Nazareth,*

27 *to a virgin betrothed to a man whose name was Joseph, of the house of David;*
and the virgin's name was Mary.

2. Salutation by the angel

28 *And he came to her and said,*
'Hail, O favoured one,
the Lord is with you.'

3. Reaction

29 *But she was greatly troubled at the saying,*
and considered in her mind what sort of greeting this might be.

4. The angel's message

30 *And the angel said to her,*
'Do not be afraid, Mary,
for you have found favour with God.'

31 *And behold, you will conceive in your womb and bear a son, and you shall call his name Jesus (the Lord saves).*

32 *He will be great,*
and will be called the Son of the Most High;
and the Lord God will give to him the throne of his Father David,

33 *And he will reign over the house of Jacob for ever; and of his kingdom there will be no end.'*

5. Questions leading to a new message

34 *And Mary said to the angel,*
'How can this be,
since I have no husband?'

35 *And the angel said to her:*
'The Holy Spirit will come upon you,
and the power of the Most High will overshadow you;
therefore the child to be born
will be called holy, the Son of God.

6. A sign is given

36 *And behold your kinswoman Elizabeth in her old age has also conceived a son;*
and this is the sixth month with her who was called barren.

37 *For with God nothing will be impossible.'*

38 *And Mary said, 'Behold I am the handmaid of the Lord;*
let it be to me according to your word.'

7. The angel goes away

And the angel departed from her.

He has freely bestowed grace on us in the Beloved.
Eph. 1.6

Zephaniah 3.14–16

Rejoice, daughter of Zion, the king of Israel, the Lord is in your midst.

Isaiah 7.14

The virgin shall conceive and bear a son, and shall call his name Emmanuel.

Do not fear, O Zion. The Lord your God is in your midst, a warrior who gives victory.

II Samuel 7

I will make for you a great name, like the name of the great ones of the earth. . .
I will be his father and he shall be my son. . .
I will establish the throne of his kingdom.
Your house and your kingdom shall be made sure for ever before me; your throne shall be established for ever.

Exodus 40.35
Num. 9.18,22

The cloud abode upon it and the glory of the Lord filled the tabernacle.

Gen. 18.14

God said to Abraham,
'Is anything too hard for the Lord?'

'Must . . .'

Some texts might give the impression that Jesus is not free, that his life is written in advance in these scriptures so that he has only to realize it: 'The Son of man must be delivered up.' 'The scripture must be fulfilled' (Luke 24.7; Acts 1.16). This is not a matter of obligation, but of interpretation.

Think of someone who exclaims, 'That had to happen.!' She doesn't mean, 'That was fated, there was nothing anyone could have done about it,' but rather, 'It was in the logic of things, as a result of a whole series of earlier attitudes or events.' To understand the event, she interprets it by going back into the past, and now – but only now – it becomes clear that things couldn't have ended otherwise.

To understand how the one who was now recognized as Messiah and Son of God could have been rejected by his people and finally condemned to death, Christians put his death in the logical context of his life, his attitudes and the position he took up over against the established powers, for God and for the poor. And they had to acknowledge that the message of this Messiah was so different from what was expected that things had to happen like this. However, they went back still further, into scripture, to locate this life and this death in the logic of God's attitude. When we studied the kingdom of God (pp. 65,78), we saw that God is not neutral, that he is on the side of the oppressed, and because of that he too was rejected by his people. So they interpreted the fate of Jesus in the light of the fate of the persecuted righteous man in the Psalms, the suffering servant of Isaiah. Such is God's character, such is that of Jesus, that he had to be rejected and die.

It is probable that the disciples simply carried on an interpretation that was begun by Jesus. It sometimes happens that someone can attach meaning to an event which he in fact hopes will not happen.

In all probability, at the beginning of his mission Jesus thought that he could fulfil it in a happy way and that the Jews would accept his message. And then he had to consider the evidence: he was upsetting too many people; things would turn out badly (see p. 85 again). Jesus did not want to die (he even fled to escape death, John 11.54). However, in faithfulness to his mission he had to face up to death and therefore, in advance, give it meaning. And he found this meaning by meditating on the scriptures: he went up to Jerusalem as the Suffering Servant of Isaiah (see p. 111) and put his death in the train of that of the prophets (the parable of the murderers in the vineyard, p. 91).

The scriptures or Jesus?

Like the Jews, the first Christians assiduously reread the scriptures, looking for a meaning in their life. Their methods of interpretation were the same, yet everything was different.

For the Jews, scripture came first: the Jews were the servants of scripture and related it to the present in order to find a specific way of putting it into practice. 'My life is the Law,' Paul could say. For Christians, the risen Jesus was henceforth the centre, the key to everything. In order to understand his mystery and his mission better, they put it in the context of scripture, which was thus also made to serve Christ: 'My life is Christ.'

We can see the errors of a certain kind of Christian apologetic which relies on the argument from prophecy. Jesus, people might say, fulfilled the prophecies: that proves that he is God. They start from the scriptures to arrive at Jesus. The first Christians started with Jesus and went back to the scriptures. Here is an example. According to Matt. 26.15, Judas was paid thirty pieces of silver; that fulfilled the 'prophecy' of Zech. 11.12. Mark and Luke simply write that 'they agreed to give him money'. Matthew is trying to understand: he sees that Jesus was rejected by his people just as God himself had been. By making the text more specific with his reference to Zechariah, Matthew is not intending to give historical information (we don't know how much Judas received) but theological teaching: Jesus is God himself, rejected by his people.

By doing this, the disciples are opening up a way to us: to give meaning to our life in the service of Christ, we too should put it in the context of scripture.

In this way we rejoin the profound apocalyptic movement. In making a study of a trajectory (see p. 105), Revelation invites us to pick up our roots in the past, the past of the people of God, of Jesus Christ, and to discover there the trajectory which today we need to extend by our lives, in faithfulness to our history and in the freedom of the Spirit.

The Beginning of the Gospel

The beginning ... what a strange title for a conclusion! The double sense of this word will help us to complete this course through the New Testament by looking in two directions. Beginning in fact signifies a point of departure and a gateway on to the future.

The starting point of the gospel is clearly Jesus of Nazareth. What can we really know about him through the texts of the New Testament?

Jesus made a future for the gospel: these New Testament texts, and also the life of Christians for two thousand years. Is the gospel closed? Can we continue to write it today?

1. Jesus, the Beginning of the Gospel

Look back on the course which we have just covered. Perhaps we began it with the idea that the Gospels would put us in direct touch with Jesus, even if we did not actually say so: we thought that by opening them, we would hear his words as though they had been recorded on tape, and would see him as though in a photograph. It's clear at the end of this study that things are not as simple as that: we have neither recordings nor films of Jesus.

Have we lost anything by that? I feel sure that you will have discovered, by contrast, everything that we've gained. We do not have words or photographs which are accurate but none the less incomprehensible because their meaning escapes us: authentic witnesses hand the words and actions of Jesus on to us and interpret them at the same time. So the New Testament introduces us to a living community, and it is with that community that we are invited to make this encounter with the Lord Jesus.

However, perhaps another question arises: through these interpretations can we really get back to the very person of Jesus of Nazareth?

Easter is not a wall

Fortunately the time is past – I'm thinking, roughly speaking, of a period between 1920 and 1950 – when scholars, astonished at rediscovering the importance of the Christian communities and their interpretative work, claimed that Easter is a wall behind which we cannot go. They thought that while the New Testament gives us a good account of the disciples' faith in the risen Christ, it no longer allows us to know the Jesus of history.

After several decades, scholars have come back to more sensible positions. Easter is not a wall but a prism, which reveals the splendours of the mystery of Jesus. Through this prism we can really rediscover Jesus of Nazareth.

Just to reassure you, if that is necessary, and possibly to encourage you to look at some of the more learned commentaries, I shall list some of the criteria which scholars have produced to help us rediscover the authentic words or actions of Jesus. We shall spend a short while on the results they have achieved.

How do we arrive at Jesus of Nazareth?

Two criteria above all are used, and they must be taken together: originality and similarity.

Originality is assessed in connection with what came before and what went afterwards. If Jesus declares in a Gospel that God is our Father, he is not being original in relation to Jewish belief. The Old Testament already said as much, so it is probable that Jesus also said so; however, this phrase could also have been attributed to him because it was common at the time. On the other hand, if Jesus addresses God as 'Abba', using a much more familiar term, almost equivalent to 'Daddy', the familiarity is original: a Jew would not have dared to invent it.

After Easter, Jesus was recognized to be the Christ, the Lord, the Son of God. When Thomas says on the evening of Easter Day, 'My Lord and my God', we can read this as the church's faith: the words are not original in relation to what was believed after Easter. On the other hand, if Jesus declares, 'Even the Son does not know the hour of judgment', we find ourselves confronted with a phrase which would seem to contradict the faith of the church: if Jesus is God, he ought to know everything. This is an original phrase which the disciples would have preferred to suppress rather than to invent. Similarly, the church would not have dared to invent a scene like that of the agony in Gethsemane where one who was now recognized to be Son of God could be seen weeping bitterly and being afraid of death, or that in which he comes to receive the baptism of John, which was a baptism for sinners.

Similarity also works on two levels. There must be a certain coherence between what is said of Jesus and what is known of his day. If a modern text tells us that Napoleon reviewed his armies as they marched past the Eiffel Tower, we know that it is a fiction. When Jesus says, 'Do not go into their synagogues', we know that the phrase has been edited after there has been a separation between Christians and Judaism: Jesus should in fact say 'the synagogues', as we would talk about going to church: to say 'We're going to their church' suggests a division between us and those who go there regularly.

There must also be a certain coherence between the words of Jesus or his attitudes. The Gospel of Thomas (a Gnostic account from the second century) ends with this exchange: Simon Peter says, 'Let Mary (Magdalene) go out from among us, because women are not fit to live.' Jesus says, 'I will make her male so that she shall be a living spirit like you men; every woman who becomes a male will enter into the kingdom of God.' Such a phrase has a strange ring in view of what we know of Jesus: it is surely not authentic. Or when the Arabic Childhood Gospel of Jesus (a seventh-century writing) shows us the child Jesus killing on the spot a friend who has bumped into him and made him fall over, we know that this is completely out of character with the way in which Jesus performed miracles and the love he showed for all men.

Scholars use other criteria: these are the chief ones. However, we should note the results of their research: it has succeeded in establishing that certain words and actions may well be attributed to Jesus. However, it does not claim in any way that the other sayings or actions whose authenticity cannot be established in the same way do not come from Jesus. This research can affirm certain points: it does not claim at all to deny those which it cannot affirm in the same way.

The main stages in the life of Jesus

Without going into details about the actions and attitudes of Jesus, we can take it that the main features of his life are assured.

Jesus began his mission with the baptism which he received at the hands of John. Perhaps he was John's disciple for a while, and then separated from him.

In Galilee, Jesus preached the imminent coming of the kingdom of God. Crowds followed him enthusiastically, recognized him as a prophet and perhaps as the Messiah. However, their expectation was so ambiguous, filled with nationalistic hope, that Jesus disappointed them. Gradually these crowds left him. The pressure from his opponents grew more severe. Jesus guessed that to continue as he was doing was likely to bring him to a violent end.

He then went up to Jerusalem – several times, if we are to believe John. His attacks on the religious system, with the Temple at its centre, aroused more and more antagonism from his opponents. His way of behaving towards sinners, the people who did not observe the Law, and women and his very free way of interpreting the Law with authority, to restore it to its primitive purity (for example, the law of the sabbath), led to his rejection.

Religious authorities among the people (not all of them) condemned him to death. They succeeded in getting the Jerusalem crowds behind them. They delivered Jesus to the civil power for execution. Pilate sought to free him, less concerned for justice than anxious to cross the desires of the authorities. In the end he yielded. Jesus died on 7 April 30 (or, by another reckoning, 3 April 33).

'True God and true man'

To ask, 'What awareness did Jesus have of himself and his mission?' may court an amazing answer. Since he is God, he knew everything. However, some texts do allow us to ask this question; for example, there is one in which Jesus declares his ignorance of the day of judgment (Mark 13.32).

Here we are confronted with a mystery; here we can only hang firmly on to both ends of the thread without knowing how they are to be brought together: Jesus is fully God and he is also fully man.

When faced with a mystery, we are always tempted to neglect one aspect or at least to favour another. And the way in which we begin necessarily leads us to stress one aspect. For centuries, theology has deliberately been framed in terms of 'from above, downwards': it presents the mystery of the Son of God made man; so we begin from the affirmation that Jesus is God, to show that he was also fully man. Contemporary theology tends rather to be 'from below, upwards': it recognizes that Jesus is fully man, and in the Gospels looks for those features in his actions and his words which show a special and unique relationship with the Father, in which we can see his divinity.

The first disciples above all stressed the divine aspect. For those who had known Jesus and lived with him, it was clear that he was a man as they were. What they had to show was that this man was God.

Later on in the history of the church, and recently in Christian education as well, this was the starting point for disciples: Jesus is God. Hence the recent reaction: there has been all the more stress that he is man. That could lead to excesses, like the theological development called 'theology of the death of God', or certain popular representations in which Jesus is no more than a hero, a revolutionary or a close friend. However, avoiding one extreme should not lead us to the other.

So the Christian affirms very carefully, with the New Testament and the whole tradition, that Jesus is Son of God from the first moment of his conception. To ask what awareness Jesus might have had is not to doubt this faith; it is simply to attempt to locate it in the growth of this person who was fully man.

It has always been accepted that Jesus grew up, that he was hungry and cold, that he suffered, that he learned to talk and to pray. But to be man – as we are even more aware today – means also to be free, to have a choice, to look for one's way, to take chances. If Jesus was fully man, he had a psychology, freedom, like ours.

We saw earlier (p. 114) that Jesus probably first thought that his mission would be successful simply as a result of his preaching; confronted with opposition, he must then have envisaged the possibility of his violent death and attached a meaning to it. He was not acting out a comedy in the garden of the agony when he was coming to terms with his passion, believing according to the Pharisaic faith which he shared that God would raise him up at the end of time on the third day. A human comparison may help us here. We know that a new-born baby is a 'man', but he or she becomes aware of the fact only gradually; and throughout our existence, events and reflection allow us to discover better who we are and what our task is. We might think that it was the same with Jesus. Fully Son of God from the time of his conception, helped by the great experiences which God vouchsafed him, like the baptism and the transfiguration, and by the power which he discovered that he had of curing bodies and transforming hearts, he gradually became aware of the fact.

In affirming in this way that Jesus experienced our human condition 'in all things save sin', we are not minimizing his divinity, but are getting a better view of this divine humility of a God who became man, fully man, that we might become God.

Non-Christian Texts about Jesus

We know Jesus through the Gospels. Few secular texts say anything about him. There is nothing surprising in that: they did not have reporters or journalists in those days, and sadly the death of a Jew in an obscure corner of the Roman empire was an all too common occurrence. Secular writers only began to show an interest when the movement which Jesus launched showed its strength and seemed likely to put the very Empire in peril (see *How to Read the Old Testament*, p. 32, 'What is a historical event'). Here are the main texts.

About 110, Pliny the Younger, proconsul in Asia Minor, wrote to his friend the emperor Trajan to tell him how he was treating Christians. Christians were multiplying to such a degree that pagan temples were deserted. He did not go out looking for Christians, but when they were denounced, he imposed the death penalty on them if they persisted in their faith.

Some explained that they had ceased to be Christians . . . They maintained that the amount of their fault or error had been this, that it was their habit on a fixed day to assemble before daylight and recite by turns a form of words to Christ as a god; and that they bound themselves with an oath, not for any crime, but not to commit theft or robbery, or adultery, not to break their word, and not to deny a deposit when demanded. After this was done, their custom was to depart, and to meet again to take food, but ordinary and harmless food . . .

I have found nothing but an absurd superstition.

About 115, the Roman historian Tacitus describes Nero's persecution of the Christians, after the great fire of Rome in 64.

Christus, from whom the name had its origin, suffered the extreme penalty during the reign of Tiberius at the hands of one of our procurators, Pontius Pilate, and a deadly superstition, thus checked for the moment, again broke out not only in Judaea, the first source of the evil, but also in Rome, where all things hideous and shameful from every part of the world meet and become popular . . .

About 120, another Roman historian, Suetonius, wrote this in his *Life of Claudius*:

Since the Jews constantly made disturbances at the instigation of Chrestus, he expelled them from Rome.

Thus Christians were confused with Jews and Christ was taken as an agitator from among them (conpare this text with Acts 18.2).

He makes another brief allusion in his *Life of Nero*:

Punishment was inflicted on the Christians, a class of men given to a new and wicked superstition.

Flavius Josephus is a Jewish historian who first fought against the Romans and then entered their service. He died in Rome about 98, having written several works presenting Judaism to the Romans.

A passage from the *Jewish Antiquities* speaks of Jesus. This text has come down to us in different forms, and Christian hands have clearly been at the original text. The version given here has some chance of being earlier than the others; it can be found in the *Universal History* composed in Arabic, in the tenth century, by Agapius, bishop of Hierapolis.

About this time arose Jesus, a wise man, who did good deeds and whose virtues were recognized. And many Jews and peoples of other nations became his disciples. Pilate condemned him to be crucified and to die. However, those who had become his disciples preached his doctrine. They related that he had appeared to them three days after his crucifixion and that he was alive. Perhaps he was the Messiah in connection with whom the prophets foretold wonders.

Alexamenos worships his god
An anti-Christian caricature scratched on a wall in Rome (end of the second century or beginning of the third). It shows a figure at prayer in front of a crucified figure with an ass's head.

2. Can we Write the Gospel Today?

Are the Gospels, the New Testament, a closed book?' Can we continue to write them today? This question will help us to understand what the canon is and how it has been formed.

The canon of the New Testament

'Canon' and 'testament' are strange words, which prompt us to look at them in rather closer detail.

Canon, from a Greek word signifying rule, denotes in various contexts the ideal norm. In the fifth century BC a Greek sculptor wrote 'On the canon', i.e. the exact proportions of the human body. The 'canon of virtues' drawn up by ancient philosophers suggested how to live a moral life. 'Canon law' is the law which serves as a rule for Catholics. The 'canon of scripture' is the catalogue of books recognized by a church as the rule of its faith.

You should not confuse the canonicity of a book (the fact that it is included in this canon) with its authenticity. An authentic book is one which has been written by the author to whom it is attributed. The conclusion of Mark (16.9–20) is not authentic (it was not written by the author of the Gospel, but added later); it is, however, canonical.

The Greek Bible translated the Hebrew word denoting the covenant by *diatheke*, which indicates the arrangements made between two parties. At the beginning of the third century, Tertullian translated *diatheke* by the Latin word *testamentum*, which produces the English word testament.

The canon of the New Testament was formed gradually, by trial and error; some books were accepted and others were rejected.

Collections of books must have been made at an early stage: first of all there was a collection of Paul's letters (already indicated by II Peter 3.15), then probably a collection of Gospels and Catholic Epistles (James, I and II Peter, I, II, III John, Jude).

In the second century, the delimitation of the canon was speeded up as a reaction to two kinds of heresy: the Gnostics produced various Gospels (like those found at Nag Hammadi in Egypt, which include the Gospel of Thomas) and false apostolic letters. At the other extreme, Marcion, in Rome round about 150, rejected the Old Testament and part of the New.

The canon as we now have it was almost fixed between 150 and 300. Evidence from this period includes the Muratorian Canon (named after Muratori, who discovered it), an eighth-century manuscript giving a list of books accepted in Rome about 180, the writings of Irenaeus (who died about 202), Terutllian (died 220), Clement of Alexandria (died before 215) and Origen (died in 254).

These lists correspond almost exactly with the present-day canon: books sometimes disputed are Hebrews, James and I and II Peter. On the other hand, other books like the Didache, the Shepherd of Hermas and the Gospel of Peter were sometimes included. The canon was fixed in the fourth century, with a few minor differences, depending on churches.

In the Greek church, Eusebius of Caesarea (who died in 340), recognized the present-day canon except for Revelation. However, in 367 Athanasius fixed the canon of the Old and New Testaments as we have it today.

In the Syrian church, the official version, the Peshitto, does not have II Peter, II and III John, Jude and Revelation.

In the Latin church, Jerome, who translated the Bible into Latin between 384 and 395 (the Vulgate), adopted Athanasius' list.

What is the basis for the choice of the canon?

Several criteria played a part in the admission or rejection of books: they had to be of apostolic origin and be Catholic or universal, i.e. accepted in all the churches. These criteria played their part, but they are not enough to form the basis of our canon: some books then thought to have been written by the apostles were written at a later stage by their disciples.

So the ultimate criterion is that because the church is animated by the Holy Spirit, it has felt that certain books 'edify' it, build it up, and others do not. The recognition of the canon as all the inspired books which lay a foundation for faith is itself an act of faith in the Spirit which guides the church. The canon is now closed: the revelation has been made. Does that mean that we no longer need to write the gospel for our day?

The Text of the New Testament

'Do we have the original text of the Gospels or the New Testament? What is the basis of the text that we have in our Bibles?' These are questions which people often ask.

In fact, we have hardly any original texts from antiquity at all. One of the rare examples is a letter written by Simon bar Cochba, leader of the Jewish revolt in 135 (see p. 121). Usually we only have copies. Thus the earliest manuscripts of the works of the Latin poet Virgil date from four centuries after him; thirteen centuries separate Plato from the manuscripts of his writings, and in the case of the Greek poet Euripides this goes up to sixteen centuries.

We are in a much better position with the New Testament. We have thousands of manuscripts, some of which are very old.

These manuscripts are written either on papyrus (the fibres of a plant) or parchment (the skin of sheep, goats or calves). They can either be scrolls or, more often, in the form of a codex (leaves sewn together like our modern books). Until the ninth century they were written in majuscules (or in uncials, i.e. capital letters), without separation between the letters; thereafter they were also written in minuscules.

Here are some important periods in the transmission of the text of the New Testament.

Down to the fourth century

Even at the end of the second century, people were disturbed about differences between manuscripts. At Alexandria, scholars made a recension, i.e. from different manuscripts they tried to establish the text that they thought came closest to the original. This 'Alexandrian recension' spread throughout the Empire.

The Greek text was translated into Latin (the Old Latin or the Itala, between 160 and 180), Syriac and Coptic.

From this period we still have:
the Rylands papyrus
(see p. 9);
Bodmer papyrus II, about 200, from Egypt: fourteen chapters from John (the beginning of John is in the box opposite);
three Chester Beatty papyri, from about 250: these contain passages from the Gospels, from Paul and from Revelation.

From the fourth to the sixth century

The great complete manuscripts of the New Testament, written on parchment, date from this period:

Vaticanus (middle of the fourth century);
Sinaiticus (middle of the fourth century);
Alexandrinus (beginning of the fifth century);
Codex Ephraem (fifth century);
Codex Bezae (fifth century), which has only the Gospels and Acts. The text of Acts differs somewhat from the usual text;
Freer Codex (fifth century), which has only the Gospels.

Sinaïticus. Heb. 13,24-25

At the beginning of the fifth century a new recension was made in Byzantium. This established itself as the common version (the Koine) in all Greek-speaking churches.

The text of the versions was unified: in 382 St Jerome produced the Vulgate (Latin). The Peshitto (Syriac) and the Armenian version date from the fifth century.

From the sixth century to the Renaissance

A great many copies were made in the monasteries.

Renaissance: fifteenth and sixteenth centuries

Greek manuscripts came over into the West after the capture of Constantinople in 1453.

The Alcala Polyglot, edited by Cardinal Ximenes, the work of a conscientious scholar, was begun in 1502 and published in 1522. To keep it out (competition was strong even in those days), in 1516 Erasmus published a text which was established in six months on the basis of only six manuscripts. The printer Robert Estienne revised the Erasmus text on the basis of Alcala. Theodore of Beza took up the fourth edition of Estienne; this is the Received Text, which was used down to the end of the nineteenth century.

From the middle of the nineteenth century

In 1859, Tischendorf discovered Sinaiticus and published Vaticanus. These are the two manuscripts which serve as the basis for the text of our Bibles as we now have it.

Differences between manuscripts are only in points of detail. Although we do not have the original texts, we can trust the copies that we have.

Writing the Gospel today?

After following this course, we have probably had to give up rather naïve ideas like: the apostles listened to Jesus, wrote down his words and actions, and after Pentecost set off for their mission to the world, Gospels under their arms. . . Jesus gathered together disciples, founded his church which existed before the Gospels and gave them their shape. . .

We have followed this course because it matches what seems to have happened. However, our approach does have an important consequence for us today.

If we had photographs and recordings of Jesus, we would be condemned to repetition, to taking them as a model to be reproduced.

If the Jesus whom the New Testament presents to us was discovered slowly by Christian communities, through their lives and their reflections, we have a future opened up to us. Our communities, today, have to continue this work of discovering Jesus through our life and our questions. The life of our churches today, the face of the Risen Christ which they show to the world, are the Gospels that we write today.

In common with many other texts, the Epistle to the Ephesians, in a passage which we studied on p. 37, reminds us of the work of Christian communities: to build up the body of Christ until it achieves its perfect form. That is what the glorified Lord has equipped his church to do, and he needs that church: the Holy Spirit and the various ministries are the gifts which he gives it. Christians must 'give birth' to Christ in the world (Rev. 12.1–6; John 16.21–22; see p. 109). And their life, expressed in countless writings, from personal or liturgical prayers to innumerable testimonies, are the Gospel of the twentieth century.

However, there is a basic difference between these 'Gospels' which we produce and the writings of the New Testament. The latter are recognized as the word of God; they form the rule of faith for Christians of all times and all places. With them, revelation comes to an end: God has told us everything in his Son. Our 'Gospels' do not tell us anything more; they simply show the way in which the first message resounds in a particular part of the world in a particular century; so they are not universal. Furthermore, they are valid only to the extent that they produce the same sound as the first writings, for which they provide today's harmony.

So Christians are not condemned to the passive reproduction of a model: they are invited to give birth to Christ in the world, to discover, in faithfulness to the first message, the countenance of the Risen Christ for our world.

Autograph letter of Simeon bar Cochba, leader of the second Jewish revolt in AD 135.

If You Want to Know More . . .

As far as possible, I have deliberately avoided referring to other books in this work; you can manage very well by using it on its own, along with a good Bible. However, if you want to explore further, you will find the following books useful.

Reference books

A wealth of information about the content of the Bible can be found in two dictionaries: James Hastings, *Dictionary of the Bible*, T. & T. Clark, and the five-volume illustrated *Interpreter's Dictionary of the Bible*, Abingdon Press. Two convenient atlases are Lucas Grollenberg, *Shorter Atlas of the Bible*, Penguin Books, and the *Oxford Bible Atlas*, edited by H. G. May, Oxford University Press: each has an illustrated text as well as the maps. There are many commentary series, with a separate volume for each book (or groups of books in the case of the smaller works in the New Testament). Three very useful series for the New Testament are the New Clarendon Bible, published by Oxford University Press, which has illustrations; the Black's New Testament Commentaries, published in England by A. & C. Black and as the Harper New Testament Commentaries in the USA by Harper and Row; and the Cambridge Bible Commentaries, published by Cambridge University Press. The Pelican New Testament Commentary series, now published by SCM Press and Westminster Press, is incomplete, but has some important volumes in it. Big one-volume commentaries are, of course, predominantly concerned with the Old Testament because that is so much bigger; they also contain articles on general topics. There are three good ones to choose from: *The Jerome Biblical Commentary*, edited by R. E. Brown, J. A. Fitzmyer and R. E. Murphy, Geoffrey Chapman and Prentice Hall; *The New Catholic Commentary on Holy Scripture*, edited by R. C. Fuller, Leonard Johnston and Conleth Kearns, Nelson; and *Peake's Commentary on the Bible*, edited by M. Black and H. H. Rowley, Nelson. A synopsis of the Gospels is a very important book to have; the most convenient is Burton Throckmorton, *Gospel Parallels*, Nelson. A concordance will help you to trace the use of words and phrases, and to look up passages about whose location you are unsure; the most up-to-date one is Clinton D. Morrison, *An Analytical Concordance to the Revised Standard Version New Testament*, Westminster Press and SCM Press.

Background information

C. K. Barrett, ed., *The New Testament Background: Selected Documents,* SPCK
   This contains translations of a wide variety of works of every kind from the time of the New Testament, giving some impression of thoughts and practices at the time.

Joachim Jeremias, *Jerusalem in the Time of Jesus*, SCM Press and Fortress Press
   A classic work, reconstructing from Jewish sources what Jerusalem must have been like.

Josephus, *The Jewish War,* Penguin Books
   This is the most accessible and readable translation of the work of a Jewish historian who survived by joining the Roman side and wrote a history of events leading to the capture of Jerusalem.

Eduard Lohse, *The New Testament Environment*, SCM Press and Abingdon Press

Bo Reicke, *The New Testament Era*, A. & C. Black and Fortress Press
   Two comprehensive accounts of the historical background and religious ideas which underlie the New Testament.

Samuel Sandmel, *The First Century in Judaism and Christianity*, Oxford University Press

Samuel Sandmel, *Judaism and Christian Beginnings*, Oxford University Press
   A Jewish scholar offers his perspective on the beginnings of Christianity and provides an important correction to many ideas we too easily accept uncritically.

Geza Vermes, *The Dead Sea Scrolls in English,* Penguin Books
   A translation with comments of the most important discoveries.

Geza Vermes, *The Dead Sea Scrolls,* SCM Press and Fortress Press
   An account of their discovery and of the most important consequences for biblical studies.

General works

T. G. A. Baker, *What is the New Testament?* SCM Press
   A compact introductory study dealing with questions of authority, etc.

Alan T. Dale, *New World,* Oxford University Press
   A basic, illustrated guide.

W. D. Davies, *Invitation to the New Testament*, SPCK and Doubleday
   Written for the author's teenage daughter.

Floyd V. Filson, *A New Testament History,* Westminster Press and SCM Press
   A simple history extending from the time of the Maccabees to the early church.

R. M. Grant, *A Historical Introduction to the New Testament,* Fount Books and Simon and Schuster
   A good non-technical study with a wealth of information, lucidly presented.

A. M. Hunter, *Introducing the New Testament*, SCM Press and Westminster Press

A basic guide to questions of date, authorship and the content of books.

C. F. D. Moule, *The Birth of the New Testament*, A. & C. Black and Harper & Row

An account of the circumstances leading to the formation of the New Testament.

Stephen Neill, *The Interpretation of the New Testament 1861–1961*, Oxford University Press

A riveting account of the rise of New Testament criticism.

Norman Perrin, *Introduction to the New Testament*, Harcourt, Brace

A textbook written along new lines.

R. Spivey and D. Moody Smith, *Anatomy of the New Testament*, Collier-Macmillan

A comprehensive analytical study of the content of the New Testament.

Robert C. Walton (ed.), *A Basic Introduction to the New Testament*, SCM Press and John Knox Press (American title: *Bible Study Source Book: New Testament*)

Easter and the Resurrection

R. E. Brown, *The Virginal Conception and the Bodily Resurrection of Jesus*, Geoffrey Chapman and Paulist Press

A discussion of the evidence using the techniques of biblical criticism.

C. F. Evans, *Resurrection and the New Testament*, SCM Press

A thorough discussion of the idea of resurrection and its significance throughout the New Testament.

Willi Marxsen, *The Resurrection of Jesus of Nazareth*, Fortress Press

A rather controversial but extremely stimulating approach.

Norman Perrin, *The Resurrection Narratives: A New Approach*, Fortress Press

The theological significance of the stories in Matthew, Mark and Luke.

U. Wilckens, *Resurrection*, St Andrew Press and John Knox Press

Biblical testimony to the resurrection: an examination and explanation.

Paul and his letters

William Barclay, *The Mind of St Paul*, Fount Books and Harper and Row

A portrait drawn from his letters.

Günther Bornkamm, *Paul*, Hodder & Stoughton and Harper & Row

A detailed all-round study which relates to his theology and his biography.

F. F. Bruce, *Paul: Apostle of the Free Spirit*, Paternoster Press and Eerdmans (American titles: *Paul: Apostle of the Heart Set Free*)

An examination of the main themes of his thought.

W. D. Davies, *Paul and Rabbinic Judaism*, SPCK and Fortress Press

A pioneering study in the connection between Paul's thought and what we know of contemporary Judaism.

Lucas Grollenberg, *Paul*, SCM Press and Westminster Press

A highly attractive account, perhaps the best introductory book.

A. M. Hunter, *The Gospel according to St Paul*, SCM Press and Westminster Press

The theology of St Paul and its meaning today.

John A. T. Robinson, *Wrestling with Romans*, SCM Press and Westminster Press

A good way of getting down to detailed study of one of Paul's letters.

Krister Stendahl, *Paul among Jews and Gentiles*, SCM Press and Fortress Press

Argues that we should beware of assessing Paul by the wrong standards.

Mark and miracles

C. F. Evans, *The Beginning of the Gospel*, SPCK

An introduction to the purpose and construction of the Gospel.

R. P. Martin, *Mark, Evangelist and Theologian*, Paternoster Press and Zondervan

Shows how Mark's thinking is related to that of Paul.

D. E. Nineham, *Saint Mark*, Penguin Books

One of the best New Testament commentaries in any language and an ideal introduction.

R. H. Fuller, *Interpreting the Miracles*, SCM Press and Westminster Press

Particularly concerned with their theological significance.

Ernst and Marie-Luise Keller, *Miracles in Dispute*, SCM Press and Fortress Press

A fascinating history of the understanding of miracles.

Matthew and the Sermon on the Mount

W. D. Davies, *The Sermon on the Mount*, Cambridge University Press

An analysis of its content.

H. Benedict Green, *The Gospel of Matthew*, Oxford University Press

Perhaps the most useful commentary on the Gospel.

E. Schweizer, *Good News according to Matthew*, SPCK and John Knox Press

Another useful guide in the form of a commentary.

Luke and parables

John Drury, *Tradition and Design in Luke's Gospel*, Darton, Longman and Todd

A provocative and questioning study.

E. Haenchen, *The Acts of the Apostles*, Blackwell and Westminster Press

A big book, but surprisingly easy to understand if you pick and choose, and very illuminating

I. H. Marshall, *Luke, Historian and Theologian*, Paternoster Press and Zondervan
A study of Luke, his thinking and his approach to history.
Neil Richardson, *The Panorama of Luke*, Epworth Press
Perhaps the best approach to the Gospel and Acts; readable and clear in its explanations.
A. M. Hunter, *Interpreting the Parables*, SCM Press and Westminster Press
A good popular book.
Joachim Jeremias, *Rediscovering the Parables*, SCM Press and Scribner
A popular version of the most famous book ever written on the subject.

Lucas Grollenberg, *Jesus*, SCM Press and Westminster Press
A vividly readable study by the distinguished Dutch Dominican.
Geza Vermes, *Jesus the Jew*, Fount Books and Fortress Press
Against a Jewish background by a distinguished Jewish scholar.
None of these books is difficult to read. It would be well worth going through each of them and comparing the portraits they give.

The Synoptic Gospels

Some useful books which deal with all three Synoptic Gospels (and in some cases with the Gospel of John as well) are: William Barclay, *The Gospels and Acts*, SCM Press and Westminster Press; F. W. Beare, *The Earliest Records of Jesus*, Blackwell (a companion to *Gospel Parallels*); A. E. Harvey, *Companion to the Gospels*, Oxford University Press; Keith Nickle, *The Synoptic Gospels*, SCM Press and John Knox Press.

John and worship

There is a richer collection of commentaries on the Gospel of John than on virtually any other book of the Bible; somehow the book seems to bring out the best in modern writers. They are not necessarily easy, but they will more than repay the time and effort you spend on them. Among the distinguished authors are R. E. Brown, E. C. Hoskyns, Barnabas Lindars and John Marsh: they will point you to yet others. More general books are A. M. Hunter, *According to John*, SCM Press and Westminster Press, O. Cullmann; *The Johannine Circle*, SCM Press; Ernst Käsemann, *The Testament of Jesus*, Fortress Press; and C. H. Dodd, *The Interpretation of the Fourth Gospel*, Cambridge University Press. For the letters see especially J. L. Houlden's commentary in the Black New Testament series. Worship, even worship in New Testament times, is a vast subject, and it is impossible to give a list of books about it here; a good starting point is J. D. G. Dunn, *Unity and Diversity in the New Testament*, SCM Press and Westminster Press. Commentaries on Revelation are also helpful here: see the series mentioned above.

The beginning of the Gospel . . .

And here is the most difficult task of all! At least you should look at:
C. H. Dodd, *The Founder of Christianity,* Fount Books
A portrait by a very famous English New Testament scholar.

ROMAN EMPERORS	JUDAEA SAMARIA IDUMAEA	GALILEE PERAEA	ITURAEA TRACHONITIS	ABILENE	PRIESTS	JESUS and the CHRISTIAN COMMUNITY	PAUL: his life	his letters	OTHER WRITINGS
AUGUSTUS	HEROD THE GREAT 37–4								
	ARCHELAUS	HEROD ANTIPAS	HEROD-PHILIP II		?6 Birth of JESUS				
	6 exiled to Gaul								
	8 Coponius Ambibulus	divorces and marries Herodias, wife of Herod-Philip I	marries Salome, daughter of Herod-Philip I and Herodias		10 Annas		Between 0 and 10, born at Tarsus		
	12 Annius Rufus								
14	15 Valerius Gratus				15 Eleazar / 18		between 15 and 25, studies at JERUSALEM, with Gamaliel		
TIBERIUS	26 PONTIUS PILATE				Caiaphas	JOHN THE BAPTIST / Baptism of JESUS / Death and resurrection			
	34 dies childless	34 dies childless	34 dies childless		36 Jonathan	36? Martyrdom of Stephen	37 Call. Preaches in Arabia, JERUSALEM TARSUS		
37	36 Marcellus M.				37 Theophilus				
CALIGULA		39 Exiled to Lyons							
41	41 HEROD AGRIPPA 1	41 HEROD AGRIPPA 1			41 Simeon / 44 Matthias	42 Death of James, Peter in prison	43 Barnabas goes to look for Paul in Tarsus / 44 Ministry in ANTIOCH with Barnabas, 'famine' visit to Jerusalem		
44	44								JAMES / I PETER
CLAUDIUS	46 Cuspius Fadus / Tiberius Alexander				46 Elionaeus / 48		45–48 First mission: Cyprus and Derbe. Paul goes to the 'Council'		
	48 Vintidius-Cumanus					end 49–50 'Council of JERUSALEM'	50–52 Second mission: Antioch to Athens. Stays at CORINTH	51 I-II Thessalonians	
54	52 Antonius FELIX marries Drusilla sister of Berenice	HEROD AGRIPPA II and his 'sister' BERENICE			Ananias		53–58 Third mission, EPHESUS (2–3 years) Macedonia, Corinth (winter 57–58)	57? Philippians I-II Corinthians Galatians, Romans	
NERO	60 Porcius FESTUS				58 Ishmael / Joseph / Annas II / Jesus / Joshua / Matthias / Phinehas		58–60 In prison in Caesarea (Felix-Festus), visit of Agrippa and Berenice	63 Colossians, Ephesians, Philemon / Timothy, Titus	HEBREWS / MARK
63 Galba	62 Albinus						61–63 Prison in ROME. Spain?		
69 Otho	64 Gessius Florus						65 Macedonia		
70 Vitellius	66 Jewish Revolt						66–67 Prison in ROME, MARTYRDOM		
VESPASIAN	70 TITUS captures JERUSALEM								MATTHEW LUKE – ACTS JUDE II PETER JOHN, I – III JOHN REVELATION
79 TITUS									
81 DOMITIAN									
96									

Analytical Index

Jesus

King, 63, 99
Lamb, 110
Lord, 37, 52, 54, 71, 76, 88
Martyr, 87
Messiah (or Christ), 58, 60, 63, 64, 65, 75, 76, 96, 111
New Adam, 51, 53
New Elijah, 85
New Moses, 85
Priest, 53
Prophet, 88
Saviour, 76, 85
Servant, 54, 63, 85
Son of David, 58, 60, 62, 112
Son of God, 58, 60, 63, 64, 71, 75, 76, 85, 99, 100, 112
Son of Man, 58, 63, 64, 75, 76, 100, 110
Word (Logos), 98

Holy Spirit, 19, 32, 51, 55, 81, 88, 97, 99, 109, 110, 119

Church

and kingdom of God, 70
in Matthew, 69
in Revelation, 106, 108
Two images, 46, 52
Various aspects, 32, 48, 84, 119

Groups, institutions

Baptists, 28
Diaspora, 25, 54
Elders, 27
Essenes, 28, 93
Festivals, Jewish, 30
Godfearers, 28
Jamnia (or Jabneh), 31, 69
Levites, 27
Nazarenes, 28
Pharisees, 27, 28, 31, 45, 69
Priests, 27
Proselytes, 28
Publicans, 27
Sabbath, 30, 61
Sadducees, 27, 28
Samaritans, 28
Sanhedrin, 30
Scribes, 27
Synagogues, 30
Zealots, 28

Some themes

Appear, make visible, 37, 39–41

Ascension-exaltation, 39
Baptism, 51, 55
Beatitudes, 65, 78
Catechesis, 12, 24, 55, 77–80
Celebration, worship, 13, 24, 36–37, 57, 93, 101–104, 108
Christian action, morality, 47, 48, 55–57
End of time, 71
Eucharist, 40, 63, 75, 87, 96, 102
Exaltation, see *Ascension*
Forgiveness, 56, 61, 76, 104
Gnosis, 93, 116, 119
Kerygma, see Preaching
Kingdom, reign of God, 65, 70, 77, 89, 92
Mary, 86, 112
Morality, see Christian action
Preaching, kerygma, 13, 23, 34, 39
Resurrection, 33–44
Scriptures, 42, 70, 81, 111–114
'Third day', 36
Universalism, 58, 69, 81

Literary questions

Allegory, 89
Apocalypse, 21, 54, 71, 105
Calling, accounts of, 20, 61
Canon of Scripture, 31, 119
Controversy, 20, 61
Gospel, 18, 57
Koine (common Greek), 82
Midrash, 21, 74
Miracle, 20, 65–68
Narratives, 21, 38
Parable, 20, 89–92
Recension, 120
Synopsis, 15, 16–17
Targum, 37
Theophany, 20
'Tool box', 21
'Tracing paper', 19, 69, 81
Type 'mock up', 72
'Upheaval', 67, 71, 75

Jewish texts

Parable of Rabbi Bun, 90
Prayer from the Jewish liturgy, 109
Philo (on Ex. 20.18), 84
Targum on Hos. 6.1, 36
Targum on Num. 24.17, 74
Targum on Ps. 68, 37
Testament of Levi, 60

The Synoptic Gospels: Texts Studied

Other Texts Studied

Table of Contents